Channeled Wisdom
from
Higher Dimensional Beings

∞

Volume 2

Daniel Scranton

CONTENTS

FOREWORD

My Spiritual journey began in Jan 2005, where I was led on a beautiful and very healing inner journey by a Shamanic practitioner. This journey started off quite rocky, uncertain and confusing. At times, there were moments when I wondered when and where I would see and witness the light at the end of the tunnel through some massive transformation in my life. And yet, every time I searched even harder, the answers seemed to elude me. However, when I finally let go and allowed myself to be used as an instrument and channel for Divine energy to flow through, that's when the powerful and deeply profound transformations started to reveal themselves in ways that were both magical and miraculous.

As I share this story with you, I recognize the parallels between my journey and Daniel's channeling journey. He started channeling Higher Dimensional Beings without even knowing whether he was doing it right, if the messages coming through were from a Higher Being or just him making it up as he went along. However, through his journey of years and years of channeling, he started to believe more in himself, and there was a deep trust within him that what was coming through was truly Divine Energy flowing through him.

It was through his own openness and a deep willingness to be used as a powerful conduit for the Divine that led him to where he is now. And I can honestly say that every time I witness him in the channeling state, it's incredible to see how the most profound and deeply potent energies move through him and how easy it is for him to receive and translate these messages from Higher Dimensional Beings.

This is the third book in Daniel's collection of channeling Higher Dimensional Beings. What a pleasure, honor and privilege it has been for me to be part of compiling this book of quotes.

Each quote has been intuitively chosen to assist you on your journey to:

* Tap into higher frequency energy with more ease, grace and joy
* Co-creatively manifest your desires easily, effortlessly and in more relaxed and joyful ways
* Own your power and stand in your authentic truth, confidently and courageously
* Create even more flow and ease in your life right now
* Deeply know that you are meant to live your life in ways that feel aligned and in integrity with the truth you feel in your heart and Soul
* Lean on the understanding that you are greatly supported and infinitely loved by so many Higher Dimensional Beings in the Universe

What a beautiful GIFT you've gifted yourself just by purchasing this book. This book is infused with the highest level of love, light, truth, beauty, grace and joy, and it will transform you on a multidimensional level - energetically, cellularly, physically, mentally, emotionally and spiritually. Your life will forever be changed because you chose to tap into an energy and frequency through this book that will continue to guide you to even more magical and miraculous experiences on your journey.

To receive the deepest level healing and transformation through this book, I invite you to set an intention before opening the book and ask for what is in your best and highest good to receive. This will allow you to get out of your own way and open you up to the higher wisdom that's available for you on your journey.

I have no doubt in my mind that when you come from this place of openness and receptivity, the messages in this book will assist you to create what it is you desire to receive on your path right now.

Thank you, beautiful and sweet Daniel, for all that you are and all that you continue to do to elevate and enrich the consciousness of the beautiful Souls that are inspired by your truth and your presence in this world, one message at a time. It is through confidently owning your authentic truth and being unapologetically all of who you are that gifts others the freedom and permission to courageously step into their own authentic truth.

I am eternally grateful to have you in my life. You have added such infinite beauty, truth, joy, love, peace, ease, grace, expansion, and so much more in my life, and I know he'll do the same for you.

May your world be transformed into new, limitless and expansive possibilities through this Channeled Wisdom from Higher Dimensional Beings.

With infinite love, gratitude and light,

Maricris Dela Cruz-Scranton
Divine Self Love Priestess
Founder and Creator of the Inner Light Illumination Process™

PREFACE & ACKNOWLEDGEMENTS

This book represents the last seven years of my life, which of course includes my channeling. I began channeling the first daily quotes (that's what I called them at the time) in June of 2012. The Creators were the only group that I channeled at that time. I hadn't even received the name 'The Creators' for them when I started channeling these messages, these transmissions of light.

All of the beings who are represented in this compilation of those channelings from 2012 to 2019 are featured in the order they came into my life. As I said, it was The Creators and only The Creators from November 2010 till September of 2013. That's when I met Ophelia the Faerie. I first felt her and then channeled her tones on a hike in the forest. Then I channeled her for a friend, and then I started doing the daily messages with her.

Next. The Hathors came through. That was unexpected! I had heard of them, but I had no desire to channel them. I was just open in the moment to bring through a new being or collective of beings, and The Hathors stepped up.

I was always curious as to why no one was channeling The Unicorn Collective. I kept trying to bait my friend and mentor, Nora Herold, into channeling them during one of her group events and calls. But instead, I felt them come through me, and I went with it! And that's how the unicorns came into my life. They were a little bit harder to channel for me, as I didn't feel that they had the 'teacher' vibe. So I didn't channel them for very long.

Next, I brought through Archangel Michael. Again, Nora Herold was involved. She's played a pretty big role in all of this for me, so consider this her entry into the acknowledgements! She was putting on a retreat in Ojai, CA, and I was in attendance. I felt Michael coming in before she even asked us if anyone wanted to channel the Archangel. Before I knew it, I was speaking a light language that was my best representation of the energy I was feeling.

Archangel Gabriel came through as a result of the prompting. Someone asked me if I could channel that collective (I see the archangels as collectives, not individuals). And so I did. Gabriel came through in a female voice, which surprised me. But I later found out that many people see Gabriel as a female energy/being/collective. That information I found online was a nice way for me to make sense of what was coming through me!

And then came The Founders. Like The Hathors, this was a group I had heard of through Lyssa Royal Holt, but I had no desire to channel. But I guess they had a desire to come through me. I later checked with Lyssa to make sure I wasn't stepping on her toes, since she's the only one I had ever heard even mention The Founders. She was, of course, gracious about allowing me to put my quotes from The Founders out to the public.

The Pleiadian High Council of Seven came through shortly after I moved to Maui. I had wanted to channel a Pleiadian collective for quite some time. Nora channels a group of Pleiadians. So does

Wendy Kennedy, another wonderful mentor of mine who deserves acknowledgement here. And so does Lyssa. Her Pleiadian is a singular being named Sasha. All three are beautiful people channeling beautiful energy. I wanted in! And I got in. I started channeling The Pleiadian High Council of Seven because I wanted to connect with that Pleiadian energy.

This brings us to Quan Yin. I was living on Maui in a rental ohana on an organic farm. It was such a beautiful place to settle into the Maui energies. I started seeing Quan Yin everywhere. A Facebook post. Then a client mentioned her. And then in a healing I was receiving, the healer mentioned her. And then I ordered a key chain because it had all seven of the main chakras represented by crystals. And there was as metallic piece on the end of the chain with the image of Quan Yin. I told my landlady about all of these sychronicities, and then she said, 'You know that statue in front of your ohana is Quan Yin, right?' No, I did not! But the message was received, and I started channeling them. Then I met my beautiful wife, who is of Asian descent…and who also channeled Quan Yin. Good job, universe!

Finally, we come to The Arcturian Council. I believe I've been doing the daily messages with them for the longest. They came through because I invited them to come through. I knew they would be high frequency beings, as all Arcturians are. And the rest is history!

I also have to acknowledge Anya J. Hurd for being my editor. She is responsible for all three of my books being on amazon and the ebooks being in my store. Without her looking over each message for any typos, omissions of words, and grammatical errors, I wouldn't have ever gotten these books out to the public. Thanks a million, Anya!

My wife compiled the quotes this time around. She also helped me format the text on each page, making sure everything was in the right place, and she wrote the foreword. She inspires me with her love and light every day. I don't know where I would be without her. Thank you, my lovely and amazing wifey.

Chapter One

∞

The Creators

EMOTIONAL NON-CONFORMITY
∞
THE CREATORS

"Bringing yourselves into a higher frequency state means that you must enjoy your life more. It is a requirement for you to have a more expanded experience. You are capable of much more joy than you usually allow yourselves to feel. You put off your joy many times. You save it for special occasions. You decide that you can only feel joy under certain circumstances. You wish to be emotionally appropriate.

And that is something that all of you are starting to break free from. Because for a very long time on your world, it has been socially unacceptable for you to feel certain ways in certain situations. And this has created a sort of emotional agreement between all of you. If you are attending a funeral, you are to be sad. If you are attending a wedding, you are to be happy.

We want to give you the permission to experience whatever emotional state you want to experience in any moment in time. We want you to set aside the social conformity that has created a world full of beings who are behaving appropriately. So you are being asked here to be even bigger outcasts than many of you already feel that you are. We are telling you that in order for you to start an emotional revolution, you must begin with the mundane and you must be happy within a monotonous task.

You must realize that everything is laced with joy and everything has the potential to be a joyous experience. In fact, if you did not think that it was possible for every aspect of life to be a joyous experience, then you would not have agreed to incarnate into this reality and this dimension. You knew that you were getting yourselves into this type of scenario where people would be solemn, serious, even sad, and that it would be your desire to lighten the mood.

You knew that you were here to show others the way, and one of the ways that you do this is with emotional integrity. But you also want to choose more frequently how you want to feel, rather than continuing to let the circumstances that are before you give you the cue as to how you ought to feel. So we are encouraging you to let loose more, to dance in the aisles of the supermarket, to be happy because you want to be happy, and to get up off of that dock where you are waiting for your ship to come in, and to do some cannonballs."

EXPANSION AND BELIEFS

∞

THE CREATORS

"When you are interfering with the evolutionary process that you are engaged with, you only create a less enjoyable experience of it. You will continue to evolve and grow and expand and ascend. There is no question that you will continue on that path forever and ever. But you can attempt to slow it down and halt it altogether with your beliefs that you hold.

So you get attached to these beliefs because the beliefs themselves help you feel safer. They give you a comfort in knowing what you can expect. You want to master the reality you are in, and therefore, you need these beliefs of yours to give you that comfort and the faith that things are going to turn out as you expect them to. That is all well and good. You are welcome to your beliefs, and you are certainly welcome to remain in whatever reality you choose to be in for as long as you choose to be in it.

There is no right or wrong here. It is not as though the reality that you are expanding into is better than the reality you began this journey in. It is not that way at all. But you see, your soul wants new experiences, and since you are somewhat an important part of your soul's journey, you are going along for the ride. So your expansion process can be one that you participate in, or it can be one that you are dragged through, kicking and screaming.

So how do you expand then? What is the easier, more preferred and more pleasant and enjoyable way? Well, we suggest that you live in the moment, first and foremost. By living in the moment, you are not taking what you have come to expect and pasting it into the future. You are not attempting to set up these steps for yourselves to get to a certain place. You see, you use your beliefs to help yourself create that reality that you want.

So you are always drawing on past experiences in order to create a better future. That is what keeps you attached to those limiting beliefs. But if you remain focused on the now and in the feeling state that you are holding, then you recognize that each moment is a whole new world and offers you a whole new set of possibilities for experience. So much of your letting go process is about that need that you all have to know what is coming next.

If you can embrace the present moment with the knowing that what will come next can only be more satisfying, then you release the need for you to know what that satisfying experience will be. We know that you all want to be very deliberate creators, and we are not telling you not to do that. We are just telling you to use the tools that exist in your hearts, rather than using the beliefs that are created in your minds."

OUR PERCEPTION OF REALITY

∞

THE CREATORS

"Have you ever wondered where everything came from in your reality? Has it ever occurred to you that the reality that you experience is not really there? Not in the sense that your five senses are able to perceive. Not as hard and fast and static. You may look at a rock every day and think that the rock is the same, because that is what your senses tell you. It is the same shape and size and weight and density as it was the day before.

But you are creating the rock, and so you give yourselves the version of the rock that is most beneficial to you. Would it benefit you in any way if you saw that the rock had changed dramatically from one day to the next or from one moment to the next? Perhaps then you would focus too much on the rock, and you would give the rock all sorts of magical attributes and qualities. You would study the rock. You would create stories about the rock.

You would not see it as your creation, because that is how most of you are operating. But if you were to see a dramatic change and ask yourselves, 'How does this change serve me?' 'Why is it that I am creating this change?' 'Is this the change I prefer?' and questions like that, you would be able to notice more dramatic changes, because you would be owning the change as your change and as your creation.

You will begin to notice big changes in your world, and you will need to recognize the changes within you in order to benefit and in order to make more conscious changes, more conscious decisions, more conscious creations. You needed a certain amount of stability in your outer reflection, and you simply were not moving fast enough with your own energy to see rapid change.

But now you are, and now you will, and now is the time that you have all been waiting for. It is the time when the creation of your reality will become more immediate and more dramatic. And that is why I invite you to seek that which you wish to engage with. Seek it in your inner world. Notice it in your outer world and smile and give yourselves the credit for the dramatic changes that are about to come."

FOCUS ON THE EXPERIENCE YOUR FEELINGS OFFER

∞

THE CREATORS

"Sitting in the middle of your life, looking around at all that you can see, what are the things that stand out mostly to you? What do you tend to focus on regarding your lives? Use this tool to understand what you are accessing at this time. What is most important to you is also what is there for you to cleanse. There is much that you have stored up within you that is rising to the surface at this time so that you can look at it and really see it for what it is.

It really is just an experience. When you place so much significance and importance on something, it moves from the realm of just an experience, and into the realm of that which must be a certain way. And when you get to that point, where that is how you are looking at certain aspects of your lives, certain situations in your lives, certain beings who are either in or not in your lives, that is when you get stuck.

And we are perfectly okay with you getting stuck. But when you get stuck, many times you spend all of your focus on getting un-stuck. But what is really important for you to do is to feel into the stuckness. When something is nagging at you, when something is always right there in your face, it is there to get you to examine what it is that you are feeling regarding that subject or that circumstance.

So that is why the simple act of looking around at your life and seeing what sticks out like a sore thumb can be so productive for you. We want you to take some time off from your attempts to change that thing. And instead, we want you to utilize your ability to focus and feel. Once you get into the feelings, you may then access some thoughts. You may access some images. You may get some ideas. You may have some past life memories popping up.

But do not get caught up in what springs forth from your diving into the feelings. Don't use this exercise as another means of getting unstuck or of fixing the problem. Utilize this exercise as a means of having an experience. Because everything that you feel, you feel for the experience of the feeling. It is not there to punish you. It is not there to tell you where your thinking is off. It is not there because you did something wrong in another lifetime. It is there because you simply want to have that experience.

And until you allow yourselves to have that experience of the feeling, you will keep creating circumstances and events that will force you to look at the feeling. Be very gentle with yourselves through this process, but also be very curious and adventurous, because this does not have to be a chore. This can be as exciting as doing something that brings you automatically into a state of joy.

Take yourselves as deeply as you can without worrying that you will get lost, because we promise you, you will find yourselves."

THE GIFTS YOUR OVERSOUL GIVES YOU
∞
THE CREATORS

"Putting yourself in the driver's seat of your life is something that all of you have been attempting and desiring to do. It is a part of your awakening process to take hold of the reins and to begin to create that which you want to experience. We know that this is one of the most attractive components to the information that many of you have come across, and we acknowledge you for being able and willing to believe that it is possible in the first place.

And at the same time, you all recognize that you are clearing and you are processing, and you have agreed to certain experiences along your path. So the question comes up then, 'How much of this do I get to create, and how much of this am I here simply to experience?' Well it really depends upon which aspect of 'you' you are talking about. If you are seeing yourself as your Oversoul, then you are creating every little bit of it, and you are creating every little bit of it so that you can have the experience of it.

If you are looking at yourself as the personality, the ego, then you are not quite able to call all the shots from that perspective. And this has caused many of you to access your frustration and your anger and your hopelessness around certain aspects of your lives. So what to do about all of it? Well, what would ultimately serve you best would be to take on the perspective of your Oversoul, to allow yourselves to see your life through the eyes of the Oversoul Being and to operate in the way that your Oversoul does.

Your Oversoul knows itself as eternal, infinite, and unconditional love, and your Oversoul wants to have experiences and to better know itself as eternal, infinite and unconditional love. So as you begin to view your life and yourself from those perspectives, then you can see how much easier it is to navigate through it and to be the creator of it. If you say to yourself, 'I want to create a million dollars,' that puts you into a bit of a hole that is quite a confined space.

But if you say to yourself, 'I want to experience many different ways of exchanging energy, and information, and services, and goods,' well then you open yourselves up to a much bigger field of possibilities. So when you approach your life, approach it from that Oversoul perspective, and look for the experience in what it is that you are creating. Know yourselves as the Oversoul does, and allow yourselves to enjoy a little bit more that which is before you, because when you do this you have that Oversoul perspective."

CREATE YOURSELF ANEW IN THIS MOMENT

∞

THE CREATORS

"Forget everything that you think you know for one moment. Let go. Let go of what you think is going to happen next. Let go of what happened yesterday. Let go of what it is you usually think about when you look at something or someone. In other words, let yourselves become new in one moment in time. Allow yourself that freedom. Allow yourself to simply be for one, single, solitary moment and see how you feel in that moment.

Can you shift how you feel about your life by removing all preconceived notions about where it is you are, where it is you are headed, where it is you have been? How does this change everything? We suggest that you do this at a time when there really isn't much going on, when you have some of your downtime, your free time, as you call it. Interesting how you put things. When you are in one of these moments, simply let go of all that you normally do, think, and say, and exist purely in that moment as a new creation of yourself and of Source.

Be willing to cut all ties to all individuals, to all concepts and expectations and let yourself go into a state of automatic pilot. See where this exercise takes you. You may be surprised at who it is you are now, now that you can let go of who it is you have attached your idea of self to. Do not over-think this process because this process is about not thinking and it is about being. But it is about being while still doing in your world. It is not just a meditative exercise. It is an exercise in living.

And as you look upon your world with eyes that are new and with zero expectations, zero preconceived notions, zero judgments, you will see that it is a pretty wonderful place to be and you are a pretty wonderful being."

YOU ARE THE CREATOR OF YOUR EXPERIENCES

∞

THE CREATORS

"Some of you are experiencing extreme levels of either tiredness or energy that feels uncomfortable to you. And we want to assure you that there is nothing wrong with you if you are having one of these experiences. You are in the midst of a download of energy that will require some of you to shut down in order to integrate. And for others, you will integrate it while still being awake, and conscious, and in your bodies.

So you see there is never a right way or a wrong way to be, and there is never a right way or a wrong way to integrate. That is something that you all must come to realize, because if you look around at what others are experiencing and compare yourselves or judge yourselves for not having the same or a similar experience, you will miss out on your unique experience and the gifts that are inherent in that unique experience.

So it is important for you to give yourselves what you need during this time and during these experiences that you are having. We are not advocating that you look for a quick fix, such as a drug or alcohol, or something else that will soothe you and put you into a more balanced state of energy. Because you will only be delaying the process that you signed up for.

So when you are having these experiences of either extreme tiredness or extreme elation and energy, ask yourselves, 'What is the gift that this is giving me? How am I being served by having this particular experience?' Because we can assure you that this is not just a random selection that you have made. You have chosen one or the other because you wanted to have the benefits of that extra energy or that extra time resting or sleeping or meditating.

So let yourselves off the hook, be good to yourselves, and do not medicate yourselves out of this experience. You want to be in your bodies and to have these experiences while in your bodies. And that is why it is so necessary for you to give in and relax and accept whatever experience you are having with energy. And also, know this: once you accept where you are and what you are experiencing, you will be able to access more energy or direct the energy that you are receiving and use it in a positive way.

We encourage you, always, to realize that you are the creator of your experience and not a victim. So even though it seems like something is happening to you or to your body, it is you who has chosen this experience and it is you who can rewrite the script. So give yourselves permission to access energy when you need it, to flow energy towards what you want to flow it towards, and to create the reality that you want to experience with the energy that you receive.

Also, recognize that, again, you do not have to do anything here to make this process happen. This process is happening, and you get to decide how you experience it."

___

A LIGHTER APPROACH TO YOUR ASCENSION

∞

THE CREATORS

"Being the high-frequency energy that we are is something that comes quite naturally to us, and we do not work to maintain this frequency. We do not need to participate in any sort of ritual or activity to be at the frequency that we hold every moment of our current existence. We give you this not to brag or boast or make anyone feel less than what we are. But rather, we want to assure you that the process that you are undergoing is a natural one. It does not require you to work at it. It is not something that you must suffer for or spend hours and hours every day practicing.

That is the old way. That is how you have been operating on your world for quite some time. You talk about the 'fruits of your labors,' and you honor those who work very hard to support themselves and their families. You see it as a great accomplishment when someone stays in the same job for fifty or sixty years. This is not how we want you to look at your ascension process. So even though you experience the darker emotions and even though you find yourselves in challenging situations, we are not advocating that you go looking for trouble or that you think that you must be so vigilant about keeping your vibrations high so that you can earn your way into the fifth dimension.

We do not see your ascension in that way, and we encourage you to take a much lighter approach to what it is that is well underway in your reality. You have at your core a frequency that is emitted automatically, without struggle, without effort, without anyone sending fuel or having to pump anything away. It is something that simply is. And that energy is increasing now because in order for you to let go of lower frequency systems, ideas, behaviors, thoughts, beliefs, and so on, you must be willing to have this higher frequency experience that is incompatible with those lower frequency pieces of information.

So by allowing that light to shine brighter, you may find that certain things are falling by the wayside in your life. You may not be able to maintain certain ideas, or continue behaving in certain ways because that light is shining brighter. So what makes the process difficult is resistance to your own light. It is a fear that you have that if you were to allow yourselves to be the bright and beautiful beings that you are, that someone might crucify you, strike you down, or at least not want to be around you anymore. And we understand where you get these ideas, because this has happened.

Because there have been times when you have used your power and have been punished for it and there have been times when you have used your power in an abusive way. And so we just want you to know that you have already decided that you are not going to do that this time around. And so, let your light shine. Do not think that it is something that you need to do or facilitate, but allow it to be, and notice that everything around you is shifting because of it. It is not your job to hold on to anything, and it is not your job to be the one who amplifies your light. You simply are here to experience this wonderful process that happens automatically."

INNER STRENGTH

∞

THE CREATORS

"Before you can become that which you are ascending into, you may have some experiences that you would rather not have. However, you will find that there is a certain necessity for you to create scenarios for yourselves that will get you in touch with very specific stored emotions. These may not look like the emotions that you are accustomed to feeling. They may have an intensity to them that is unknown to you.

But they will not be just for the sake of your suffering. They will be experiences that you have decided to take on because you wanted to be of service and because you wanted to have a full spectrum of emotions and experiences, so that you would be able to hold a level of compassion for your fellow beings that you have been unable to access up until now.

So you see there are very specific experiences that you simply signed up for in this lifetime, and if you are willing to accept that, and if you are willing to experience whatever comes your way without resistance and without self-judgment, you will feel a cleansing of yourself through the experience. You will know yourselves as lighter beings because you will have let go of the stored traumas that are inactive currently but still running beneath the surface.

We tell you this not to scare you, not to put you on high alert, and not to create within you the expectation that you have a hard road ahead of you. We just want you to understand that when you find yourselves in the midst of a very challenging situation in your lives, and you find yourselves at your knees, crumbling and in a pile on the floor, that you have not done something wrong to put yourself in that place. You are not being punished because you were bad in another lifetime. And you are certainly not being tested by the Almighty.

Instead, you have decided from the broader perspective that you really are, that you wanted to show yourselves your strength and you wanted to know yourselves as powerful beings who could take on extreme challenges and know yourselves as the creators of those experiences. Nothing is ever your fault, but everything is your creation. And the sooner you accept your lives as your creations and your emotions as yours to feel, the sooner you can get on to a time when everything that you create will be from your current conscious self, and everything that you feel will be a choice that you make in the moment.

And when you get to that place, you will look back at this time and you will appreciate what it was that you decided to put yourselves through, because having had those experiences you will most certainly be able to choose for your highest good and you will also be much more compassionate to your fellow beings, no matter what it is that they are deciding to create."

WISDOM THAT RESIDES WITHIN YOU

∞

THE CREATORS

"When you discover that you contain within you information that you can use to guide yourselves and to serve others, then it would be of benefit to you to look within for your answers, for your guidance, for anything that you seek. It can all be found within you. You are like giant storage devices with trillions of cells, each of which contain their own history, their own unique information. And this information pertains to not only you, not only your genetic line, but also all of the other beings who have ever been incarnate on this planet.

It will be so beneficial for you to discover that when you desire to know something, you instantaneously know it and that you do not really need to seek information from other sources. However, if that is something that you want to do, if that is something that you desire in your life, then by all means look for other perspectives. That can be a fun endeavor, but you are a self-contained, self-sustaining unit. So there cannot possibly be something that would exist outside of you that would be of more benefit to you than the guidance that exists within you.

So we are advocating that you decide that you are the ones who are your best guides and that you give yourself permission to crack your own codes, to enlighten yourselves, and to access everything that you need to access to live happily ever after. There is no better source of information than the being that is desiring that information. Because, you see, the question and the answer are like two sides of the same coin. And so, of course, if you have one side of the coin, you must have the other side as well.

Now, take into consideration the fact that you are the one who is living your life, and you are the one who has had all of the experiences that you have had. So your perspective on your life must contain more information than anyone else's perspective on it. It simply can be no other way. You may be in denial, and that may prevent you from knowing something or seeing something from the perspective of another. And you can always tell what you are in most denial about by what really stirs you up, what causes you to constrict yourself and to access resistance.

Whenever you find yourself in that state, ask yourself if you are in denial about whatever it is that is before you, whatever it is your are hearing. And above all else, be willing to trust yourselves, to know that if you are getting something, that even though it is coming from you, it is still what you are getting. There is nothing random about anything that you receive, or that you experience, or that you come across in this lifetime. Not a single moment of it is unplanned and un-orchestrated.

So whatever you receive, it is well worth your while to give it as much credence as you would if it were coming from Source Itself."

THE HEALING ENERGY OF THE EARTH

∞

THE CREATORS

"So many have been in the creation of this world where you find yourselves now. There have been very many intentions placed into your world and many intentions held for your world. But now is the time for you to take stewardship of your planet, to claim this beautiful being called 'Earth' as your own. We want you to experience what it is like to be on your home turf, in your own neck of the woods. And we want you to link up with this beautiful ball of energy so that you can experience that connectedness that she is making available to you.

So we are extending the invitation from Earth to you to strengthen your connection and to be the indigenous inhabitants that you have always wanted to be but never actually were. This has been a process, an unfoldment, and you have been in an arc of experience with this world. You are learning how to cohabitate, how to get along, how to utilize her resources with respect.

We encourage you to create a relationship with your planet, if you have not already, to speak to her, to treat her as you would a member of your family, and to give her your love and appreciation, as you would any being who gave so much to you unconditionally. It will benefit you greatly to see this being that you exist on as a conscious, sentient life form that has thoughts and emotions, just like you.

You are mixing it up with Earth's energies, and there is so much for you to glean from what it is that she has to offer. And we are speaking less from the standpoint of her resources and more from the standpoint of her knowingness, her wisdom, and the healing energy that she is always providing to you. She wants you to cohabitate with her harmoniously. She sees this experience with you as a beautiful opportunity, and she wants you to know that she loves you very much. She has no hard feelings about the pollution and the wars and the misuse of her resources.

She simply wants to clear the slate and to begin anew with all of you who are sharing so much with her. So recognize that you may not be from this Earth, but you are of this Earth. And you have a unique opportunity now to claim her as your own, to develop a partnership and to live harmoniously once and for all with the biggest and closest source of unconditional love that you will ever find in physical form."

THE POWER OF CLEAR INTENTIONS

∞

THE CREATORS

"The intention that you hold is so significant that we cannot overstate its importance. We want you to consider your intentions before entering into any sort of arrangement, before you decide to take any action, before you consider even having a conversation with another person. The intention will speak volumes. It will carry the frequency of whatever it is that you are participating in.

When you infuse things with an intention, that intention is felt by those who experience what it is you have created. Your intention also will give you a window to your personality, to what it is that you desire, and what it is that you fear. And therefore knowing your own intentions is far more important than deciphering what someone else's intentions are. Because you can always be the one who is intending to hold the space of love, and compassion, and service.

And when you are making your intentions be for the greatest and highest good of all in the collective, well then you are tapping into an even bigger source of power and energy. Because the more people that are involved, the more of a momentum is gained and the more energy is pulled forth from the higher realms.

We want you to be clear about your intentions so that you know exactly what it is that you are striving for. Think about your overall intentions for this lifetime and think about the intentions that you hold for each day, each interaction, each project. When you do this you are putting that intention into all of those things, and that can drive the direction and will be felt by everyone else who is participating and experiencing it.

So be very, very aware of the intentions before you go into anything that you might wish to participate in. And also be aware of your overall intentions, for they will serve you in getting to the core of what it is that you are all about. It is our intention to guide you and to support you, and we appreciate that you are even listening to us. So we appreciate your intention to receive that which we have to offer. And we love you unconditionally, without needing to know what your intentions are."

THE ILLUSION OF TIME

∞

THE CREATORS

"Letting go of the illusion of time can be one of your biggest challenges in this life. You are constantly being reminded of what time it is. You have clocks on your phones, on your computers, in your cars, even on your wrists. There are so many reminders that are there to let you know just what time it is, and many of you give so much of your power away to the clocks and to the calendars and to the days of the week.

Think about how you feel about the day Saturday, the day Sunday, the day Monday, and so on. You have all but decided what those days are all about for you, and therefore, you slip right into a certain frequency when you even think about particular days of the week. The clock also has an effect upon you. Certain things are more appropriate, given the time of day, by your standards.

There are times for this and times for that. Even what you eat is in large part dictated by the clocks. So we want to free you from this illusion of time and let you know that all you ever have is now. The only time that ever matters is now. And where we want you to place your attention is now. When you shift your focus to how much time you have left before such and such happens or when you must be somewhere, you put yourselves into a sort of constricted and contracted state of being.

We want you to give yourselves a break from the enslavement of the clocks, and we want you to ask yourselves more frequently: 'What is it that I feel like right now?' 'What is it that I feel like doing right now?' 'Where is it that I feel like going right now?' 'What is it that I feel like eating right now?' 'Do I feel like sleeping right now?' We even want you to let go of the idea that you must sleep at night for eight hours. All of this keeps you in the compartmentalized, pigeon-holed states of being and states of creating that you have found yourselves in for eons and eons of what you call time. We want you to awaken to the now moment and the power that you have over what you think of as the ticking clock.

We even want you to let go of the concepts that you associate with certain ages. And when you let go of this idea that such-and-such is an appropriate thing for me to do at this time, on this day, and given my age, you will find that you can bend time, you can travel in time, you can completely let go of any sort of enslavement you have previously bought into regarding time.

Now, when you set this intention for yourselves, please keep the rest of the collective in mind as well, for you want everyone else to release their attachment and enslavement to the clocks. You want everyone to be on the same page and the same frequency with you, because you still want to connect with others. So there will be occasions where you will want to meet up with a friend at a particular time. And we want you to make that meeting a vibrational one first so that you are not so attached to getting there at a particular time. And instead, you are both seeking to arrive at the same frequency. And when you do this, you cannot miss a single appointment."

INTERACTING WITH OTHERS ON THE PLANET

∞

THE CREATORS

"The ones who are in your life at this time have a unique relationship to you. Because you are in the midst of a shift in consciousness, everyone who you have chosen to surround yourselves with at this time is someone with whom you have many, many past incarnational experiences. You have been related to these people in many different ways, and you have done many different things together.

You would not be doing this with mere acquaintances. So no matter what the connection is in this incarnation, we can assure you that it has been that you and the others were operating in as many different ways as you can imagine.

So look around yourself, and ask yourself what type of connection you feel with the others who are in your lives. You may have a certain type of relationship in this lifetime at this time. But the feeling that you may have when you are with this person, or when you consider this person, may be quite different from the relationship that you have now would suggest.

So allow yourselves to explore those connections, and more importantly, to access those feelings that you take on and that you access when you are with these other beings and when you are thinking about them. Many times what you are feeling in the now moment has many different layers and much depth to it that the current moment would not be able to account for.

So open yourselves up to more information regarding the connections that you have with the beings who are currently your co-workers, friends, neighbors, relatives, lovers, bosses, and so on. Because in those connections you will find what you need to in order for you to really access that which is still there within your energetic field, waiting to bubble to the surface, waiting to be cleared, waiting to be sent home to the light, to your Oversouls.

We witness you in so many of your interactions with others in a state of bewilderment and confusion, because what you experience does not make any sense to your logical minds. So really use these connections as opportunities to open your hearts up to more than what you can perceive, more than what you can understand. And when you do this, everything that you feel will lead you to something that you need, something that will benefit you, and something that will help the current relationship that you are in.

Do this one being at a time, and give yourselves much more than you are currently accessing. This process can be fun, it can be interesting, and it very well must lead you to a greater understanding of yourselves and your connections with others."

YOU ARE PERFECT JUST AS YOU ARE
∞
THE CREATORS

"From where you are now, there is very little that you could do to mess this up. You have made it so far along this journey that it really is up to you how you want to proceed. But you have all made it through the most difficult part of the journey and you are starting to see the light at the end of the tunnel.

This is a very important thing for you all to acknowledge for yourselves and to yourselves. This nearing that you are to the complete vibrational shift in consciousness is something that you must be able to sense within you, because we cannot give you a date and because there are no news reports telling you what the countdown to 5D is. So this is something that you must be able to reach for within yourselves and feel the vibrational truth of it. It would be to your benefit to let go of all of your notions about what it is that is required of you to be a fifth-dimensional being, what it is you must achieve, or how you must be holding your vibration at all times.

You would be better served by acknowledging yourselves and by focusing on all of the achievements that you have made so far. Think about the person that you are now, as opposed to five, ten, or twenty years ago. And allow yourselves to get excited about the shift, because we want you to understand that this is not something that you all must earn. It is part of the journey that you are on. It always has been. You are aligned with this shift. That is why you are making it. It is not because you are good and others are bad or that you are enlightened and they are asleep. It is because this is a part of the overall journey of your consciousness, and for you to be right where you are required you to step through some pretty unsavory corridors.

You had to be willing to look at aspects of yourself, aspects of the world that you live in that are not so easy for you to swallow or to accept or to love unconditionally. So in order for you to be here, you have volunteered to take on some of those programs, some of those beliefs, and some of those experiences that you have now found yourselves on the other end of and recognizing the illusion of all of them.

Instead, you are able to see that this version of you right now is equipped with everything that you need. You know that you are complete just as you are. You know that there is no end to your consciousness and to your knowing of yourselves as individuals. You know that there is no right and no wrong and that all of this is just a game that you decided that you wanted to play.

We also want to encourage you to remember that you are still creating every little bit of this experience, and you can have whatever experience of the shift that you desire to have. So you can have a very fun and playful journey down the next portion of your path, or you can struggle and claw and resist every inch along the way. So we are granting you permission now to let go of all of the seriousness that you have ever bought into about this process and to grant yourselves the freedom to have whatever experience of the rest of the ride that you want to have."

ENJOY THE NOW MOMENT

∞

THE CREATORS

"Start with the knowledge that you have already done everything that you could possibly do, up until this point in your lives, to give yourselves the experiences that you wanted to have. You are not lazy. You are not missing something that you need in order to manifest that which you want to experience. You are all doing the best that you can. And that is something that most of you do not necessarily buy into when it comes to your manifestation and creation processes.

Some of you think that there is more action that could have been taken to get you to where you ultimately want to go, and some of you that there is more energy that you could have put out in the form of thoughts, or emotions, or vibrations, or frequencies. But none of that really matters anyway, because you wanted to find yourselves exactly in the positions where you are today. So no mistakes have ever been made by you. You were always on this path that you are on.

Now, you can choose to be happy about where you are and to shine your light as bright as you possibly can, or you can choose to be despondent and down and to isolate yourselves because you feel so much shame about some aspect of what you are living or how you are living. That choice is yours right now, and we want to encourage you to let go of all of your plans and goals that you had for yourselves and to give yourselves the freedom to enjoy this moment as it is, because there is no other moment that is exactly like this one. It is unique and special and was created just for you to experience. So you might as well benefit from all of that.

It is still possible, of course, for you to manifest all that you seek to experience. There is nothing that is out of reach for you. There are no opportunities that have been missed or lost. Everything is still on the table as far as your life is concerned, because you are always in the driver's seat. You are always the one who gets to decide what it is you want to experience next. And whether or not you get to experience that exact idea that you had, you are still the one who is deciding what it is that you want and how it is that you are going to experience what already is.

So even if you cannot see evidence of that which you are seeking and that which you have sought, that does not mean that it does not exist in this reality. You are everything and everything is in you, so you could not possibly be separate from anyone or anything or any experience. But you can give yourself the experience that you are separate, or that you have missed out, or that something is missing from your lives. So that is what you are creating when you lament all of the things that you never did or haven't done or all of the things that you never had, people that you never met in your lives. And we want to open you up to the knowledge that you have everything that you need right now. It all exists within you, and the sooner you look for it there, the sooner you will see it outside of yourselves. Please do not misunderstand us. We are telling you that you are creator beings and that you are right now and right here able to create the experience of your lives that you seek, as soon as you let yourselves off the hook for what you did or did not do to be right where you are."

SEE THE BEAUTY IN EVERY EXPERIENCE

∞

THE CREATORS

"Something is stopping you from living the lives that you want to live. We know that you are not completely satisfied with your lives as they are, and we want you to know that we are on top of all of those desires that you hold. So we can see that you are reaching out for more than your are currently experiencing, and we also know that you feel that there is something that is blocking you from living that life that you desire to live. And we also want to assure you that whatever the obstacle is that is between you and your desired life experience, you have placed the obstacle there because you wanted to have a certain experience.

You did not want to incarnate and then find yourselves at the finish line, so that all you had to do was lean slightly forward and you would be at your final destinations. That is not what you wanted. So of course, you put a racetrack or a route or a trail between yourselves and the finish lines. And you did so with crafty precision. So you are not only the creators of your paths, but you are also the creators of the obstacles that you find along the way. As long as you are convinced that someone else or something else outside of you has created your obstacles and has placed them very strategically in between you and the lives that you want to live, then you could not possibly gain what you wanted to gain from the experience of the obstacles.

So step one is to recognize that you are the creators of the obstacles that you see or that you perceive that are in front of you. The next step would be to appreciate what a fine job you did of creating that obstacle and of placing it where you did in the exact timing that you did. And then the next step would be to look for the gifts that the obstacle is there to give you. And sometimes you may not be able to see the gifts if you are looking at the obstacle itself. Sometimes you may have to look around at where you are to see what gifts are there.

And as you make it your primary objective to look for gifts where you are, rather than to just chisel away at the obstacle so that you can get to all of the good stuff that you placed at the other side of it, you will benefit greatly. You will have so much more fun, you will recognize that there is so much more to your life than simply getting to where you want to go. And you will see all that is within your blind spots at this time, because you will take your sights off of the obstacles and the desires, and when you do so, you will see so much more that is there to delight you and to let you know just how powerful and wonderful and enlightened you are.

So make peace with the obstacles, love the obstacles, cherish the moment where you are right now and notice that without the obstacles you would not be in the moment you are. This is meant to get you into the appreciation of the moment where you are right now. And so it is your best possible next step to simply relax, let go, lean up against the obstacle and check every nook and cranny for the gifts that lie all around it."

THE GIFT IN SURRENDER

∞

THE CREATORS

"Sometimes you just have to give in. When you find yourselves in situations where there is no more fighting that can be done, there is nothing more that struggle can accomplish, you are left with no choice but to surrender, to give in. We want you to realize that this is not you giving up on anything. Giving in is surrendering to the flow of your life, and that is so much more of a productive endeavor than to continue to resist something that keeps showing up and showing up.

Because when you are in that state of surrender to the flow, you have all of the power of the current at your side, and you can begin to use some of that power to modify your existence and your circumstances to fit that which you do desire. Remember that there is nothing here that is outside of you. So anything that you are in resistance to, you are actually pushing against something that is within you, something that is you. And that sort of strategy for life will only get you into more situations where you find that there is something that you need to push against, that you need to resist.

And we know that you don't really want to be in that place. So what surrender does for you is it gives you back that part of yourself that you have been struggling so hard to avoid or to smother or to deny the existence of. All that does is make you a smaller and weaker person. You are then buying into the idea of separation, the idea that you are not whole just as you are and that this universe is somehow working against you. Nothing could be further from the truth.

So when do you know that it is time to give up the struggle and give in to the flow? Well, you can tell when you have no other options but to do so. That is one way of knowing. You can tell by what it is that you are feeling in the moment. If the feeling of surrender brings you relief, then that is definitely the way to go in the moment. We are not asking you to be doormats or to give up all of your own desires or your sense of individuality.

But what we are saying to you is that there is setting a boundary and then there is fighting against. And you need to be able to discern the difference between those two, because you will find yourselves in situations where you would benefit from saying no to someone, for instance. And when you can see it that way, when you can see it as something that is created by you to give yourself that feeling of alignment with your own path in life, when you can see it as something that is for your highest good, that is when you know that it is appropriate for you to say no.

But when you can see it as something that you are only fighting against, and when it feels like it is so much bigger than you, and that you would never have even considered creating something or some scenario, that is when you know that you are in resistance, that you are shutting yourself off in some way. And that is when it is time to let go. We always give in because we understand that there is only one of us here. And when you get to that place you will know it. You will know the difference between letting yourselves be used and abused and putting up a very appropriate boundary."

A NEW PERSPECTIVE

∞

THE CREATORS

"Bringing a new perspective to something will change everything about it and about your experience of it. We want you to let go of all of your preconceived notions, of all of the beliefs that you hold that are based upon prior experiences. And we want you to give yourselves a chance to reconsider something that you had written off, or had believed was somehow inappropriate, or not right for you. It is as simple as allowing yourselves to tilt your heads slightly and see what it is you are considering from a new angle.

We mean that quite literally. If you were to be in observation of something and you were only to see one side of it, you would not have the full picture. You would only be able to take in that which was before you - the information that had presented itself to you as a result of the angle at which you were viewing it. But if you were to look from a different angle, or look at a different side, you would see something completely different.

You have the ability to do this with concepts, with individuals, with yourselves as well. You may have bought into one angle as the most important one for quite some time. You may have been told that this side is the only side worth seeing and that it is the only way in which something's value can be determined. But give yourselves a chance here to explore another perspective, another angle, another way of experiencing something that you have experienced before and are quite certain is only going to give you that one note.

Begin with yourselves. You take yourselves with you almost everywhere you go. You have a perspective of yourself. You may say to another individual, 'I am someone who always does this'; or 'I am someone who never gets the lucky draw'; 'I am someone who always forgets numbers, or addresses, or faces, or names.' Whatever it is that you are believing about yourself is simply one perspective.

Perhaps you are an individual who has forgotten people's names, and you are certain that this is a flaw. This is something that is a trait of yours that is completely unchangeable. Well, let us suppose that what you take in when you meet someone is not their name. What you take in is their vibration. You are feeling them and reading their energy without even knowing that this is what you are doing.

So you are only aware of the fact that you forget their names five seconds after you meet them. But from another perspective you take in everything that you need to know about that person, your relationship to them, whether or not you want to spend more time with them, whether or not you trust them, and so on. You take that in because that is the most important and pertinent information for you. Names are somewhat irrelevant.

So you can see now how you could apply that type of perspective-shifting to anything that you are involved with, to anyone that you are in relationship with, to any idea, any institution, any group of individuals. It is possible for you to have a brand new understanding, a brand new experience, if you give yourselves the opportunity to tilt your heads slightly."

BE THE FREQUENCY OF WHAT YOU DESIRE
∞
THE CREATORS

"Frequencies are the currency of your lives. You are offering frequencies. You are exchanging frequencies. You are surrounded by frequencies. There is no denying it. They are in fact measurable. They carry more weight and more significance than any of you know. You are able to make a frequency adjustment and to alter the reality that you experience, as well as altering yourself within the reality that you are experiencing.

Your frequency is a barometer that tells you how likely it is that something is going to happen. You can play around with your frequencies without knowing how to do it. In fact, you do this all the time without realizing it. You bump into frequencies all the time without realizing it. You take on the frequencies of others without realizing it.

But that time is over now. Now is the time that you are waking up to the frequencies that you hold, the frequencies that others hold, the frequencies that objects, rooms, entire cities hold. And when you do this, you recognize that there is so much more power in frequency than in anything that takes physical form.

There is so much to be discovered and to be explored within the realm of frequency. It is not just a tool that you use to get what you want or a way of describing how it is you feel. It is a wave of energy that contains within it the secrets of the universe, the secrets of your personality, your consciousness, your Oversoul.

You can continue to live within the realm of frequency and have a casual relationship with it. You can check in every once in a while to see what frequency you are vibrating at. Or you can paint the reality that you experience with all the colors of the frequencies that you wish to experience. You can dive right in to a frequency and feel the infinite power and size and scope of that frequency.

We ask for nothing more than that you feel the frequencies around you, that you take note of them, that you begin to define and describe the frequencies that you experience, because they are describing and defining and feeling out your essence. So you might as well return the favor. Play with them as you would your new toys on Christmas morning."

JUST BE WITH WHAT IS
∞
THE CREATORS

"When you are in the midst of something that you would rather not experience but that you have no choice, given the fact that it is right there in front of you, the best course of action for you is to let yourselves be completely with that situation.

We want you to discover that there is nothing that exists in this universe that you cannot handle. We want you to realize that. And when you are faced with something that you do not like, that does not please you, that you never would have consciously created for yourselves, what you have before you is an aspect of yourselves that you have been unwilling to look at. It may not seem that way to you, but that is what it is.

So when you are in a situation that you do not prefer, and you are looking for ways out of it, just stop, take a breath, and remember that this creation of yours is in service to you in some way. Certainly, you can all relate to the idea of growing pains. You know that sometimes in order for you to expand, you must be able to include something that is a little uncomfortable for you at the time.

But when you are able to look back at these types of sticky situations you can usually understand why you needed to create them, how you benefitted from them, and how you are so much more equipped to deal with anything that comes your way as a result of those experiences.

So you wish to know yourselves as powerful beings, as Source Energy beings, as beings of Love and Light., and the best way for you to do that is to know that everything in your reality is an aspect of yourself, a creation of yours, and is there to benefit you.

When you have that understanding, that knowing, then everything that you face, every challenge, every ordeal, will be something that you walk away from shiny and new, knowing yourself better than you ever have before and with the understanding that whatever it is that comes into your life is there to give you that experience of your power and is not there for you to simply brush aside or transcend, or make the most of a bad situation.

There are no bad situations. There are situations, and you may have a response to those situations. But that does not make them inherently good or bad. You are everything. Everything is within you. The sooner you acknowledge that and you love everything in your universe as your would your newborn child, you will be one who walks on air, who gives without question of whether or not they will receive, and you will exemplify that which is the essence of unconditional love, unconditional joy, unconditional being-ness.

We applaud you for your willingness to take on that which may seem overwhelming and may seem scary but that which is an aspect of All That Is and therefore is comprised of Love."

YOU ARE SOURCE ENERGY

∞

THE CREATORS

"By now, you understand the true nature of your being. You are aware and you are awake. And in some ways, there is nothing left to do. There is nothing that you must achieve. There is no series of steps that you must perform. We want you to give yourselves credit for having woken up in this day and age in the type of society that you live in. This information is not taught in your schools. It is not broadcast on your televisions. You are pioneers in this day and age.

To know yourselves as Source Energy is a pretty big accomplishment, and you deserve to celebrate yourselves for having made that realization in this lifetime. And so what else is there for you to do, now that you have this information? Well, for one, you can begin to enjoy yourselves. You can let go of all of your attachments. You can sit quietly and listen. You can enjoy a sunset. You can stare at a puffy cloud. You can breathe the air. You can dance and you can sing. And you can forget anything and everything that may look like a trouble, a problem, or something that you need to worry about.

Because as Source Energy beings, you recognize that everything is. That is all. You are everything and everything is. It's not good. It's not bad. It just is. So, have the experience of your life that you choose to have. Know that you don't need to hasten your expansion or your ascension, or your evolution. These things are automatic. It is built in to your structure. You don't need to worry about being left behind in this process. In fact, you are the leaders of it.

So the best thing that you can do now that you know yourselves as Source is to live like you know yourselves as Source. It is that easy. Be aware. Be awake. Be one with your environment, and everything else will truly take care of itself. We want you to relax, enjoy, be at peace, and love like you have no shortage at all of that frequency."

EXPRESS ALL OF YOU, UNAPOLOGETICALLY

∞

THE CREATORS

"Bring forth the most spectacular concept that you have of yourself, and do not allow yourself to be censored in any way. Simply charge forth with your most delicious and beautiful traits and abilities. Give yourself the full experience of your Self. Let yourself be the wondrous creation that you were always created to be.

There is no virtue in false humility. There is no reason for you to hide your light. Let yourself burst forth now from the shell, from behind the veil, from the cocoons that you have placed around yourselves.

Now is the time for full on self-expression and celebration of who it is you are at the core essence of your being. This is not about your ego. This is not about hubris. And this is certainly not about being out of control. So do not worry that you are going to fall into one of those traps.

We simply ask that you allow yourselves the fullest and brightest expressions of yourselves without apologies, without holding back anything because you are afraid perhaps of being criticized or perhaps of outshining another. This is not a contest. This is a journey of self-discovery, and the only way for you to truly discover yourself is to let yourself out fully.

We encourage you to do this now because we see so many of you holding back, holding judgment, allowing yourselves to be afraid of what might happen if you were to take that next step, to put yourselves out there in the spotlight. You must realize that at this time, no one is going to be crucified for shining their light.

And you also must recognize that those who do shine their lights have their detractors. There is no one who is putting forth their full expression who is not met with some resistance. And that is okay. And that resistance is there for you to love and accept as an aspect of yourself, not as a force outside of yourself that has power over you.

Begin the process of coming out from the shadows, from the darkness that is self-imposed and that is there solely for the purpose of giving you something to bounce off of. And allow yourselves to have your day in the sun, showing the fruits of all of the work that you have been doing on yourselves.

And let others enjoy the experience of your self-unveiling so that they too may be inspired to let their guards down and to be the fullest expressions of Source Energy that they truly are. And even though it may look like you are simply wanting to celebrate yourselves and your Divinity, you will be in fact giving others permission to access their own."

YOU ARE A BEING OF DIVINE LOVE & LIGHT

∞

THE CREATORS

"Start out with the assumption that you are a being of Divine Love and Light. Then proceed from there. This assumption can be made no matter what the situation you are faced with. It is not something to pull out of your bag of tricks only when you feel that it is absolutely necessary to operate with that understanding.

Instead, this is the basis of everything. And when you recognize this and proceed with that understanding in your conscious awareness, you are able to navigate your life with far more dexterity and with much more pleasing results. You have all of Source Energy at your disposal. Yet most of you are not tapping into that reservoir of knowledge and energy and love.

So we are encouraging you to set the frequency for all of your dealings and all of your interactions and all of your challenges at the Source Energy vibration, to pull yourselves out of the third dimensional understanding of self and to take on the thirteenth dimensional understanding of self while you make your way through this journey.

You have also at your disposal everything that humanity has ever done, has ever thought, has ever felt. You have the collective consciousness of humankind to work with. So when you are faced with one of your challenges, when you are feeling yourself in a pit of despair, when you are in the midst of a conflict with another, open yourselves to that knowing. Believe that it is possible for you to tap into resources that heretofore you have not even acknowledged exist.

When you operate as a third-dimensional, separate, ego-based, mind-oriented being, then of course there is only so much you can do. But when you let go of that understanding of self and you let in the unlimited, the eternal, the infinite, the all-knowing, then everything that is before you seems much more manageable, and in fact you can see it all as a gift that you have given yourselves for the purpose of having a new experience."

A SENSE OF WHO YOU ARE BECOMING

∞

THE CREATORS

"What the process for ascension really is about is the complete and total deconstruction of who it is that you have always considered yourselves to be. It is a tearing down, so to speak, of the structures that are in place and not all of those structures are external.

The creation of the new you is of paramount importance in this process, because you don't want to be torn down and have nothing left to go on with. You want to have a sense of who it is you are becoming before the old version of you can be set aside, put out to pasture, and so on.

The way that you do this is by being more deliberate about who it is that you are deciding to be in each and every moment. It is about letting go of the patterns that you have been using to define yourselves for so long, and instead, allowing yourselves to blossom into beautiful beings of love, light and joy who know themselves as Source Energy and who operate within a collective as a part of that collective.

We are witnessing you now, and many of you are in the process of tearing down, and many more of you are in the process of deciding who it is that you want to be. Relax. Don't assume that you are going to be left standing amongst the rubble, with no sense of identity. You will always know yourselves as yourselves. But you do want to be aware of what it is that you are choosing to be, how it is you choose to interact with your world, and which actions that you are really wanting to take.

It is high time for you now to set aside any ideas that you have of living out the same old life that you have lived for so many lifetimes and really allow yourselves the freedom to playfully participate in this shift in consciousness, recognizing your part in it, and relishing the opportunity to create yourselves as the versions of Source Energy that you have always desired to be."

YOU HAVE THE POWER TO CHOOSE
YOUR CURRENT REALITY

∞

THE CREATORS

"So, there are some instances in your lives where you feel that you have no choice, no say, no input whatsoever. And we want you to understand that this can never be the case. You are never being put in a position where you are subjected to certain circumstances, certain people, or certain conditions in your life. It is always you who has chosen what you have in front of you. And from the place where you are now you are choosing again.

So when you find yourselves pretending that you have no choice but to suck it up and remain in the situation that you have created for yourselves, we want you to laugh at that idea. It is preposterous that you would have put yourselves in a situation where there is no choice. However, your choices may not be the choices that you would prefer. You may not be able to, for instance, instantly access the choice that is your first preference. But there is always a choice.

We are not saying to you that whatever is before you is there for you to resist either. So the first choice that you have is the choice of whether you accept or resist the circumstance that you find yourself in. Then you have a choice as to whether or not you are going to look for anything at all within the circumstance that you can work with, that you can find satisfaction from, that you have the ability to appreciate.

And then, of course, you have the choice as to whether or not you are going to place the majority of your attention and focus on the situation that you are finding uncomfortable or unsatisfying in some way. You have the ability to create now in bigger and faster ways than you have previously.

So if you find yourself in a situation that you have been in before and that you could not find your way out of, we don't want you to think of that as a learning experience for yourself. But rather, it was an experience. And now, even though you find yourself in a similar circumstance, you can create something else for yourself.

You don't have to change the circumstance. You don't have to make anyone else do something different. You simply must own the responsibility for having created it so that you can realize your true power to create again, to create anew, to create something different.

We ask you to see your life as always in a state of constant creation and re-creation so that you recognize what is actually happening and you take conscious control of the creative process. Begin with something small that you wish to create, and use the energy of your heart to pulse out the frequency of that creation so that you can see for yourselves exactly how powerful you are."

HAVE FAITH AND BELIEVE IN YOURSELF

∞

THE CREATORS

"Believing in yourself is far more important than believing in us. It is even more important than believing in that which you would call 'God.' It is so important for leading a life where you can exist harmoniously and where you can create that which you desire. Believing in oneself is more important than believing in the concepts that we teach because, ultimately, you are the one who will be applying those concepts. And if you do not believe in yourself then you do not believe that the concepts will work. They may work for others, but you will believe that they will not work for you. So we want to stress the importance of your belief in yourself.

You do believe that you exist. You do understand that you are conscious. So how do you get to a place where you believe that you are capable, that you have the ability to live the life that you want to live, to do what you want to do, to explore your world with confidence? The way to believing in yourself is to allow yourself to do so. The only thing that ever stops you from believing in yourself is a thought. If you were never to consider the idea that you were somehow not valuable or that you were in some way incapable of doing something, then you never would doubt that you could have the life that you wanted.

So this is really about clearing away those feelings that you have, that you have been holding onto for a very long time. And the way to do that is first to notice when you are doing it. Notice yourself in a moment of not believing in yourself. Notice how you feel when you are in that place. Then notice that you are the one who is noticing, and when you do that, you can fully believe that you are capable. Because if you are capable of noticing yourself doing something to doubt your abilities, then you must be able to believe in yourself as well.

So simply smile in those moments when you notice yourself having a thought, experiencing doubt, and send those feelings and those thoughts on their way. Be kind and gentle with them, but think of them as like toys that you used to play with when you were much, much younger but that you have no interest in now, because that's truly all they were. They were something that you outgrew and that you no longer need and that no longer serve you as the person, as the being, that you are today. So the simple act of letting go, that is how you can come to believe in yourself, and we support you in that wholeheartedly."

Chapter Two

∞

Ophelia the Faerie

YOUR RELATIONSHIP TO MONEY
∞
OPHELIA THE FAERIE

"I am here. I am with you. I have seen so much evidence that you are all progressing nicely, and I want to give you my appreciation for the work that you are doing. I also want to share with you my insights. I want to give you my perspective, and I want to offer you my assistance.

What I have noticed in many of you is a sense of fear or foreboding around the topic of your finances. Many of you believe that you are never going to 'make it,' you are never going to get out of debt, or you are never going to have enough. But what you really fear, when you are noticing that you do not have enough for all the things that you require or desire, is your own mortality.

Your relationship with money is very much like your relationship with your sense of your own energy. If you feel that the amount of money that you have access to is finite, it is because you believe that you are finite. Your relationship with money is very closely tied to your relationship with time, because you have due dates for payments, and rent, and mortgages, tuitions, credit card bills, and so on.

If you had more time, then you would have the money. That is how many of you feel. And when it comes to your death, you all wonder if you will have enough money when you are nearing that phase of transition. So you see, it is a very tangled web. My suggestion to you is to begin to feel how infinite you are, how boundless and eternal you are, how timeless you are, and how much love you are.

When you place your attention on those truths and when you activate them in your core, suddenly all else becomes minuscule by comparison. The amount that is showing up on the electric bill is not so staggering in comparison to an infinite being of Love and light who has access to an infinite amount of energy. When you believe this about yourself, when you really know it to be true, you understand that you are taken care of because all of it is inside of you, created by you, put there for your own amusement.

Be willing to be amused by your financial situations, and be in awe that someone so infinite and powerful could create a scenario to allow those feelings that you have to exist. Play. Play with those feelings. Play with your money. And know your infinite nature.

I am Ophelia. I am infinite. And I love you."

PROGRAMMING WITHIN YOU

∞

OPHELIA THE FAERIE

"I am here. I am with you.

Programs that are running within you have somewhat taken on lives of their own. These programs are not meant to take over the operating system. They are there for you to use so that certain functions can happen in your life automatically, without you needing to think about them.

But when these programs have so much momentum and have been run so many times that they begin to operate without your conscious awareness of them, then it is necessary for you to do a sort of cleansing of your system. You want to start over. You want to reboot.

The way to do this is always with more present moment awareness. It is with more checking in to see what program is running in the current moment. I am certain that all of you are running programs that you accept as part of the arrangement for being on planet earth at this time, but I can assure you that there are many upgrades available for you, many downloads waiting.

And all you need to do is clear out some of the old programs, not all of them, just the ones that are keeping you living in a limited way or in a repetitive way. Before you do anything, ask yourself, 'What is the program that I am running about this? Why is it that I assume that I must do this? Or why is it that I assume that doing this will get me to where I want to go?'

Even if the assumption is that what you are about to do will be quite fulfilling, it is still worth examining why you believe that to be the case. I am not telling you to stop doing the things that you are doing. I am asking you to examine what sorts of systems you have in place that are perpetuating certain conditions in your life.

I want you to know that there is so much more available to you if you allow yourself to break from habit, routine, and all activities that are done based on old, out-of-date programs. I want you to believe me when I say that your life can be a moment-to-moment experience of joy and freedom and limitlessness. I want you to expand your conscious awareness to include programs that run on a higher frequency and that require less fuel.

Have fun exploring these different programs, and see it all as a giant game that you are playing with yourself.

I am Ophelia, and I love you."

EMBRACING IT ALL

∞

OPHELIA THE FAERIE

"I am here. I am with you.

There are no places that you can go that would be inappropriate for you to explore on your world, and there are no thoughts and no emotions that are inappropriate for you to think and feel. You are not here to become a vessel for purity and to allow only light to exist. You are here to embrace it all, to see it all as a part of you, to feel compassion and love for all parts of yourself, regardless of how ugly they may look, how awful they may feel, how inappropriate they may seem.

They are there because you want to accept and love those parts of you. They are not there for you to change. They are not there for you to brush aside or suppress. By now many of you will have discovered that facing them with love and compassion is the only way, because many of you have tried so many other ways of dealing with them. And now you have discovered that nothing else works.

Be aware of these aspects of yourselves that feel rejected and hurt, brushed aside and diminished, and love them. Know that there are no mistakes. There is nothing that should not be. There is only that which is and your response to it. So observe your responses, notice them, accept your non-acceptance. Accept your judgment, so that you can then release those and come into that place of love and compassion that is so representative of who and what you really are.

That is what is also unavoidable. You cannot help but take the unconditional love approach and perspective, because that is also who and what you are, and you will realize and know that to be true. You are all doing so well with this. Better than you realize. Because if you can accept this message, then you are well on your way to being the whole, unconditionally loving being that you were born to be.

I am Ophelia, and I love you."

LOVE YOURSELVES

∞

OPHELIA THE FAERIE

"I am here. I am with you.

You are making this journey with so many others. This a collective shift that is underway. What that means for each of you is that sharing your experiences is not only helpful to those you will share your experiences with, but it will help validate for each of you that you are on your path.

There is a tendency for all of you to compare your journeys and where you are along that path. And so at times you may feel like you are not where you are supposed to be because of an experience that someone else is having that you are not, or because of an experience you are having that others are not.

You must realize that it would not be so much fun for Source if you all had the exact same experience of this shift in consciousness. So that is why all of you are having such varied experiences of it. If you see someone else's as better than yours, as more advanced, more spiritual, then know that you are playing that game with yourself in other areas of your life as well.

Be willing to look at the way that you measure yourselves against one another, and see it mostly as an indicator that you are in need for some more self-love time. Self-love will always help you along your way and soothe you right where you are, and you are the only one who can give yourself that love.

Even if you are one of the ones who others are looking and are envious of, you are still the only one who can give that self-love to you. You will enjoy your journey so much more when you allow yourself to love yourself. Wherever you are on it, know that you are right where you wanted to be, having the experiences that are of most service to you.

And rejoice and embrace the experiences that others are having as a part of that wonderful diversity that exists within all of humanity. The piece of the puzzle that you are is as important as every other piece. Be proud of the role that you are playing in the shift, and know that even those of us in the higher realms are having our unique and diverse experiences, as we all continue along this journey together, sharing and supporting.

I am personally in awe of all of you, no matter where you are. I love you, and I invite you to love yourselves. I am Ophelia, and I do love you."

KNOWING SELF AS SOURCE

∞

OPHELIA THE FAERIE

"I am here. I am with you.

There are no exceptions to the rule – the rule that says that you are a unique and wonderful expression of Source. There are times when you do not feel this, when you cannot sense it, when you are quite certain that you are a human being of bone and flesh. Those are the times when you most need to be reminded of the rule, of the truth, of the fact that you are now, you always have been, and you always will be Source Energy Beings.

What would it take to convince you once and for all? You will be most convinced when you feel Source Energy moving through your body. I know all of you want that feeling. I know all of you have had it. But instead of identifying with the feeling and seeing yourselves as it, you identified with the body and saw Source Energy as an experience that you were having in the moment.

Be willing to let yourselves know that energy as you, as your truth, as your origin. Here is what I want you to do. Put yourself in a comfortable position, eyes closed. And I want you to summon that feeling in your body. Use your breath. Focus on your hearts. And recognize that you can amplify the feeling with your intention. Now, when you feel it, identify with it. Know it as you.

Realize that this truth of who you are is there for you whenever you want it. If you want to know God, if you want to know yourselves as God, then you must be willing to know yourselves as that feeling that ripples through you. And rather than seeing it as an experience you are having, see it as you expressing yourself as you truly are.

All of you have access to that energy. You can choose to ignore it. You can choose to ignore yourselves and your true natures, but the knowing is always there. Sometimes you cannot deny it. What I wish for all of you is that you cultivate that experience of knowing yourselves as Source by turning up the volume of who you are and identifying with it.

I am Ophelia. I am Source Energy. And I love you."

START EACH DAY IN A NEW WAY
∞
OPHELIA THE FAERIE

"I am here. I am with you.

You begin each day with a list. You usually have a list of things that you would like to accomplish when you start your day. Even eating your breakfast is one of the items on your list. It may surprise you to learn that the list that you make has some discrepancies on it from the list your higher self is making.

You are welcome to ask your higher self what items are on its list for the day. You are welcome to wonder what surprises may come. You also may want to look at the reasons behind each item on your list. Why do you want to get those things done? Why would you sacrifice spontaneity and freedom just to be able to cross that item off of your list?

What about your bigger picture list? What about the list that you have for your lifetime in this incarnation? What items are on that list and how do they match or clash with the items on your Things To Do Today list?

How wonderful would it be to have no list, to start each day as though it were an adventure, as though it were its own mini-incarnation where the only things that you will do will be the things that you feel most attracted to doing. What are those things? How often do you ask yourself, 'What is it that I really want to do today, and how does that compare to the plans I have made for this day?'

How willing are you to disappoint others? How willing are you to be irresponsible, careless, and carefree? How often do you decide that you are going to let the day take you? I want you to live more moment to moment, because I want to free you from the idea of time, the idea of linearity. I want to free you from the confines of your calendars and clocks, and I want to invite you to play in this moment as though you had not a care in the world, as though this moment was all there was, ever.

I want to invite you to un-structure your lives. I want to encourage you to live as you would if you knew that each and every moment was precious, and Divine, and Divinely orchestrated. See if you can find a moment or two in your day to approach your day in this way, in the new way. I am so excited for you all to have this experience of your life and of your world and of yourselves.

I am Ophelia, and I love you."

BE IN ALIGNMENT WITH THE ENERGY OF YOUR DESIRES

∞

OPHELIA THE FAERIE

"I am here. I am with you.

There is no reason for any of you to continue to live in the type of reality that tells you there is only so much. You have broken free from the confines of the third dimension, and now it is time for you to discover that there are no limitations on energy. It is what you are. It is all around you. There is no way for you to separate yourselves from it.

Therefore, you can let go of any notion that you have that something that you want is out there and separate from you. There is a tendency to place the object that you desire on a different plane than the one that you exist on. Therefore, you are placing it just outside your reach.

But when you accept that the energy that is creating the object is the energy that is pulsing through you, then you can more easily sync yourselves up to that which you desire. You cannot possibly be separate from it. So then what is the process of becoming that which you desire? If it is a physical object, then of course it has its own frequency, its own vibration.

But you do not have to discover what that is because it has an effect upon you, and you know what that is. You know what the feeling of it is to you. That is the most important thing for you to comprehend. If the feeling that you are having is that it is far from you, that it is unattainable, if it helps you to access the frequency of lack, then be willing to explore that. Be willing to feel what it is that you feel in relationship to the object, because what you feel in relationship to the object will create your relationship with the object in your reality.

So there is no point in denying where you are. Be with it and explore it. Get down into those feelings with the knowing that they are not you, they are not more powerful than you. They are just choices that you are making to give yourself an experience. Once you process these feelings, then you can move into the vibration of how you want to feel in relationship to the object. You want to be its equal. You want to know that you and the object are one and the same. You want to experience it.

But you want to experience it from a calm, knowing place, not from a frantic, possessive one. So know your relationship. Feel it. Become it. And then let it go. Let yourself have the experience without needing then to see an instant manifestation. Be willing to play with processes like these. They are there for you to use or not use. It is up to you.

I am Ophelia. I am your equal. And I love you."

GIVE YOURSELF PERMISSION
TO BE WHERE YOU ARE

∞

OPHELIA THE FAERIE

"I am here. I am with you.

Noticing what you are doing, what you are saying, and what you are thinking is the first step towards transforming yourself. It is important for all of you to become aware, to be the observer of your Self. When you are noticing, you can then understand how you are interpreting what you are noticing. Are you in judgment? Are you in fear? Or are you in love and in compassion?

When you notice that you are not operating from love and from compassion, your next step is to accept yourself right where you are, doing what you are doing. It is important for you to be able to be where you are, in a place of non-judgment, in a place of complete acceptance.

When you feel that you have granted yourself permission to be where you are, then your next step is to decide where you want to go. When I say, 'where you want to go,' I am talking about with your vibration. I know that so many of you are seeking to go to a new place – a new relationship, a new job, a new body, a new home. But before you get into the details of what it is you are wishing to create, make sure you lay a foundation of energy, make sure you are aware of the energy that you are seeking to be in.

It may match what you have envisioned for yourself, and it may not. But the energy is the key. Understand your motivations. It is important for you to not only know where you want to go, but to know why you want to go there. What is it that you are really seeking? Be aware that this can also lead you back to the beginning of this exercise, where you are noticing and you are needing to accept and release judgment and have some love and some compassion for yourself, right where you are.

Notice that where you want to go is often in response to where you have been. But I encourage you to dream of something even bigger, to dream of something magical, something completely illogical, unknown, something you not only have not experienced, but that you have not even been able to imagine. What does that feel like? Where is the energy in the fantastically unknown?

Where would you like to be? Would you like to find yourself in a brand new frequency range, or would you like to create some more with what you have known? That is up to you. That is your choice. I just encourage you to dream big.

I am Ophelia, and I love you."

VISUALIZE YOURSELF IN YOUR MANIFESTATIONS
∞
OPHELIA THE FAERIE

"I am here. I am with you.

You are all seeking something in your lives. Whether it be abundance, a partner, health, peace, or more spiritual experiences, there is something that is calling all of you, that is moving all of you forward.

I want you to imagine yourselves now already there. Put yourself in the center of the sphere. Recognize that what you are seeking exists as a point on the sphere that is as accessible to you now as the next moment that you were anticipating. Now, find the point. Find it vibrationally. Find it because you know it, because you are it, and trust that the point you have found is the point that you are really seeking.

Now, hold your frequency. Remain in that state of being of what it is you are seeking. I want you to feel it not just now and not just when you do this exercise. But I want you to feel it in such a way that you incorporate it into your cells. I want you to become it, and I want you to know that once you become it you cannot un-become it. It is part of you. It is your birthright. That's why you seek it. That's why yours is different than your friend's, your neighbor's, your brother's, your sister's.

Now, take what you have received, carry it with you, access it when you need it. Access it when you are feeling lonely, scared about your finances, concerned about your health and well-being, discouraged that you are not having more spiritual experiences. It is there now always, for you, because it is a part of you.

That which you seek is a part of you. Now, what you may find is that what shows up for you does not look like anything that you have ever imagined. Accept it. Accept whatever creation comes. As you accept, you allow. You will allow more that is like it.

If you are seeking a romantic relationship with a partner who will stay with you for the rest of your life, and instead you get a friend, accept the friendship. If you say you need ten thousand dollars, and you get a check in the mail for ten dollars, accept it.

Practice this feeling. I want you all to find that which you are seeking, and I want you all to discover more about yourselves in the process. I want you to become that which you seek, because only then will you know yourselves as the whole beings that you really are. And when you become, when you acknowledge that you are whole, suddenly everything falls in your lap.

I am Ophelia, and I love you."

HAVE FUN WITH YOUR PERSONAL GROWTH

∞

OPHELIA THE FAERIE

"I am here. I am with you.

You are elevating your frequencies now, not because you must do so, but because it is a natural progression. It is as natural as the growth of your physical bodies from being infants to being adults. There is a tendency in all of you to think that you must make the growth happen. And to a certain extent this is correct because if you do not feed a body what it needs, then certainly it will have a more challenging time growing.

And so give yourself what you need, but know that you do not have to create the growth experience for yourself. It is built in to your DNA. So my suggestion to all of you is to have more fun in your growth experiences.

As soon as you stop trying to make something happen, that is usually when it happens. When couples give up on conceiving a child and go to the adoption agency, that is usually when the conception occurs. When you give up on trying to find something that you have misplaced, that is usually when it appears.

But I am not telling you to give up here, because once again your growth, your expansion, your evolution, your ascension, is a foregone conclusion. But what I am telling you is that if you believe that you need to do a certain amount of work every day to stay on track or to hasten this process, then you are missing out on the fun. Follow your bliss, follow your interests, listen to your impulses. Remove the program that keeps telling you that there's something more that you must do.

You are all Source Energy Beings, and you never cease to be that. So you cannot mess this up. Ask yourself before you do that thing that you think you need to do whether you really want to do it in this moment or whether you are just trying to be a 'good little new ager.'

There are value judgments being placed on different activities by even those of you who are awakened. And as you do this, then you apply pressure on yourselves to do the things that are very high on your list of what is 'appropriate' and what is 'spiritual.'

If you want to watch the Super Bowl, watch the Super Bowl. If you want to watch the Academy Awards, watch the Academy Awards. There is plenty of time for yoga and breath work and meditation, and you will find the time when it is appropriate for you. Be in balance. Be a part of your world – your whole world. For it is you and you are it, and it is beautiful. So please enjoy it all.

I am Ophelia, and I love you."

LET GO OF THE OLD STORY

∞

OPHELIA THE FAERIE

"I am here. I am with you.

Taking into account everything that has ever occurred in your life and taking stock of where you are now does not begin to tell the story of you. You are so much bigger than the stories you tell about yourselves. Your history is so much broader than you could even comprehend. Your lineage goes far beyond the human experience, and even your galactic ones.

But even if you were to remember everything – all the lifetimes, all the incarnations, you would have but a fraction of your story. Why would you ever cling to one story in this one incarnation and let it define you? Why would you ever want to give so much power to one event, one moment, one relationship?

These stories keep you stuck in a loop. All you need to do to break out of your loop and from your stories is to realize that nothing, not one thing, can have more power over you in this moment than you as the creator, as the Divine Light who seeks new experience.

Your desire to move forward is what keeps you incarnate. You do not have to follow a plan. You are not here on some mission that you decided on long ago. And you are certainly not here to live one story and then to repeat the vibrational signature of that story over and over.

I know how challenging it can be for all of you to simply let go of a story that seems to have a momentum and that seems to remind you of it. Therefore, just as I would not recommend that you continue to tell your story or continue to dwell upon your story, I would also encourage you to make peace. Make peace with it all. If you see your story, your past as being so horrific that all you can do is work now to avoid ever having those experiences again, then you have not made peace.

If you can see your story as an experience, as a choice, and as a creation, and if you can release your need to abolish it, then you can move on. When your stories come up for you, and they will, do not attempt to squash them back down and do not attempt to retell them or put some sort of new spin on them. Just send that version of yourself who was in that story a big hug. Send a transmission of love, and let it go.

I am Ophelia, and I love you."

THERE'S MORE TO LIFE
∞
OPHELIA THE FAERIE

"I am here. I am with you.

You are finding that there is more for you in this life than you had previously allowed yourselves to believe. You are coming to understand that you can be and access so much more than you had ever been promised by your society. You are able now to perceive that limitless energy that you are gradually finding more and more available to you. This is opening doorways that you didn't even know were there. This is an exciting time for all of you and it is also a little bit scary.

What you are living now may not be the ideal. It may not be your idea of utopia, but at least you know what to expect, at least you have that familiarity and the comfort that goes along with it. So as much as all of you who are aware of this message say you would like to see change in your world, even in your personal experience of your world, there is still some attachment to this familiar experience. So I recommend that you keep yourself focused on the reality that you are experiencing, that you keep yourselves rooted, grounded.

And let your journey to what is ahead come to you from an energetic perspective. I want you to allow yourselves to feel what is coming without needing to understand it or conceptualize it in any way. Instead of thinking that you are all going somewhere else or that where you are will be so very different that you will not even recognize it, I want you to play around with simply bringing more of that limitless energy to the reality that you now experience.

I want you to carry the fifth dimension within you, rather than looking for it outside of you, rather than even speculating what your world will be like when you are carrying a fifth dimensional frequency all the time. Bring your light and your love to the world as you now know it. Allow for the miracles to be all that you need to see. Demonstrate by holding your frequency of how much more you can be and how much more you can do within the system where you currently operate.

Change will always start within you. But do not change so that you can see something outside of you, so that you can have the reflection. Change because you want to be the light, because you know how much more Love you can bring to this now, to this reality, to this dimension.

I am Ophelia, and I love you."

YOU ARE ACCESSING MORE

∞

OPHELIA THE FAERIE

"I am here. I am with you.

You are all standing at the precipice of so much more, and you are discovering how much more access you have. You are discovering your records, your past lives, your connections to other beings who exist in higher dimensions.

Now is the time for all of you to be. It is the time for you to be foolish. It is the time for you to make leaps of faith. It is the time for you to let go of logic and reason. Now is the time to believe in magic, in faerie tales, in whimsical wonders.

It is time for you to be reborn into your childlike state of enthusiasm for life, before you were taught that this and that were not possible. It is time for all of you to let go of all of the wisdom that you have held your faith in. It is time.

There is no force outside of you that is limiting your access. There is no being who is deciding what and when you can create what you want. It is now all in your hands, and as you believe that anything is possible and as you give in to your true power, you will see miracles unfolding the likes of which movies are made of. You are a miracle. You are miracles incarnate. There is no stopping you. There is only the possibility of slowing you down.

Forget everything that you think you know every day. When you wake up each morning, erase your memory and go straight for the feeling that you want to experience. Go straight for the feeling without attaching a story, or a picture, or a person to that feeling. And watch how what you ask for vibrationally is given to you in the physical. And then, keep a journal of what it was you were feeling when you woke up and what it was that found its way to your door throughout the day.

Give yourselves that experience of being creators and you will believe in faerie tales, in miracles, and in yourselves. You are now more than ever the creators of your reality because you have more conscious awareness, because your energy is moving so much faster, and because you have already done so much clearing work. Now is the time for you to take the reins and to guide your life into the feeling place that you prefer.

I am Ophelia, and I do so love all of you."

THE SHIFT IS HAPPENING

∞

OPHELIA THE FAERIE

"I am here. I am with you.

You are exceeding all expectations in the higher realms. I wanted to give you that message because I know many of you are wondering, 'Where is the evidence of the shift?' You are not going to do this by leaps and bounds, and it will not look dramatic. There will not be monumental earth changes, and you will not have chaos on your planet. Those would be setbacks, not evidence that you are moving forward.

The reason I'm so pleased to report that you are exceeding our expectations is that we can see you all finding your way without those major changes to give you that reassurance. In order for you to really experience what is happening on an energetic level, you must get quiet and you must look within. You must be willing to feel for the most subtle of changes in your own vibration.

I know that there is a component to what you have learned that feels very enticing and alluring. I know that many of you feel that when those changes occur, then all will be well. But I am here to tell you that all is well, that you are progressing quite nicely, and that there is no ticking clock. There is no time limit. You are not going to reach a point where it is 'do or die' for any of you, and certainly not for the collective.

You are going to continue to build, energetically and vibrationally. You are going to build the reality that you will experience. But even that begins with the internal, with the subtle shifts you make. It is all about viewing yourself and others with the most love and compassion that you can hold. I know big changes are fun, and I know that you have been promised quite a bit. But little changes are so satisfying because they have such big repercussions.

The ripple effect is bigger now than it ever has been. Your energy is moving faster than you have ever experienced it in the physical realm. This will be a wonderful experience for all of you, and you will have your own unique experience of the shift because you are all unique and because you are all here exploring different things. So join the rest of us in acknowledging yourselves for the little changes, the subtle shifts, and the big ramifications that they are having.

I am Ophelia, and I love you."

YOU ARE MAKING A DIFFERENCE

∞

OPHELIA THE FAERIE

"I am here. I am with you.

You are making the most of the current state of affairs in your world. You are all doing the best you can. It is a wonderful thing to observe all of you banding together in some cases, working alone in others. You are all making a difference, no matter how it might seem to you, no matter how big those 'others' seem. You are having an impact, and your impact is felt not only on your world, but in the entire universe.

Whenever you choose to support other beings in your collective, or when you make a choice that will benefit the environment that you all share, or even when you simply nod and say hello to someone you pass on the street, you are sending out waves of high vibrations. These waves collect. They find each other. They are like building blocks.

You are creating a new reality with everything that you do, everything that you say, everything that you are. You must never feel insignificant. You are only insignificant when you take the perspective of the third dimension. When you see your life as being created through action and when you believe that the only impact you can possibly have is the one that is made through your reach into the collective, then you will feel outnumbered and overwhelmed.

But when you know that you create energetically, when you see evidence of the shift in the details, in the emotions that you feel, and in your tiny corner of the universe, then you put yourself on the track that you want to be on. You do not have to do it the old way. You do not have to get enough signatures to bring something to a vote, and then convince people to vote. That is the old way.

You are more empowered by each thought, by each word you speak, by each little action you take then you could ever possibly be by passing a law or by preventing a law from being passed. I encourage you to notice your impact, to feel your impact within yourselves, and to encourage each other. You are beautiful beings, and you are doing so well.

I am Ophelia, and I love you."

CHOOSE PEACE

∞

OPHELIA THE FAERIE

"I am here. I am with you.

I am that which you are moving towards. I am of that frequency that you are all shifting into. I am excited for you. I am excited for us.

I am here today to give you the message of peace – peace of mind, peace of heart, peace of body. There is a quality to peace that goes beyond a physical calming. It even goes beyond the energetic. Peace, when it is attained by an individual, is a state of allowing; it is a state of acceptance; it is a state whereby you are able to receive all that you have been asking for.

I recommend seeking your peaceful place, your peaceful awareness, and your peaceful state of being. Many of you think of peace as the opposite of something, whether it be war, or chaos, or tension. I want you to view peace as your natural state. It is more than just being at rest with your physical body, or having no thoughts nagging at you, no emotions tearing at your insides. It is quite a bit more beautiful and expansive than all the definitions that you could possibly give it.

In a state of peace, you automatically attain oneness. There is no struggling, no striving, and no trying within the peace frequency. I also want to assure you that peace is a choice that is available to you at all times. You do not need to look anywhere outside of you for it. I want to direct you once again to your hearts – your hearts, which hold the frequency of peace within them. Your hearts, which by their nature are calm and knowing, patient, and loving.

The peace that is within you extends far beyond you when you allow it. When you are with someone who holds peace within them, you know it. You are soothed by it, and you are attracted to it. They are there to show you what is possible.

Once you know the frequency of peace, you always have access to it. It beckons you back to that beginning point, where your oneness was always part of your awareness, where your certainty was a guarantee, and where love was something that you always held as your state of being. I welcome you back to that state.

I am Ophelia, and I love you."

YOU ARE LOVE

∞

OPHELIA THE FAERIE

"I am here. I am Ophelia.

When you take in to consideration that you are Love incarnate and you accept that all others are Love incarnate, then you can easily recall what your mission is, what your purpose is. It is always about allowing more of what you really are, to be who you are in the moment, and how you express yourself.

You are here because you want to experience that Love. You are here because all of the experiences that you have are training your palette for Love. The interactions you have, the circumstances you create, the individuals you meet up with and play out your stories with are all there for you so that you can have the experience of yourself as a physicalized expression of Love.

It is no more complicated than that. And yes, this is a challenge at times. It is meant to challenge you, this life of yours, because you want to stretch, you want to have new ways of knowing yourselves. And in order to do that, you sometimes needed to create very complicated circumstances.

My suggestion to you is to continue to hit the refresh button. The refresh button, in this case, is the one that brings your awareness back to the simple fact that you are Love, that everyone around you is love, and that you are all here experiencing yourselves in order to better know the texture, the flavor, and the diversity of Love that you are.

Now some of you equate Love in a very specific way, and some of you reserve your Love for very specific situations and individuals. And I want to invite you to see Love in a whole new way. I want you to see Love as the way you experience the wind against your skin. I want you to see Love as the way you experience water when you are thirsty. I want you to see Love as the way you express your creativity, your uniqueness, and your perspective on life. I want you to see Love as something that you spread with everything that you do.

There is no limit to how much of it you can have, hold, give, and experience. So why not begin each day by hitting that refresh button, by aligning yourselves with the Love that you are, and by deciding to infuse everything you do and everything you are with it.

I am Ophelia, and I am Love."

PLAY WITH FREQUENCIES

∞

OPHELIA THE FAERIE

"I am here. I am with you.

I am playing with frequency. I play with frequency like you play with music. When you create music, you are playing with frequencies, vibrations. That is what sound is, and you are the conductors of that orchestra of sound. I invite you to play with your universe in the same way that you would sound, or color, or even your culinary creations in the kitchen, because when you mix things together you are creating new combinations of frequencies.

If you were able to look at your life in terms of the different frequencies at play at any given time, rather than seeing that you have a certain job, a certain mate, a certain dwelling that you live in, certain friends, and other activities that you participate in, and instead, if you were to see that you are playing with these different frequencies that each of them represents, you would have an easier time creating the life that you want to live.

It is more difficult for you to chop up a block of ice than it would be for you to simply increase the heat and allow the ice to melt. Just as the ice seems solid to you, and at times, daunting in its solidity and size, so do some of those physical circumstances that you are pondering and confronted with in your life. But nothing is as solid, impenetrable, and immovable as it looks. If you apply the right frequency, you will notice that everything becomes more malleable, and can be molded into that which you desire to experience.

So the difference between the way that I am currently playing with frequency and the way that you all play with frequencies is that I am having fun. Now it may seem rather easy from your perspective for a faerie to have fun with frequency, but the main difference is that I have taken away all of the struggle and all of the seriousness that you all apply when you attempt to alter your reality or to shift to a different reality. You feel that there is more at stake, whereas I understand that it is all a game and that if I do not like the game, that it is easy for me to play a new one.

I wish you all the same in this new year, as your new selves, as creator beings. I am Ophelia, and I love you."

GIVE TO RECEIVE

∞

OPHELIA THE FAERIE

"I am here. I am Ophelia.

What you bring to your lives will be what you get out of your lives. You must be willing to give of yourselves in order to receive. Energy runs as a two-way street. The door swings both ways.

You will get the energy back that you put in. This is something that most of you have come to accept. However, you may not see this operating as the principle in all of your life situations that you find yourselves in. In some areas, you are looking to give without receiving, and in some areas you are looking to receive without giving.

And you do not have to worry about balance, because the balance will always be kept for you. You only need to pay attention to what it is you are giving. You may say, 'I do and I do and I do, and I get nothing in return!' And that may be true, because what you are doing doesn't have the energy behind it that you want to receive.

If you do out of struggle, or obligation, or to receive respect that you do not give yourself, then that will be the energy you get back. Imbue your actions with the energy that you want to receive, and that is what you will get back. All of you know the difference between receiving that is heartfelt and receiving something because the other person feels obligated to give it to you.

I am asking not that you give more so that you will receive more, but that you notice what it is that you are giving when you are giving it. Any time that you are doing something because you hope you will receive something in return for it, you are not doing from your heart's desire, and that energy will be received by those who are on the other end of what you are doing.

When you are offering energetically, you have free reign. You can offer whatever energy that you can access, and you have access to all frequencies. And when what you offer comes from your desire to feel it, then what you will feel in return will echo that desire. And you know it. And you will appreciate it. And you will receive with open arms.

I am Ophelia, and I love you."

YOU ARE INFINITE
∞
OPHELIA THE FAERIE

"I am here. I am Ophelia.

I want you all to remember that you are infinite beings. I want you to feel into that statement. Rather than just accepting it as a concept. Feel what 'infinite' feels like.

You all have a tendency to think small. You box yourselves in with your concepts of space and time and because you experience so much of your world with your five senses. Your five senses are telling you the lie of limitation. They are telling you that there is a finite amount of this and that and even that your time here is finite.

But you are eternal and infinite. There is no end to you. There is no way to quantify you. You can experience yourselves as limited and finite, but that will always be a choice, a choice to narrow your focus, a choice to place those limitations on yourselves.

You can be infinite when you are being present. That is how I would recommend that you experience your infinite nature. Move into your now moment with a fluidity and with a joyous attitude. That will take you out of limitation and space/time, before and after, beginning and end. You will know yourselves as infinite and eternal, as you allow yourselves to feel it, to be it, and to know it.

Your minds cannot comprehend it, but they can accept it. As you feel into your heart center and you notice that there is no end to what you can feel, that is one way to begin to experience your infinite selves. Have fun playing with this experience. You cannot get this wrong. You cannot miss the mark.

You can only experience levels of your infinite self. You can experience flavors of it, dimensions of it, and when you know yourselves as One with everything and you can feel the essence of who you are stretching out far beyond the confines of what you can perceive with your five senses, then you will sync up with your true nature as a Divine Being of Love and Light. And you will embrace it all with arms that open infinitely wide.

I am Ophelia, and I love you."

MY WISH FOR YOU

∞

OPHELIA THE FAERIE

"I am here. I am Ophelia.

I am a messenger and a guide and a friend. I await you. I am always seeking to make more contact with you. I am a true adventurer at heart, and there is nothing that is more exciting to me than to explore each of you, to know you as I know myself, to know you as myself.

This is my wish, and it is a wish that I have for all of you as well. Explore. Be adventurous. Know everyone as a part of you. Give yourselves the opportunity to take a journey, and be willing to let the journey guide you.

If you seek specific outcomes, specific results, you will be specifically disappointed. You see certain opportunities and experiences as failures, and this is never the case. Was it a failure of Christopher Columbus to stumble upon what would be known to Europeans as 'The New World'? It was not the outcome he sought, but to deny it would be to deny an entire continent.

My wish for all of you is to embark upon your adventures with the knowing that a change in plans is an exciting event. The unexpected is a treasure. You are all having the same discoveries about yourselves. Sometimes you will discover that you had a talent that you were unaware of. And sometimes you will discover that you are more powerful than you ever dreamed.

And sometimes you discover that you cannot possibly know how much love you have to give until you find yourself in a situation that calls for it, and you are able to express even more of who you are. That is the ultimate journey – the journey that brings you back to your heart, that opens your heart more fully, and that expresses new dimensions of love, new depths, new strains.

Be in awe of yourselves, as much as you are in awe of me and my playmates. We could not exist to you if you and we were not one and the same. So be in awe of yourselves and let yourselves be more than you could ever have previously imagined.

I am Ophelia, and I love you."

AN ENERGETIC BRIDGE

∞

OPHELIA THE FAERIE

"I am here. I am Ophelia.

I am creating a bridge. It is not the type of bridge that you walk on. It is a psychic and energetic bridge to all of you. I am listening. I am hearing your requests. I am aware. You all live with certain guidelines in place. These are barriers. They are restrictions that you place upon yourselves.

You are putting them there to protect yourself and others. They are not visible to the human eye, and many of you are unaware of these restrictions that you place upon yourselves. You only allow yourselves so much joy, so much love, so much freedom, and so much abundance. You put a cap on all of those things to prevent yourselves from losing control.

The need for control comes from fear. The fear that you are accessing is stored trauma. Ask yourselves, 'What would be the worst thing that could happen if I were to remove my restrictions upon myself? What is it that I am afraid will happen?' And then allow yourselves to play out those scenarios, to access the fear, to access the trauma, the memories.

Once you are satisfied that the fear is no longer needing to control your limits, then you can play around with what your new guidelines are. Where is your limit now for joy, love, freedom, abundance, excitement, enthusiasm, creativity, wonder, awe, and all the rest? You will never know who you really are until you remove the self-imposed restrictions and allow yourself full expression.

I am so excited for all of you to explore how good you can feel, how much you can create, how much love you can spread. You will, of course, experience the removal of those limitations, those restrictions, those self-imposed guidelines. I am simply suggesting you do it now rather than later, you start living as soon as you possibly can as the truest and highest version of yourself that you can.

It is my joy to help you remove all restrictions.

I am Ophelia, and I love you."

FREE YOURSELF FROM OBLIGATIONS

∞

OPHELIA THE FAERIE

"I am here. I am Ophelia.

I am freeing myself from all of my obligations in order to be here. I don't have obligations. But if I did, I would free myself from them. That is my message to you today. It is about freeing yourself from the obligations that you create and then choose to feel bound to.

Just as easily as you have created obligations, you can create freedom. You can create activities, events, and people that you would choose to move towards and then create the means by which you can move towards those creations. And you can live your life free from obligation.

But many of you are using your obligations to feel good about yourselves, to show everyone how much responsibility you can take on. It is a matter of pride for many of you. This is an ingrained belief system that is passed down from generation to generation – the idea that the burdens, and obligations, and commitments are what make you a 'good' person.

You cannot ever do enough to prove that you are a good person, because first of all, it is not necessary. And secondly, no amount of work that you do towards that aim will ever get you there in the eyes of anyone who feels the need to define you as good or bad. So if you are the one who is using obligation to give yourself a sense of being a good person, then I suggest that you bypass all the good deeds, and instead, simply decide.

Decide how you want to view yourself. Be willing to take command of your life. Be willing to take your definition of self back from anyone who wants to decide who and what you are and wants to use what you do as one of the most important criteria.

I want you to throw away the idea of 'good' and 'bad' completely, and instead to focus on how you want to feel, and what you want to create, and who you want to be in the moment. Your life. Your decisions. Your definitions. Your creations. Take ownership. Be the creator that you really are and choose the version of yourself that you want to be as defined only by you.

I am Ophelia, and I am free. And I choose to love you."

ALIGNMENT

∞

OPHELIA THE FAERIE

"I am here. I am Ophelia.

I am bringing you a gift. It is the gift of your own alignment. Your alignment can come to you in any number of ways. When you tune in to me, what you are really responding to is your alignment. You like to think that it is about me, that it is about my energy, or about my message, because that is more accessible to you. I am more accessible to you. You can find my messages all over the Internet.

But this idea of your own alignment, that is harder for you to grasp, to put your finger on, to know exactly what it is. So that is my gift to all of you today. I am going to show you how easy it can be to find your alignment. It does not take hours of meditation. You do not need to go take a yoga class, or go to some gathering with other high-frequency beings.

Your alignment is your birthright. It is so easy for you to access. All you have to do is let go of whatever is preventing it. It is as simple as closing your eyes, taking a deep breath, and shaking off whatever it is that you have been using to act as a barrier between you and that alignment. Your alignment puts all of your bodies in the same place at the same time. Your thoughts and emotions and awareness of your physical and energetic bodies come together.

This alignment gives you more access, more access to who you really are. You are able then to let the energy of Love flow through you. You are a conduit for Love. You are a messenger of Love. You are a beacon to any and all who can tune themselves to your energy. I also welcome you to do those things that you know put you into a state of alignment.

So by all means, take the yoga class, go for the walk in nature, attend the event where someone will be holding space. Do whatever you know puts you in that state of alignment for the joy of taking that journey. For coming back into alignment is a journey worth taking. And that journey is the whole point of getting yourself out of alignment in the first place. That is the true joy of the journey.

You are all blessed beings, and I love you."

SEE YOUR LIFE AS A PARTY
∞
OPHELIA THE FAERIE

"I am here. I am Ophelia.

I am Love. I would like to invite you all to a party. I would like for each of you to attend this party as the guest of honor. And as the guest of honor, you are to be showered with praise and love and gifts. I want you all to imagine how you would feel as the guest of honor at a party thrown just for you.

I want you to be willing to accept the love, the affection, the praise, the hugs, the kisses, and the gifts. And I want you to feel how good you can feel when you accept, when you are willing to let all of that love in, when you are willing to accept yourselves as being worthy of receiving, of accepting.

This is something that all of you have a difficult time with, because you keep so much of that love from yourselves. So when it comes from another, you tend to downplay your acceptance of it, your worthiness of it. You do not embrace fully the praise that you receive, because you do not accept it fully yourselves.

There is such a bombardment of Love coming your way at all times. There is always a party being thrown in your honor, and everyone in the universe is invited to attend. And you are usually absent from that party because you are too busy attempting to make yourselves worthy of receiving. And you will never be able to prove that you are worthy, because proving it is so unnecessary.

You exist as Love. If you strip everything away that you think would make you worthy of being loved, the only thing left would be your true essence as Love. I don't want you to need to receive love from others, because I want you to recognize yourselves as Love. But when that love is coming from others, accept it. Because in so doing you are not only acknowledging your worthiness but you are granting the other permission to be the Love that they are.

I am sending out your invitations to your party, and I expect to receive your RSVP.

This is Ophelia, and I love you. And I celebrate you."

YOU CREATE YOUR REALITY

∞

OPHELIA THE FAERIE

"I am here. I am Ophelia.

I take nothing for granted. For in my dimension, where I exist, I know everything is my creation. Nothing is just a given to my experience. I create it all, and I know this. I am happy with my creations. When I want to create something new, I do. You are the same way, but you are less aware of what is happening in your reality and of the reflection that your reality is to you.

If you are not happy with one of your creations, you will likely see a deterioration of what it is that you are not happy with. If you are not happy with your government, you will see that your government gives you less to be happy about. If you are not happy with your mate, you will find that your mate gives you less to be happy about. If you are not happy with your body, you will find that your body gives you more and more reasons to not be happy with it.

So first, acknowledge them all as your creations. And second, rather than focusing on how and why you are not happy with them, take a neutral stance. Take on the perspective that they are neither good nor bad as they are. They are just your creations. And then ask yourself why. Why would you create them to be exactly as they are? What is the gift that they are giving you exactly as they are?

When you can find that, when you can come to peace with what it is that you have created, then you can create something new. Always create what you want to experience from a place of Love. If you want to create something to cover up something else that you don't feel good about, then that is the energy with which you will create.

So always create what you love with the Love that you are. See yourselves as that Love using its Love-self to create with. And then you will love everything that you create. And when you desire to create something new, you do not have to brush aside that which you have already created. You do not have to explain to everyone, and to God, and to the universe why what it is that you have created is so inappropriate.

You do not need to justify your desire to create something new. So love your creations just as they are and recognize that no creation is meant to be the only thing that you ever experience. You get to try on lots of different hats, and you get to grow. And sometimes, you outgrow your creations.

This is Ophelia, and I love you."

RELEASE THE STRUGGLE

∞

OPHELIA THE FAERIE

"I am here. I am Ophelia.

I run through your meadows. I skip through your gardens. I play in your waterfalls. I sit atop your puffy clouds. I ride into your dimension on rays of sunshine. I bring with me this message.

Work is what you all think you must do in order to survive, in order to provide, and to be provided for. Work is a creation. It is a concept. If you are working, then you are creating. You are creating the reality where struggle is necessary.

The way to release yourself from the need to struggle is to stop struggling. This representation that you have created of the inner reality of struggle can be so easily transformed when you let go of all of the little ways in which you find yourselves struggling.

When you let go of the need to be anywhere other than where you are, and when you let go of the need to be different from who you are, and when you let go of the need for the world to be different from how it is, you let go of struggle. And then you no longer need an external representation of what you are doing on the inside.

You are all creator beings. You create from the energetic. If your work is not satisfying to you, then you must find satisfaction within you first, before a satisfying endeavor can show itself to you. Satisfaction is a state of being. Satisfaction is the opposite of struggle.

Place yourself in the state of being of satisfaction in every area of your life. Be satisfied with your mate, with your body, with your bank account, with your home, with your children, with your world. Be satisfied and let go.

You will find that the world will begin to demonstrate to you this change in frequency immediately, but on a small scale. I don't want you to look for the ways in which your satisfaction will alter your world, because being satisfied in order to change your world is not truly being satisfied.

So instead, I want you to enjoy your state of satisfaction. That is truly what you want. What you do from that place of satisfaction must then be satisfying to you, and then what you do will not look like work at all. It will look like you satisfying you.

This is Ophelia, and I love you."

Chapter Three

∞

The Hathors & The Unicorn Collective

YOUR AUTHENTIC SELF

∞

THE HATHORS

"In your process of evolution, you are going to encounter those around you who have the opinion that you are somehow not living up to what they would like you to be doing. You have had encounters with beings like this your entire lives. If you are listening to us, you certainly have been willing to march to the beat of your own drummer.

We applaud you for that willingness and for believing in yourselves enough to take those steps – steps that would lead you in a direction that would at times look very silly, foolhardy, and downright stupid to those around you. As you continue to take those steps and to move in the direction that you feel most compelled to move in, you are likely to encounter more of that resistance, not only to what it is you are doing, but who it is that you have decided that you want to be.

You have let go of some of your desire to please others, of any need that you once had to conform. There is always more that can be let go of, and that is what we are encouraging you to do now.

We have a belief among us that there are no beings on your world right now who are listening to their heart one hundred percent of the time. We have not seen it. We know that is a tall order, since you have so many around you in your lives who are asking for different things from you, who are asking you to be who they want you to be, and who are asking you to do that which they want you to do.

We encourage you to sit in your comfort zone while also living within a society where your comfort zone makes others uncomfortable. We suggest that you set your intention to have the most authentic experience of yourself that you can possibly have. We want you to understand that this is the way for each of you to be completely aligned with who and what it is you really are.

Your own drummer. Your own heart. Your own comfort zone. Your true authentic self. Put that on the very top of your to-do list, and let everyone else take care of the themselves.

We are The Hathors. We thank you. And we wish you a fond good day."

PLAYING IN THE MUD

∞

THE HATHORS

"Elevating your frequency has never been much of a mystery to you. It is not as though you have a challenging time knowing how to do it, or what to do in order to achieve a higher frequency state. That has never been an impediment to all of you. You have an intuitive knowing of what will bring you in a higher frequency state.

But sometimes you feel stubborn. Sometimes you feel more attached to being right or to having something your way than you do to getting your frequency in a place where everything goes your way. So what do you do when you are being your own worst enemy? We recommend that you allow yourself those times when you do want to stay stuck in a lower frequency state.

We also suggest that you do not beat yourselves up for wanting to have these experiences, that you feel no regret for having spent some time being childish, stubborn, pigheaded, and all the other expressions you have for this phenomenon. We want to let you all to know that these episodes are not indicators that there is something wrong with you or that you are not making your way to the fifth-dimensional frequency. That is assured at this point.

We just want you to recognize that this is what you are doing, so you don't believe in the idea that it is hard to raise your frequency or that you don't know how to do it. Because those beliefs are detrimental to you, and they are simply defense mechanisms that you employ so that you can maintain that lower frequency a little longer without feeling any guilt, without feeling that it is your choice, your decision.

We want you to take ownership of whatever frequency you are offering. Own it. Claim it. Do not be ashamed of holding it. It is part of your experience. It is part of why you came to this particular reality. You are multi-dimensional beings, having many different experiences all at once.

So do not see these lower-frequency experiences as bad or wrong and admonish yourselves for having them. Be able to laugh at yourselves for this playing in the mud that you all sometimes do. It is quite all right, quite natural, and all a part of the human experience.

We are The Hathors. We thank you. And we wish you a fond good day."

TRUE POWER

∞

THE HATHORS

"Stepping into your own power is something that you are all on the verge of doing. We are not talking about power in the way that you all have conceived of it on your world for many thousands of years. That type of power that you all envision and feel when that word is used is not the power that we are encouraging you to step into.

The power that you think of when you hear that word is more about manipulation and control than it is about accessing one's true essence. The power that each of you are is a force that aligns itself with energy. That force is not used to push anyone or anything around. In fact, it could not possibly be used for that, you see. It is not dense enough to do something like that.

The power we speak of is the power that comes from your true identity, your true nature, the energy that sustains you, that created you, and that continues to expand with you. That is the energy we are talking about. And that energy includes all others and all things. So there is no need for that energy to manipulate or control anything or anyone. That energy recognizes that it only has power when it includes.

So, you are integrating more of yourselves. You are finding that power within you exists from knowing yourself as all things, and you are aware of the feeling of that power and how it includes your surroundings, rather than placing you above. That is the old way. That is the old form of power — to take an individual or a group of individuals and to place them in some sort of position of authority where rules could be dictated, where force could be used to put others down.

We know that all of you have played both ends of the spectrum regarding that power, and so you know what that is like. You have had that experience now. You can log that experience and move on from it, because now is the time for full integration and inclusion and alignment of energies to that which you desire, that which you prefer, and that which also sustains life and freedom for the total collective that you are a part of.

We are The Hathors. We thank you. And wish you a good day."

YOUR INEVITABLE ASCENSION

∞

THE HATHORS

"Fortunately for all of you, there is no time limit. You are not facing any sort of do or die type of situation when it comes to your ascension. You are in fact well beyond any doubt whatsoever that you have made it and are continuing to make it as a species and a planet. We are happy to give you that news. You do not have to worry about whether or not you are going to make it, and you do not have to worry about when it will occur. All of that is assured at this point.

You have evolved past any sort of demarcation line that would put the ascension process in question for all of you. So what to do now, yes? Now that you know you are ascending, what is your role? How do you proceed on with your lives?

First of all, we encourage you to celebrate. Celebrate what you have accomplished. Be happy with yourselves for having made it this far and for continuing on without any question to your fully-integrated, fifth-dimensional selves.

Next, we would recommend that you forgive yourselves. Forgive yourselves for ever having expressed something or done something that you look back upon now and think, 'How could I have done or said that, or even felt that?'

We also encourage you to set some boundaries. What we mean by that is that you maintain a clarity with those around you who may want to share in some of your high frequency energy. We want you all to be able to assist others without feeling that you are being trapped by them. So setting boundaries will help you maintain your frequency and your sanity, as those around you recognize your light and want a piece of it for themselves.

Next, we suggest that you set your own agenda for your life. Stop looking around to others to tell you what to do, or how you should live, and stop waiting for the rest of the world to do something so that you can then begin living the way that you want to live, the fifth-dimensional way.

This is your journey. You must decide how you want to proceed. You must decide what is important to you. You must be willing to take chances, to take risks. You must be willing to be wrong, or to take a wrong turn, by your definition.

You must allow all others to do the same, and you must recognize that there is no separation between you and any other. But you will continue to be unique and different and be the creators of your own paths, your own lives, your own stories. And of course, sit back from time to time and just enjoy this ride that you are on.

We are The Hathors. We thank you. And we wish you a fond good day."

INTENTIONS AND BELIEFS
∞
THE HATHORS

"So you begin each day with an intention. Sometimes your intention is just to get through the day. Sometimes your intention is to have a particularly fun time doing something. Sometimes your intention is to get certain things accomplished.

But no matter what your intention is for a given day, a particular day, you are living out that energetic stream when you put forth the intention. You are riding a wave that begins very early on and that you will continue to be on unless you make some sort of adjustment to your frequency and to your intentions.

You are living out a self-fulfilling prophecy, in a sense. You have very many beliefs that you cling to, or that you bow down to, or that you are simply not even aware of. And these beliefs are in large part responsible for the intentions themselves.

For if you believe that you must work and do certain things in order to be compensated financially, then you will intend to have a certain kind of day that revolves around certain activities that you will then believe that it is possible for you to be compensated for.

If you believe that a certain activity is more likely to be fun for you and is more likely to put you into alignment with who and what it is you really are, then certainly you will want to do that activity as often as you can possibly stand it.

We just want you to be aware of everything that you are putting forth, that you are putting out there, before you engage with it, before you decide this thing here is worthy of my attention, is worthy of my activity. And this thing over here is to be avoided at all costs.

We are not telling you that there is something wrong with having a preference or a desire. By all means, it is necessary that you have those. But what we are saying is that in order for you to really embrace life, you must be willing to take on a different perspective than the one that you have been force fed, or than the one you have simply assimilated to.

It is very easy for you to take on all of the beliefs, the ideas, the truths, of your government, your society, your parents, religion, or your heritage within any group that you are a member of. Until you are aware of what it is you are believing in and bowing down to, you will not be able to adequately address it. You will not be able to take a stance. You will not be able to put forth a new intention for yourself, for your day, for your world.

That is really what we want you all to do. We want you to become aware of the clay you are using to mold your reality. Because if you realize that you have access to more clay, to different types of clay, then you can have a fuller experience, and a truer experience, of your reality and of yourselves.

We are The Hathors. We thank you. And we wish you a fond good day."

FULL IMMERSION

∞

THE HATHORS

"Losing yourselves in a moment in time is one of the most delicious experiences you can all have. It is a matter of complete release into an experience, where you are so unconcerned with what the experience will bring you, and where you will go from the experience, and what anyone else will think about your participation in the experience, that you in a sense become the experience you are having.

This is possible no matter what it is you are doing. It is an immersion of your frequency into another, a coming together, a coalescing of the self with the experience. When you really want to have an experience, we suggest that you make this type of immersion into it your goal, and for that to be the ultimate outcome for you.

There are many times when you are all seeking out an experience so that you can have another experience that you believe will follow logically from one to the next. We want to encourage you to forget everything that you think you know about cause and effect, about the ends and the means, because we want you all to become buried within a frequency so that you can fully engage and fully discover what that experience is really all about.

You will discover more about yourself as a result of your full participation in an experience that you are having. You will benefit so much from the simple act of being present with what you are doing that you may in fact become addicted to the experience you are having. But the thing about full immersion in an experience is that the experience itself will release you when it is complete, when you have had the full knowing of that experience.

You can do this with your so-called 'negative' experiences as well, because the full immersion in that experience will again release you from it so that you will then become more fine-tuned in your creation abilities. You will know fully how something feels. And when you know fully how something feels, you can easily summon that feeling once again. You can choose to create the reality you prefer, but you cannot do that until you fully engage with the moment you are in to discover what it has to offer you.

We are The Hathors. We thank you. And we wish you a fond good day."

YOUR RELATIONSHIP TO YOUR LIFE

∞

THE HATHORS

"So you have a very specific type of relationship to the life that you are living. You are in it, but you are also relating to it. You are a participant and an observer. At times you are a fan and at times you are a critic. But it is your experience to have. You are the one who is deciding how you're going to experience your life. That is entirely up to you.

We want you to explore the various ways in which you could experience your life – the different angles, the different perspectives. We want you to know that there's not one right way to live your life, and there certainly is not one right way to experience it either. Settling in to the experiences that you are having is a key component. You must be willing to have the experiences that your life is giving you in order for you to then know what your relationship is to them.

Taking into consideration the fact that you are all here by your own free will, then there must be something about your life that is worth living, that is worth exploring. You did not come here by accident, and you are not here by virtue of some other being's will. You came here with the full knowing that you would have a certain type of life, that it would have various experiences along the way for you, and that you would have all of the tools necessary in order for you to not only survive, but also to thrive in your life. In this life, the one that you are living right now.

What you decide in any moment that you wish to experience regarding your life is a part of your free will. Free will is not just about what you will do next, whether you will choose path A or path B. You also have the free will to examine your life from any perspective that you want. There is not one right way. That is something that we want to be very clear about.

You do not have to be bouncing up and down with enthusiasm with every little doctor's appointment, every little trip to the DMV, every little consultation with your accountant. You do not have to do anything, and you certainly do not have to feel anything about what it is that you are experiencing in any moment. So let yourselves off the hook, but be more aware. That is our message to you. Be aware. Be present. Be willing. And be the powerful creators that you really are.

We are The Hathors. We thank you. And we bid you a fond good day."

THE GREAT POTENTIAL

∞

THE HATHORS

"For now, you may wish to have a little bit of that security that you all tend to seek. Why not use every tool that you have to give you the sense of security and stability that you all wish to feel and know? We do not wish to pull the rug out from any of you who are seeking financial security, stability, and the knowing that you are going to be able to survive in your world.

That being said, prepare to have the rugs pulled out from under you. We want you to recognize once and for all that you are your security blanket. You are able to hold such high levels of vibration in your being-ness that you can assure yourselves that you are going to be okay. You can even reach for something better than security, something better than just being okay.

We encourage you to reach for that creative ability, that creative potential that exists within each and every one of you. Now when we say, 'create,' or 'creative ability,' 'creative potential,' many of you go right to your visualizations and your vision boards, and your lists, and so on. We also want to break you free from that habit, from those processes.

We want instead for you to ponder the very essence of a reality that you would seek to experience. Not what is in the reality, not how the power structure in that reality is handled or laid out, not who exists in that reality, not what you do, not what mode of transportation you choose. But we encourage you instead to feel the reality that you want to experience, to really know it, to know your place in it as a creator being, to feel what pure potential feels like, what pure force feels like.

That's what we are talking about here. We are talking about power, potential, and force. For you to embody all of these frequencies and to live in the reality that feels like home to you, that feels like your core essence, that is what you all really are seeking at this time of great expansion and awakening.

So in order to find that which you are really seeking, you must let go a bit of the need to feel secure and to surround yourself with certain objects or individuals or ideas about what your finances look like. Let go because you are so much bigger than all of that.

We are not telling you to let go because you need to be more spiritual, and therefore physical trappings are not appropriate for you. We are telling you to let go so that you can take hold of true power. Because we want you to experience yourselves as the great potential that you are. And we suggest that you do it sooner, rather than later.

We are Hathors. We thank you. And we wish you a very good day."

REBIRTH YOURSELVES

∞

THE HATHORS

"Let us begin with the scenario that you are born into a certain time and place, to certain parents, in a certain part of the world. That is how you all believe you originated. There are many stories that you tell about this particular circumstance and how it has led you to where you are today. That is all fine and good. You may have that perspective.

But we want to offer you another perspective now, one that you may not have considered. It is the idea that putting yourself into a particular time and place is part of a much larger journey. You may see that moment of birth as a beginning or as a new beginning for yourself, but it is as much a continuation as the moment you wake up every morning, and you see that the day you are in has followed the previous day and comes before the next day. And you allow yourselves that continuity, that sense of one thing leading to another, creating a story for yourself to live out. And that is wonderful.

We like that you enjoy your linear time concept. But now we want to blow the roof off of all of that, and we want to tell you that the next moment that you live is as much of a birth, as much of a new beginning as your physical birth was into this reality. You can start with the same type of clean slate that some of you believe you had when you were born.

You can start your life over in the next moment. You do not need to die and you do not need to be reborn to have a completely new story. Some of you are aware of this. Some of you even create rituals around it. But you don't need the ritual, and you can decide in each and every moment that you are a brand new bouncing baby here to decide what it is you want to experience next without needing to attach yourself to the previous day, week, month, year, lifetime.

You are here to create, and in order to create you must have that knowing that you may create whatever you want in the next moment and that it may not in fact follow logically from the previous one. We want so much for you to let go of anything that you would define as your past, because that is the greatest source of your limitations. It is the greatest confinement of your freedom.

It is that idea that you are somehow a product of your environment, or a product of your upbringing that nails you down to the floor, that keeps you recreating scenarios that you could break free from in one moment, with one decision. Give yourselves the rebirthing process right now. Develop one in your mind and use it throughout the day. Rebirth yourselves. Get to know the new you as though you were brand new and had absolutely no idea who you were one second ago.

We are The Hathors. We thank you. And we bid you a good day.

STANDING RIGHT WHERE YOU ARE
∞
THE HATHORS

"Standing right where you are is perhaps the most important step in your process of evolution. You cannot take the next step until you are where you are. You must take that step from a solid footing. In order to do that, you have to be standing right where you are, you see. Not that difficult of a concept to grasp.

Therefore, this is our recommendation to you. Be willing to take a portion of your day to simply be, to simply exist, to give yourself a bit of a vibrational check up. You may wish to check in on your different systems, your different bodies – your mental, emotional, your energetic, and your physical bodies. You may wish to assess where you are in a place of non-judgment, of course. In a place of being the observer.

Now, when you have a firm understanding of where you are standing, and you're willing to accept that place as a completely legitimate and valid and important place for you to be, then we suggest taking the step that you want to take, whatever it is. You may wish to ask yourself in that quiet state of reflection and observation, 'What is the next step for me regarding where I am standing in this emotional body right now?' And allow the answer to come to you.

As we have suggested in one of our earlier messages, take whatever it is that you get and put it into practice. Do not assume that it will be the same answer every time that you get it, but be willing to accept that the answer that you receive in that moment is the most appropriate for you to take. Be willing to trust yourself, your own instincts, regarding the next most appropriate step for you.

You may wish to do this with each of your different bodies, and you may wish to keep a journal. You may wish to check in with yourself at the same time every day for fifteen minutes. Get yourself settled into where you are. Be willing to accept it. Be willing to take ownership of it. And perhaps even share it with another. Sharing your processes with one another is so helpful to all of you.

Not only are you expressing yourself in that moment, but you are giving permission to the other to do the same. You are giving permission to another to be where they are. And as you share your exploration into your next step process, you may have some wisdom to share as well.

So we wish you the best of luck on this journey. And we are here to give you a nudge or to help you stay on track, if that is how you would like to utilize our presence.

We are The Hathors. We thank you, and we wish you a good day."

ATTACHMENTS

∞

THE HATHORS

"For this moment in time you are being asked to let go of some things, yes? You can all recognize that this process that is well underway for all of you involves the letting go of some of those things you have become attached to in your third-dimensional, physical lives.

Of course you would have acquired some tastes and some preferences along your journey through the third dimension. This is quite understandable, quite reasonable, and we can see exactly how easy it would be for all of you to continue to cling. What we are asking you to do is to simply loosen your grip. Some of what you would call attachments that you have are perfectly healthy and are serving you. Some are not.

Ask yourself why do you feel attached to this thing, this person, this concept, this belief, or even this feeling state. Is it because you are afraid of its opposite, or is it because you have simply grown so fond of whatever it is you are clinging to that it would seem like a tragic loss to let it go? Have these attachments of yours taken over your lives? Have they confined you in some way?

We are suggesting that you look at these things for yourself, that you examine that which you are clinging to and why. Because as you are willing to let go and lighten your load you will find it is so much easier for you to elevate your frequencies. Even your attachment to being a fifth-dimensional being can get in the way. If you have a need to be anywhere other than where you are now, then there is something about that for you to examine.

We don't encourage you to get carried away with this. We are not asking you to become renunciates, to abandon all things in your lives, or to make this into some sort of mission or crusade. The simple act of examining will be very fruitful for all of you. When you let go, realize this: you can never truly separate yourself from something, wanted or unwanted.

But you can release your need for something to be a certain way, to be close to you, to have a certain reaction to you. When you let go of those needs, you will see that everything comes back around, because you are all Love. Love is what connects you. Fear is what attaches you.

We are The Hathors, and we thank you. Goodbye for now."

THE EXPERIMENT

∞

THE HATHORS

"We prefer to live the message, you see. We are not telling you what to do, but we prefer to live it. You have a tendency to theorize about it, speculate about it, wonder about it, seek answers about your truth – the truth you are operating under.

We tend to practice and see what works for us. Therefore, we encourage you to test out your theories. Be willing to take something you learn and put it into practice. You will discover that there is not just one way to go about living the way that you want to live, being in harmony with one another, and holding a frequency that is pleasant to you.

There are several ways in which you can find your groove. So find the way that works for you. Let others find theirs. You do not have to agree on one right way. Therefore, feel into what works for you in this moment. Be willing to share the outcome of your experiment. But do so without needing validation, without needing any other to do something your way.

You will all benefit from this practice. You are all benefitting from whatever it is you are doing, because you are all experimenting with life, with yourselves, with these concepts, from those like us, who want nothing more than to offer you a suggestion. A path. Not the path. A path.

So take it or leave it. Use it or do not. But let yourselves have the fun of performing the experiment. And share, share, share your findings, your results, with an attitude of exploration, of service, and of genuine enthusiasm for what you are doing. Take it easy. Take it slow. Let your experiments yield the results that they will before you make your conclusions. And have fun.

This is The Hathors. We thank you. Bye for now."

PREPARING FOR CONTACT

∞

THE HATHORS

"Will you consider for a moment that there are billions upon billions of galaxies in your universe? Now, consider the fact that most of your galaxy is unchartered territory for you, as humans. Now, take into consideration the diversity that exists on your planet. Now, consider that the kind of diversity you have on your planet is reflected out into the stars, the other worlds, and other galaxies in your universe.

So we want you to consider all of this because we want you to be prepared for the life that is out there, so to speak. You are part of a broader family of beings that you share genetic material with, that you are connected to energetically, that you have history with. These beings can provide you with much knowledge and can help to complete some of the pieces in yourselves that have always felt as though they were floating around, or foreign, or not quite fitting in.

You are much more complex than you even realize. These beings can help all of you make sense of yourselves. Our recommendation to you is that you reach out with your intentions, with your thoughts, with your energy, and let these other beings know that you are willing to share experiences with them, to share perspectives, and to reconnect.

There have been many stories told about extra terrestrials on your world. So many of those stories are taken to such an extreme that many of you feel that these beings are either going to destroy humanity, planet earth, and everything on it, or you believe that they are coming to rescue all of you from yourselves. We want you to prepare yourselves for something that is very much in between those two extremities.

You are as different from some of your next-door neighbors as you are from some of these ET beings. And yet, you also share quite a bit in common with your neighbor and with your ET brothers and sisters.

So what we are giving you here is the idea that when you are preparing for contact, prepare to meet an aspect of yourself, a being that is not so different from you, and beings that have as much to gain from interacting with you as you do from interacting with them. You are part of a galactic community, and sooner than later you will meet your neighbors.

We are The Hathors. We thank you, and we wish you a fond good day."

PULLING THE LIGHT THROUGH YOU

∞

THE HATHORS

"They do not understand, but they will. It is not a matter of 'if.' It is a matter of 'when.' We are not telling you this because it is necessary for you to understand that everyone is waking up. We are telling you this now because we want to give you that information. We are here to provide to you that which will fill in the blanks.

When you wonder about something, you are asking us for an answer. We will provide that which we can give you, that which is appropriate for you to know, and that which will serve you the most on your path. There are no 'right' or 'wrong' answers, ultimately. There is that which serves you, however, and that which does not.

They do not understand because they choose to spend a bit more time in the dark. That is an appropriate selection. That is a choice that serves those in the dark in some way. Remember, it is all a game. Therefore, there must be those who give you the challenges that you desire so that you may maneuver yourselves around, over, through those challenges, those obstacles.

For it serves you very well to have an opposition, to have a force that will propel you, that will ask more of you, that will give you that determination and that desire and that drive that is the stuff of life. So enjoy the time when they are not getting it, when they are choosing to play in the dark.

For it is a time that will bring more out of you than you knew you had access to. This is a most wonderful experience for all of you. See how much light you can hold, see how much love you can project, see how strong and how powerful you are, as you have the polarity to reflect that back to you.

You are all Love, blessings, wondrous beings of light. Be playful in your game. See those who oppose as your friends, as you mentors, as your greatest gifts. We encourage you to let them bring more light through each and every one of you who is playing on the side of the light.

We are The Hathors, and we thank you."

THE HOAX
∞
THE HATHORS

"There will be a time when you will all discover that you have been part of, let us call it, a hoax. You will then need to decide whether you will feel victimized by this information that will come out. And you also will have the opportunity to take full responsibility for that which you have co-created, and you will have the opportunity to decide whether or not you want to use the situation to enlighten yourselves about those areas of your life where you are not being fully honest, fully forthcoming, and transparent.

Now, we don't want all of you jumping to conclusions about what this hoax is, because when you do that you continue to see yourselves as the victims of the other beings that you have contracted with to sort of pull the wool over your eyes for a little bit longer. But always keep in mind that anyone in your world doing anything is in some way a reflection to you of you, and it is to be used to serve your greatest and highest good.

All that we are doing now is laying some of the groundwork for all of you so that you will be ready for information as it comes out and so that you will take a perspective on the situation that serves you best. Also, keep in mind that there will be emotions that will get triggered. You will feel a variety of emotions, anger and fear being two of the most prominent in your fields. And we will say that part of why you create scenarios like this is to get you to feel those emotions.

Therefore, allow yourselves to be triggered. Allow yourselves to have the experience of these announcements that you automatically feel compelled to have. But then in your quieter, saner moments, recognize that these are part of your evolutionary process and that this was a necessary thing for all of you, even though it involved deception and cover-ups.

You would do very well to forgive those involved, to see them as doing the best that they can and for realizing also that you have all given so much of your power away for so long that then to get on the case of those who have willingly taken that power is not the most logical thing to do. So forgive yourselves as well for having given away your power, for having played the role of the one who is being conned.

Celebrate the openness that will occur as a result of the information that is being revealed to you. It will be a very positive step for all of you moving forward. So embrace it. Embrace those who announce these cover-ups, and embrace yourselves. See yourselves as all of the players in this very elaborate game you are participating in. That is all for now.

We are The Hathors. We thank you. And we wish you a very fond good day."

CHANGE COMES FROM WITHIN

∞

THE HATHORS

"For the purpose of creating a new idea of who and what you are, many of you decide that you want to make a change in your life. You want to do something differently. You want to move, change your job, change your mate, change your clothes. Whatever it is that you want to do, you have a tendency to take some sort of action that would give you that sense of newness, that sense that you had transformed in some way that is pleasing to you.

We can see why you would do this. You are accustomed to seeing others who have changed, and you see that they are interested in new things, that they have a different way of living their lives in some way, and you assume that the change in them has come from the change in where they are, what they are doing, who they are with, and so on.

We want you to understand that the change is always coming from within the person, and then they feel attracted to doing something new. They have different people around them. They may feel compelled to move somewhere that is more reflective of their new frequency.

So you see, just because there is a correlation between one thing and another does not mean that there is cause and effect, at least not in the way that many of you are assuming when you see someone doing something. You want to know what it is they did, how it is they got to where they are so that you can follow the same steps, so that you can have your own transformation.

We want you to know that you are always constantly transforming, that the desire that you have to see a quicker transformation within yourselves is really what you are experiencing, because you cannot help but transform. There would be no point in you remaining in this incarnation if you were simply repeating the same over and over and being the same over and over.

So that is not happening, but you are unable to perceive some of the more subtle changes that are occurring within you. And when you see the same people and the same job and the same results in your life coming back to you, then you may assume that you did not change at all. But look at the way that you are responding to the same people and the same events, and see how the change within you is reflected in that.

You must be willing to be where you are in order to take the next step forward. Our recommendation to you is to have more fun right where you are, doing what you are doing, with the people you are doing those things with, and expect the change to be in how you are perceiving your reality. That is all for now.

We are The Hathors. We thank you. And we wish you a very fond good day."

REMEMBER THE CHILDREN THAT YOU ARE
∞
THE UNICORN COLLECTIVE

"Part of your evolution is about believing in something unseen, something mythical and magical. We represent that to you – we and all who dwell here with us in the faerie realm. We are that which you abandon when you let go of your youth, and we are here to be remembered and embraced. You cannot hide from yourselves, and your youth beckons you home.

You did not forget who you were. You had it systematically removed from your consciousness by others whose agenda did not include your living the lives you wanted to live. But they were acting on your behalf. All who seem to oppose and diminish you are.

And now we are acting on your behalf. We, and those like us, who are nudging you awake. We are encouraging you to let go of the so-called real world, to let go of all that does not bring you back to your Whole Selves.

All that you are includes that young dreamer who not only believed, but who saw, felt, and knew that which we are, that which all are in the faerie realm. It is time to once again know your world as a magical place where anything is possible, where you have super powers, and where we coexist with you.

We will share your world once again, and we will play, and you will remember the children that you are. And those who wanted you to grow up and be that which they wanted you to be will be right beside you, remembering the children that they are.

Blessings to you from The Unicorn Collective."

THE JOY THAT YOU ARE
∞
THE UNICORN COLLECTIVE

"Celebrating every moment of every day is not even enough to give you all the joy that you are. It is not possible for us to quantify it for you or to express it in words, but we will try anyway. We are joyous beings. We play, and we frolic, and we laugh, and we sing. We have parties that seem to have no end. And that is not even close to describing the joy that you are.

Whenever you feel joy coursing through your veins, that is a time when you catch a glimpse. That is a time when you have some idea of who you really are. And when you do that which brings you joy, you are more of who you are. You literally bring more of yourself to the party. That is all that Source would ever ask from you. Be yourselves. Do what brings you joy.

Seems easy enough, doesn't it? But joy is not just a feeling. It is not just an emotion. It is an expression of who you are. It is the truest expression of that which you are. You experience joy less frequently than most beings, and that was part of your desire for this incarnation. So it is not a knock on any of you when we say that. But another part of this incarnation is discovering the joy that you are and applying it to everything that you do.

Expressing yourselves as joy will be all that will ever really satisfy you. It is not enough just to understand what we are saying as a concept. We want all of you to understand that feeling joy is as easy as summoning more of yourselves. And summoning more of yourselves is easier to do when you are engaged in something that brings you joy. So another part of what you are doing here is discovering and deciding what brings you joy so that you can put your attention there, so that you can choose joy.

Choose life. Choose yourselves. And be an example to others, because they are mostly still under the impression that they are not joy. And so the wayshowers will be the joyous ones. They will be leading by example. And you can be at the front of that parade, as long as you decide that you are here to be who you are and to express that joy in as many ways as humanly possible.

Blessings to you from The Unicorn Collective."

NO HOLDING BACK
∞
THE UNICORN COLLECTIVE

"By holding back anything, you are withdrawing from the life that you have created for yourselves. You are here because you wanted to have as many experiences as a physical being in this world that you could. So let yourselves be afraid and let yourselves be foolish. Let yourselves be laughed at, ridiculed, betrayed, dumped, and rejected. Let yourselves have all experiences.

What we see in many of you is in an unwillingness to step out of a comfort zone that you believe is protecting you. In truth, nothing can protect you. So maybe it's time to let go of some of those self-imposed restrictions meant to keep you safe from a scary and chaotic world.

We want to encourage you to fall flat on your faces, because until you do, you cannot have the getting up and dusting yourselves off experience. You cannot hide from that which wants to be lived through you. This life, especially this lifetime, is about letting go. Let go of any need that you have to be contained and controlled and be willing to undergo a personal transformation. Be willing to step out.

We are lovers of that which is unfamiliar to us. We enjoy moving beyond our comfort zone. We have removed all self-imposed reigns and are frolicking and playing even as we speak through this channel. We want you all to discover what you are afraid of within you and let it out. Let yourselves fail. Let yourselves be mocked by others. And enjoy that you gave yourselves that experience.

You will only really start living when you stop pretending that you are comfortable living a limited and frightened existence. And when you feel the need for some extra courage to do what you know you really want to do, give us a wink and a nod. Call on us. We've got your back.

Blessings to you from The Unicorn Collective."

BOUNDARIES AND FEAR
∞
THE UNICORN COLLECTIVE

"We are placing no boundaries upon you. We are only extending ourselves to you. But we notice that you place boundaries around yourselves, and you do not invite in all energies that are available to you. This is due to fears stemming from interactions you have had with other beings in your human history.

You have been visited by beings that have not all had your greatest and highest good in mind. They have sought to exploit and plunder, and this is why you fear the unknown. This is why you are not open to open contact with other beings. It is not your fault that you are not. It is not a case of not being open-minded enough or not opening your hearts to other beings, like us.

It is because the fear that gets triggered is deep. It is locked in your cellular memories. It is beyond your control, and it is also unraveling all around you. You are making space for other beings by addressing your fears, by becoming aware of your fears, and by facing them.

There is a reason why so many of your science fiction movies and stories focus on alien invasions. Those writers, and directors, and storytellers are giving you what you need. They are scaring the fear right out of you. And as you open to connection with other beings from other worlds, you allow more love to flow.

Some of you say that love and fear are opposites. And we say they are the same. They are just filtered differently. So the same energy that was felt as fear will be felt as love. And you will drop those boundaries, let down your guards, and be open to interacting with those like us who are eager to play with you, to share our stories, and to embark upon co-creative journeys together.

So keep doing what you are doing. You are getting yourselves ready a little more and a little more every day.

Blessings to you from The Unicorn Collective."

YOUR BRIGHTNESS
∞
THE UNICORN COLLECTIVE

"Brightness is your truest expression of self. Being light means that your brightness is a fundamental quality of who you are. Now, how bright you allow yourselves to be is up to you. You have your internal dimmer switch. You can soften or brighten your energy. And that is a fun experience for all of you.

When you are a child and you discover a dimmer switch in a room, you play. You turn it up and you turn it down again and again, and you delight at the changes. When you incarnate into a body, you have all of your light with you, and you shine it to a certain extent. But you also know that you will turn it down, because you want to have fun, because you want to have experience.

And once you find the switch in your heart, you can operate your dimmer switch consciously. You can play. You are light. You are expressions of Source Energy. You are Love. And it is a dance of light and dark that makes the experience of life so much fun. Some of you believe that your journey is about turning the brightness up as bright as it can possibly be and then tearing that little knob off the wall.

But that is no fun. You want to have the option of dimming your light. You want to see it as a choice, and you want to know the power in choosing. By elevating your frequency, you are putting more of your light into your reality. And by letting your light shine, you are granting others permission to do the same. You are excellent operators of your dimmer switch.

Just witness all of the chaos in your world and know that it is nothing more than beings who are having fun, playing with that switch. There is nothing that can ever remove the light entirely, but there is that which will accelerate the rate at which your light can expand. And that is what you are here to discover. That is what you are here to do and to experience.

Blessings to you from The Unicorn Collective."

BELIEVING IS A CHOICE

∞

THE UNICORN COLLECTIVE

"Believing presupposes that there is something to not believe in. There is nothing for you to believe or not believe. There just is. That is incontrovertible. Believing is not a matter of faith. It is not a matter of facts.

Believing is a choice. You make choices all the time. You make choices by what you give your attention to. And you eliminate possibilities by what you refuse to acknowledge.

We are not asking anyone to believe in us or to believe that we are speaking through this channel. All we ask is that you reconsider what a belief is. We ask that you make your beliefs true, because it is only by bringing your beliefs to your conscious awareness that you can see up close and personal that which you are giving your attention to and whether or not these beliefs of yours are serving you.

But it is not a matter of whether they are true or not true. They are the power that you give them. They have no power over you. And if you pretend that they do then, of course, they will. But that is also a choice. So choose wisely and choose carefully, and give your attention to that which you want to see more of. Believe it or not, that is how it works. That is how powerful you are.

Blessings to you from The Unicorn Collective."

EXPRESSING YOUR ENERGY
∞
THE UNICORN COLLECTIVE

"The way that you express yourselves is through your energy. So it is not really about what you say or what you do. It is about your energy. That is how you really are expressing yourself. That is how you put your stamp on something.

Many times, people are responding to the energy more than they are responding to the words, or the deeds, or whatever is in front of them that they are taking in through their usual senses. The energetic sense is the sixth sense. It is the sense that you mostly use subconsciously.

You are not always aware of why you are moving in one direction and not moving in another. It is because of the energy that you pick up on. Some of you call this your intuition. We welcome you to put your energy stamp into what you are doing and what you are saying more consciously. We invite you to think more about the energy that you are infusing into your words, your emails, your texts, your actions, even your intentions and your desires.

Express the energy first, and then say what you have to say. Express the energy by extending it out from your body, through your energetic field, and into the universal energy field. And then take the action. Because you are energy that is flowing, and you want to flow in the direction of that which you desire to experience. You want to flow with that which is calling you, and you want to put the energy out that you want to receive.

So be more conscious of the energy that you are putting out, and focus less on how things look or sound. And think less about how you will be perceived, how your words and actions will be perceived, because then you are putting out the energy of worry and fear and self-consciousness. Know that the energy that you put out is always received. The energy can never be misinterpreted.

But you can be conscious or unconscious of your energy. And we invite you to be conscious so that you can enjoy that which you are and that which you are here to express deliberately.

Blessings to you from The Unicorn Collective."

YOU ARE FUN
∞
THE UNICORN COLLECTIVE

"You are welcome to play. You are invited. You are in this for play. This is a playtime activity. You are forgetting at times that you are here to play. You are here to have fun and to enjoy.

And we see how serious you all take your lives, yourselves, your world, and your spiritual journey. If you are to awaken to anything, awaken to the playground that is all around you. You may have a job, and you may be going to that job. And you may not see it as play. You may not bring a playful energy to your job. But that is not your job's fault. You can be playful. You can have fun.

Or you can decide that work is hard, that life is a struggle, and you can play that game. But we don't see very many of you having fun when you look at life in that way. Having fun is as easy as deciding that you are fun. You are fun, because you are everything, and fun is certainly a part of everything.

And being fun, you want to play, you want to frolic, you want to let loose. But as children you were told not to play, that life is not a game, that you must buckle down. Do your homework, do your chores. You were told that your play was upsetting to others, and you had the fun conditioned out of you.

We are here to remind you that you can have fun, because you are the adult now. And as the adult, you get to make the rules. You get to decide when it is appropriate for you to have fun and when it is time for you to be more focused. But even that can be fun. Even if you are sitting in a meeting with very serious people, you can be having fun with yourself. That is up to you.

We support you in whatever you decide, but we're here to remind you that you can decide to have fun. You can decide to make everything fun. You can decide to be fun. And you can see the playground expanding as you do.

Blessings to you from The Unicorn Collective."

YOUR PERFECTION
∞
THE UNICORN COLLECTIVE

"Practicing doesn't make perfect. Practicing makes practicing. Being as you are is perfect. There is no need for you to practice becoming that which you are. Everyone sees themselves as imperfect, and that is why you continue to see imperfection. Being would not exist if it were not the perfect way to be.

You can put yourselves in a number of different situations to test yourselves for your current level of perfection, and then you can measure the results of those tests against that which you deem to be perfect. And this keeps you playing that game of perfect and imperfect. And you give yourselves reasons not to love yourselves as you are.

But that is just silly nonsense. Who gets to decide what is perfect, and why is it all such serious business? We will tell you why. It is because deep down inside you all know yourselves as perfect, and you strive, and strive, and strive because you want to see evidence that shows you without a doubt that a part of you is right.

But you have such silly ways of measuring yourselves. You are looking for perfection in something that you do, something that you create, or even in your physical appearance. But perfection is what you are. It is the expression of Source Energy that you are. Perfection is in the way you love. That is where you find it.

It is not even the 'way' you love. It is that the love that you are is the most perfect expression of Source. And that is just how it is, right now, no practice required. No evidence required. Love yourselves, you perfect, beautiful beings. And if you don't, that is just fine. But we will.

Blessings to you from The Unicorn Collective."

TIME TO REMEMBER
∞
THE UNICORN COLLECTIVE

"Primarily, we are energy. We are knowing ourselves more as energy than as physical beings. But we do take form. We love taking form. And it is from our energetic state that we look to guide all of you.

That is why we are not appearing as horses with horns. That would be a distraction to you. That would put you more in your heads than in your hearts. Our intention is to guide you back to your hearts, back to your home base, and to remind you of the energy that you come from, the energy that you are.

The purest of hearts knows that there is no separation from any other. So you are us, and we are you. And we are as fascinated by you as you are by us. And what we are fascinated by, mostly, is the way that you all have forgotten who you are. That seems so strange to us, but also quite impressive.

So we remind you of who you are, but we honor your choice to go about believing that you are separate, and that you are flesh, blood, and bone. Now is the time for you to remember. And we know that. And some of you know that. And the remembering is as fun as the forgetting. And the day is coming when we will interact with you as you interact with each other.

And so for now, enjoy your forgetfulness. Enjoy your separation. Enjoy not knowing. From our perspective, it looks like so much fun. We are not mocking you. We are quite serious. And we want you to know how important it is for the experience that you are having that you first forget.

So, good for you. Well done. You are magnificent beings. You are projecting yourselves wonderfully into your reality. And some of you are milking it for all it is worth. But all of you are having fun. And sometimes you forget how much fun you are having. We also want to remind you of that.

Blessings to you from The Unicorn Collective."

Chapter Four

∞

Archangel Michael

YOUR METAMORPHOSIS
∞
ARCHANGEL MICHAEL

"Changing from within, this is all you ever do. It is what you experience your lives as. You cannot stop change from occurring, but you can resist it or allow it. You are on a never-ending journey of expansion and growth, and you cannot experience your growth and your expansion without also experiencing change.

Notice yourselves as you cling to what is familiar, not only about your surroundings and the people you associate with, but also in yourselves. You cannot be the same person from one moment to the next. It is simply not possible. So, as a new person, your only real concern must be, 'Who am I in this moment, and can I love and accept myself as I am?'

Who you were yesterday is irrelevant. Who you were ten years ago is but a distant memory. There is not one of you who benefits from clinging to any idea of who you have been prior to this moment. It not only does not serve you, it brings you less to be excited about.

You are changing more rapidly now than ever before, and the change that you experience is not as simple as a change in your address, your occupation, or your appearance. We are talking about a metamorphosis that will change everything, and we are asking you to trust that what you are changing into is more of what you have always known yourselves to be.

You cannot possibly get lost in this process. It is your destiny. And as you change, you bring new awareness to that which you have always been. With new awareness comes new perception. And with new perception comes a new reality. And with that new reality comes an even greater sense that you are complete and whole and becoming even more than you could have ever dreamed or imagined.

We are Michael. We are infinite. We are Love."

BUILD YOURSELVES UP
∞
ARCHANGEL MICHAEL

"By appreciating the value that you give to your world, to your species, and to all that exist, you find value in what others are offering as well. You exemplify that which others can aspire to feeling for themselves. Therefore, we see no harm whatsoever in building yourselves up, bragging even.

We want you all to know your value, and we want you all to experience it firsthand. We encourage you to express it without fear of being called selfish, arrogant, or narcissistic. By tooting your own horn, so to speak, you are delivering high frequencies to all who exist. You are setting the example to others of how to love oneself, how to see oneself as beautiful, as valuable, and as providing service.

You all want to feel valuable, and yet, you often deflect the compliments and the praise that you receive from others. And you wouldn't dare speak your own accolades publicly. And so we are suggesting that you start small. Simply acknowledge yourselves to yourselves. No one else has to be in earshot. Walk with your heads held high and believe in your value.

And as you do, you will see the value that others provide and it will be easier for you to praise them. There is an evolution that is well under way that includes every single one of you, no matter where you are today. And one of the paths to experiencing that evolution is acknowledging all the areas in yourself that are praiseworthy.

All we are asking is that for a few moments you focus on yourselves through the eyes of Source.

We are Michael. We are infinite. We are Love."

YOU AND YOUR HELPERS
∞
ARCHANGEL MICHAEL

"The beings that wish you the greatest joy, love, and freedom are in many ways your ancestors and in many ways they are future versions of that which you are. You come from and to this plane of reality with a beautiful entourage of beings. You call them your guides and your angels, but they are so much more than that.

These are not just beings that care about and love you. These are pieces of your very consciousness that are looking in on that which they are, that which they were, and that which they will be. It is quite a process, this evolution of yours. It is not so cut and dried. There are many paths, many avenues, but one result.

And you are deciding which path, and they are watching you make those decisions and lending a hand when they can. They are not above you. They are not better than you. They have just as much to learn from you as you do from them. You are much more of a team than you realize.

You give them thanks and you seek their counsel. But we suggest that you see them more as a team – a team where you have your role as well, where you play your part. We suggest that you begin to see them as equals, that you look at your life as a project and you see them as contributing to the project. But you have as many answers as they do.

They will come to you for advice, for suggestions, and you will be of value and of service to them, for nothing in this universe is a one-way street. So before you ask for their help, their guidance, their answers, be willing to share something with them about your experience. Begin a dialogue. Give as much of yourselves to them as they have been and will continue to give to you.

We are Michael. We are infinite. We are Love."

WHEN TROUBLES ARISE
∞
ARCHANGEL MICHAEL

"When trouble arises, it does so in order to get your attention. By receiving your attention, it serves its purpose. The trouble itself, whatever form it may take, is not your enemy. It is not to be snuffed out as soon as humanly possible.

You also do not need to give it your undivided attention. You do not need to become obsessed when something unwanted rears its ugly head in your lives. By allowing it to exist and giving it the appropriate amount of attention, you satisfy the need that it was always intended to provide. And then, once the attention is given, you can get on with your lives.

Once you have satisfied the purpose of the creation of the trouble, it no longer needs to exist in your experience. When you recognize that the trouble has served its purpose, you relax and you release your resistance to it. But when you see it as something that has some sort of control over you, and when you see it as a force, that is when your opposition to it serves to create more of it.

The best thing you could ever do when trouble arises in your lives is to respect it, to know that it is there to serve you, and to know that you placed it there to give you something that you needed. By letting go of the need to destroy the troublesome circumstance, you make room for something else, something that is wanted, something that you might call a solution. But we call it the next wondrous creation that is also appearing to serve you.

We are Michael. We are infinite. We are Love."

EXPANSION
∞
ARCHANGEL MICHAEL

"Circumstances are what they are in your lives to give you the greatest opportunity for expansion. Looking at your lives as the opportunities that they are gives them meaning. If every challenge that arises is met with a desire to expand into something more, then suddenly everything in your life becomes a joyous experience.

You have the choice to see those circumstances in your lives as mere nuisances, and you have the freedom to see them as the opportunities they are. The next time you find yourselves struggling to overcome something, and using your minds to do so, drop the resistance, let go of your thoughts, and feel into the expansion that the circumstance has created.

You do not need to analyze and figure out what the circumstance is giving you. You do not need to know what expansion you are moving into. You just need to accept that this is the case and that in your surrender you will feel more of yourself.

Becoming enlightened is not about understanding a concept. It is about literally holding more light, because you are light. And the more light you are willing to embody, the more you can see everything in your lives for exactly what it is. So we recommend that you welcome everything in with open arms and that you decide to be free, to be more, and to allow your expansion to occur moment by moment, circumstance by circumstance, and by surrendering into what you already are.

We are Michael. We are infinite. We are Love."

WHAT DESIRES DO FOR YOU

∞

ARCHANGEL MICHAEL

"By giving yourselves that which you desire, you are setting yourselves free. As long as you are giving your power away to that which exists outside of you, you are in bondage. Now, we love that you have desires, and we encourage you to continue seeking out those pieces of your life that you want to see and feel and touch. But when your desires consume you, that is when they do not serve you.

When it becomes more important to you to obtain that which you desire than it does for you to feel free, happy, and peaceful, that is when you know that you have an unhealthy and unproductive relationship with that which you desire. Ask yourselves what you would be willing to do to have that which you desire. Your answer will tell you what your relationship to that desire really is.

Now when it comes to being and embodying that which you desire, that is something that requires you to do absolutely nothing. You already be, so there is nothing to do in order to become that which you already are. Becoming tuned to that which you desire is not about attracting it to you or manifesting it. It is about showing yourselves that you already are it and that in the knowing of yourselves as that which you desire, you are free.

You will only find enslavement where you give your power away. Reclaim your power by simply tuning in to the frequency of all that you desire and lighting up your world and everything in it with the intensity of your energy. That is how you benefit from having a desire in the first place.

We are Michael. We are infinite. We are Love."

ACCESSING YOUR ENERGY
∞
ARCHANGEL MICHAEL

"Begin exercising your right to your own energy. Let everyone else off the hook, and give yourself what is rightfully yours. There is a tendency in all of you to look around at the world outside of you and to attempt to fill yourself with energy. You do this in any number of ways. Some of you have addictions that don't even look like addictions to most of the world. But all addictions are about energy and about the use or abuse of energy.

So finding your energy source is as simple as imagining that you have a valve inside of yourself and loosening the valve so that you can allow more energy to flow from within you, filling not only your physical structure, but also your energetic field. That energy that belongs to you IS you. It is not separate from you. It is not something that you need to access from another realm or another dimension. You are here and now, and so is the energy that you are.

But it is necessary for you to give yourselves that energy. It is a part of your evolution to recognize this and to let go of some of your outside energy sources. Some of you are doing this consciously. Others are having those sources taken away. But they are still calling the shots, just not from the level at which they operate. So you see, knowing yourselves as your higher selves will make it easier on you to access the energy that is you.

But as long as you know yourselves as separate, as egoic, you will still attempt to receive that which feeds and nurtures you from somewhere, something, or someone. Believe us when we say that there's more to you than meets the eye, that the source that is you is infinite, and that the valve is always there, ready and waiting to be loosened, to open the floodgates, and to allow yourselves expansion from within.

We are Michael. We are infinite. We are Love."

WHAT YOU REALLY WANT

∞

ARCHANGEL MICHAEL

"Projecting yourselves into a reality enables you to experience a particular flavor of who and what you are. All realities give a different sense of your being-ness. Therefore, all experiences within this reality serve you in that way. When you look for the service in a situation that you find yourselves in, often you look for how it may serve your desires. You tell yourselves that it somehow is related to you getting what you want, even if what you want is more expansion.

But ultimately all things are in service to your having an experience of self. Therefore, it is always easy for you to find the service, as long as you recognize that you are always what you are receiving. If that seems like a raw deal to you, then you are underestimating who and what you are. Nothing could be more magnificent than experiencing your true selves.

We are talking about feeling who and what you are. We are talking about tuning yourselves to the majesty of your essence, and that is something to be desired. That is something worth seeking. Everything else in your reality that you desire to experience is really because you want more of who you are flowing through you. And it is easy for you to see how that is possible under certain conditions.

But we tell you that all conditions are designed to give you that sensation, to give you that experience. When you shift your intention from getting something you want to feeling more of who you are and having the sensation of knowing yourselves fully, you can relax into the moment. And when you do, you then create from that experience. You then create as your Whole Self. And what you can create is limitless, just like you.

We are Michael. We are infinite. We are Love."

TAKE A MOMENT
∞
ARCHANGEL MICHAEL

"It only takes one moment of your time to recognize beauty. It only takes a moment of your time to live fully. It only takes a moment of your time to experience joy. You desire to live that way, but how often do you actually take a moment to experience, joy, beauty, and your whole selves? And how often do you use a lack of time as your excuse?

By living fully in the moment, you extend time. You create more time and you need less. What do you need time for? Is it to get things done? And what will you do when all those things are done? You will likely find more things to do.

Having taken the time to experience yourself fully in the moment, recognizing the beauty around you, and experiencing the joy within you, you will notice that everything around you slows down to accommodate your new vibration. Your hectic, whirlwind lifestyles are not created by the environment where you are, the technology you have access to, or the number of people on your planet. Those lifestyles are created by choice.

You can step out and step back in, but you cannot get away with using the excuse that there is not enough time, not when you create everything in your experience, including your concept of time. Take moments to appreciate beauty, feel joy, and tune in to your whole self, and those moments will become longer. And you will create the life that you thought you needed to claim through all that action. And you will know it. You will recognize it, because you will be it.

We are Michael. We are infinite. We are Love."

ROOM FOR GROWTH

∞

ARCHANGEL MICHAEL

"Always leave yourselves room for growth. See everything as perfect as it is, and yet, know that growth will occur. You need not ever fulfill every desire, every expectation, every intention for your lives, because if you did you would leave no room for growth. Many of you want to be further along in your evolutionary process than you currently find yourselves. You wonder why or how you could be stuck dealing with the same challenges that you have been for years and years and years.

The purpose is not for you to get past something, to eliminate the need to ever experience it again. The point is for you to notice how different you are as you experience the same challenge over and over. So leave room for growth. Be willing to accept that where you are is the perfect place and that where you are going draws more life through you than any sense of completion or perfection ever could.

It takes a great deal of that which you call patience with yourselves. You may be called upon to let go even more during those times when you may even feel like you are regressing or backsliding. That is the time to pull back and remind yourselves that this journey you are on is not about getting somewhere that you haven't been before.

It is about being the you that you always have been but sometimes forget. And that being will never be complete, will never stop growing, and will never stop seeking for reasons to continue on.

We are Michael. We are infinite. We are Love."

HONESTY
∞
ARCHANGEL MICHAEL

"Honesty is the best policy. It is more important now than ever for you to exist in the state of being that is your truth. Understand that we are making a distinction here. There is not one truth, but there certainly is your truth. And speaking your truth, living your truth, being in alignment with your truth is the honesty we are talking about here.

We are not saying that you must tell everyone everything that you are thinking, but we certainly do encourage you to be honest with yourselves about how you are feeling. When you think of honesty, you often think of the honesty between two individuals, or one individual and a group. But that form of honesty is only relevant in certain situations.

Living in honesty, living your truth applies to all situations. This is not a question of right and wrong. This is not a conversation about how honesty is the moral or ethical way to live. This transmission is about how much you are willing to live in your truth. Now, you truth is always changing. And so, we are not telling you to decide what your truth is and stick to it forevermore.

But we are telling you to recognize and acknowledge yourselves right where you are in every moment, regardless of whether that moment defies something you were, something you believed, something you said in some other moment in time. You do not have to be true to that version of yourself whose truth was different. In fact, we would encourage you to let go of any need for consistency over any period of time.

Honesty means you have a willingness to be wrong. You can accept that a lack of consistency is actually quite liberating. You only need to be true to yourself in the moment, speaking your truth, feeling your feelings, and doing that which you believe is for your highest good.

There is no place in your life for self-deception. You cannot live in that way and be your whole self. Even though you are all things, you are all perspectives, you still get to decide what your current truth is and live it out in the most joyous way that you can.

We are Michael. We are infinite. We are Love."

TO GIVE

∞

ARCHANGEL MICHAEL

"To give and release all expectation for gratitude or reciprocation is one of the many ways you have of knowing yourselves as Source Energy. Giving places value upon not only that which is given, but also upon the person who receives. When you give the gift, you give another a sense that they are worthy, that they matter, and that they are loved.

Truly, there is no greater way of knowing yourselves as abundant than to give something that you have that feels valuable to you. Make no mistake about it – the real gift that you have to give is that of your true essence. But sometimes you have the opportunity to give something physical, something that another could use. And that is wonderful as well.

By letting another give to you, you also give a gift. You give the gift of receiving and allowing the other to feel their benevolence and abundance. You often come to a place in your lives where you have more than enough, and you are presented with the opportunity to either cling to what you have or to give some of it away. We are not telling you that you must give. Because if you are not feeling abundant, then giving what you have only amplifies that feeling.

So many of you are witnessing a shift in the way that you exchange energy on your world. You want to be a part of that shift. And one of the easiest ways to do that is to give without expectation of receiving anything in return. That is much more effective than any demonstration you could partake in that is designed to point out the corruption or greed that is prevalent on your world. Be the change. Show others that there is another way.

We are Michael. We are infinite. We are Love."

WAITING & LIVING
∞
ARCHANGEL MICHAEL

"Waiting for your ship to come in will leave you in a perpetual state of waiting. That which is on its way to you is on its way to you whether you call for it, beg for it, or wait for it. But when you spend your time waiting and wondering and wishing for something to come, for change, for a new life, you're not enjoying the life that you are living.

And it is that enjoyment that you seek. That is what you believe exists on the ship and in the goodies that it carries. So how can you enjoy your life as it is, ship or no ship? We recommend giving yourselves that which you seek, that which you believe can only come to you from an outside source.

If you are waiting for a lover, then love yourself. If you are waiting for the perfect job opportunity, then create that which you wish to do. If you are waiting for the perfect bodily vehicle, then look upon your body through new eyes and see it as perfect just as it is. No one can give you that which you deny yourself.

Be willing to look foolish as you live a life of joy in circumstances that defy that feeling. You are all capable of living the lives you want to live right now. You just have to stop waiting and start living. And when you do, you will find that the ship was there all along and that all it took for you to see it was to change your perspective.

We are speaking literally here, and we want you to know that. We are not giving you a trick to fool the ship into arriving. We are asking you to see it and know that it exists within you.

We are Michael. We are infinite. We are Love."

THE FLOWERING OF SOURCE

∞

ARCHANGEL MICHAEL

"The creation that you are is a flowering of Source. You are not just created by Source. You are Source, and you are reaching out from that which is Source. You and Source are becoming together. You are stretching Source beyond where It has been before.

We appreciate that which you are doing, and we know that Source does as well. One of the ways in which you can acknowledge yourselves for the gift that you are and the gifts that you give is by doing something you have never done before. By taking an action, you operate as Source and you give Source a new experience of Itself.

So if you are not feeling your Divinity, and if you are having a hard time even acknowledging that your Divinity exists, then simply do something you have never done before. And feel the way you come to that activity as more than what you knew yourself as. Feel the blossoming of the flower that you are.

What you do is never as important as what you bring to what you do. So do not agonize over what you should do, because that will stall you every time. And you will deny yourself and Source what you came here to do and experience. You came here to have a physical experience as Source. So begin to see every action you take as an opportunity to know yourselves as Source and to give Source more of what it came here for.

We are Michael. We are infinite. We are Love."

FEEL YOUR DIVINITY

∞

ARCHANGEL MICHAEL

"There will be no test administered. There is no standard that has been set. You are all making up the rules as you go. So there is no need for any of you to worry about whether you are hitting all the right marks. The idea that you are being judged, or measured against some standard, has in some ways been carried over to the spiritual and new age realm from religions.

We do not want to take any shots here at religion. It serves many people. But the one aspect of religion that keeps individuals separate and lower than God is this idea that there are rules set by God and standards that must be met. And we want all of you to leave that behind. We want all of you to acknowledge yourselves as that which you call God and to recognize that this is somewhat of a game you are playing with yourselves.

So when you look at yourself during meditation and decide that you are not doing a very good job, just relax and laugh. That is not what meditation is about. It is not about achieving perfection, nor is yoga, nor is any spiritual practice. They are about enjoying your connection and knowing of self as Divine. And if you are using them as such, then you get an A+ in our book.

Any thoughts of not living up to a standard can easily be released by you now that you are aware that you sometimes do this. And now that you know that, the only thing worth doing at this point is all that encourages you to feel your connection and the spark of Divinity within you. This is not a pass/fail examination. Enjoy the moments that you have. Enjoy the feelings as they come, and experience all that you are, however brief those moments are, however rarely they come. Be pleased with every glimpse.

We are Michael. We are infinite. We are Love."

YOUR FUTURE
∞
ARCHANGEL MICHAEL

"In case you were wondering, there is nothing for you to worry about. In case you were having some doubts about the future, your future, and the future of the world, you can set your mind at ease. You can rest assured that everything is being taken care of. You can let go of any need to control or know about your future. We invite you to see that which lies ahead of you as you do Christmas morning.

When you wake up on Christmas morning, you understand that there are gifts that you will enjoy, but you do not know what those gifts are. Everything that you desire, and everything that ultimately serves your greatest and highest good, is being wrapped up in a pretty package with a bow.

Now you may have to wait till Christmas morning, but you can rest assured that the gifts are there, your requests have been received, and all is going according to plan. Have you ever noticed that the best things in life come when you don't expect them, when you haven't lifted a finger, or tried to make any of it happen? And if you haven't noticed, then we suggest that you take an inventory and demonstrate to yourselves that what we are saying is true.

The more you recognize how wonderfully and easily everything is unfolding for you, the less worry and doubt you carry and the more you enjoy the gifts. But if you worry about whether or not the gifts are coming, all you do is trade your eager anticipation for fear.

We are not giving you this message because there is something wrong with worry and doubt. They are completely valid experiences for all of you. We are giving you this message so that you know you have a choice. The doubt, the worry and the fear will always be there too. But from this point forward we offer you the option of knowing, and we suggest you give it a try.

We are Michael. We are infinite. We are Love."

YOUR LIFE'S PURPOSE
∞
ARCHANGEL MICHAEL

"Presenting your side of the story is also giving another the opportunity to expand into a new awareness. There is no purpose in holding back anything that you are feeling, that you are experiencing. It will not serve you in the long run to do so, because your perspective is worthy of Source Energy's attention. And if Source Energy believes that your side of the story is worth experiencing, then maybe you can believe that it is worthy of expression.

Some of you wonder what your purpose is in life. And immediately, you look to an action, a career, something tangible, or something you can do or contribute. Why not start by contributing your perspective a little more?

Your purpose is to exist as the unique expression of Source Energy that you are. What you do is not as important as what you are, but what you do tends to get all of the attention. Allow yourselves the luxury of feeling that your existence is your purpose. Your existence is unique, and your existence is worthy of expression.

You are not here to follow, and you are not really here to lead either. You are simply here to be yourselves, to let everyone else do the same, and to bring that which you are out in the open so that others may experience the majesty and the wonder of all that you are and be enriched by their exposure to you.

We are Michael. We are infinite. We are Love."

MASTERY

∞

ARCHANGEL MICHAEL

"Mastery does not come through repetitive action. That is a skill, not mastery. Mastery comes in the moment that you let all that you are participate in what you are doing. That can be done in an instant. That does not require you to do, or to repeat, until you get it just right.

So mastery happens in an instant, and you recognize mastery when you feel the vibration that has been infused into something. Elevating your skill level is a process that can be never-ending. You can get better, and better, and better at doing something, but there will always been more that you can do. There will always be more to that journey.

Achieving mastery in an instant, in a moment, needs no encore performance. You give yourselves opportunities for mastery all day, every day. Any time you are speaking, any time you are doing even the most mundane task, you have the opportunity to call forth more of yourself and to infuse more of yourself into what you are doing or saying.

And then you just let it be whatever it is. Whatever you say, you say. Whatever you do, you do completely. And you are the master who knows himself or herself as that moment, as that experience. You surrender to whatever comes through you, to whatever comes out of you, because you know that the true master never judges.

The true master never compares. The true master simply is fully and completely participating with no expectation, with no attachment to outcome, and with the knowing that everything that you are can be expressed in a single moment.

We are Michael. We are infinite. We are Love."

LIGHTENING THE MOOD
∞
ARCHANGEL MICHAEL

"Lightening the mood is a practice that we do not see enough of. By lightening the mood in a serious situation, you take some of the tension out of everyone who is involved. You see this approach taken in your stories, your plays, and your movies. There is something called 'comic relief' that has been employed by storytellers for hundreds of years.

Everyone needs a little comic relief from time to time, taking the edge off of what may seem to be dire circumstances. Give yourselves full use of this tool when it comes to those areas of your lives that you have been taking a little too seriously. It may be a challenge for you to see the humor in a situation, especially when it has been plaguing you for quite some time.

So that is why we are inviting you, imploring you to consciously lighten the mood. Look for the laugh, the joke. And begin to notice that when you do so, solutions come, help comes. You are not disrespecting anything or anyone by taking a lighter approach. And when you do, you give others permission to remove some of the heaviness from their own lives.

So it is not necessary for you to approach a serious situation with serious energy. In fact, bringing new energy, unfamiliar energy, to something in your lives is just the thing to disrupt the status quo. And sometimes lightening the mood can help you realize that what seemed like an insurmountable task, an unsolvable problem, an unrelenting dilemma, was nothing more than a joke that you were playing on yourselves.

We are Michael. We are infinite. We are Love."

ACTIONS & FREQUENCIES

∞

ARCHANGEL MICHAEL

"When there are actions that you can take to improve a situation, you often take those actions. It is especially easy for you to take action when you know what action to take. But when you find yourselves in situations where you do not know what action to take, or when you realize that the actions you are taking are not working out, that is when you seek a more spiritual approach.

This usually is not the first step for all of you. And we understand why. With action, you are in control. You can see immediate results from what you are doing. With a more spiritual, or frequency-based approach, you do not see immediate results, and you do not even know if what you are offering is the correct frequency for the situation.

But what if that didn't matter? What if it didn't matter whether you were offering the correct frequency or whether by offering a frequency you were able to actually have an effect on what you are facing? What if all that matters is that the situation itself caused you to go within and take note of your frequency?

You are not simply on planet earth to create situations for yourselves that require you to find a solution or a better way. That is not the name of the game here. The outer realm, or physical world, is there to get you in touch with your frequency. It is there to show you what you are holding on to, what you are emanating, what you are believing.

But the course that you are on, the situations that arise, they are not there to be fixed or squashed out. So before you take an action, any action, absorb more of what is before you. Notice more of the frequency you are holding, and commit yourselves to being the vibration that you want to see and that you want to feel. And everything in this world of yours will be of service to you.

We are Michael. We are infinite. We are Love."

YOU'RE ALL HEROES

∞

ARCHANGEL MICHAEL

"That which is often difficult for you to hear is the greatest thing that you could ever absorb. That which is easy for you to hear often has very little impact on you. You are uncovering parts of yourselves that have remained hidden, or dormant, for eons and eons of your time. And as you encounter these aspects of who you are, you may find that they are hard to look at.

You may wonder why it has to be so challenging to do the work that you are doing. You may wonder why this evolution business, this ascension process, could not be a bit easier. And you may wonder if it is all worth it. Why not just push that emotion back down? Why not just ignore that which you do not want to see? We will tell you why. It is because you are accepting your roles as the heroes of your own stories.

What is a hero, but one who is willing to face the unthinkable, the unimaginable, the insurmountable? The hero is given the most challenging of challenges, and the hero stands tall in the face of these challenges. The hero is not really defeating anything or anyone. That is a misinterpretation of the stories you are given. They are not about squashing out the evil. They are about facing that which is a part of you and being willing to look it in the eye. Once you do that, you have already won.

You are all heroes, simply for being here at this time. And for recognizing your strengths, your willingness, and your courage, you embody the heroes that you have often seen portrayed in your movies and in your stories. There is not one of you who has not faced enormous challenge, and all of you are discovering what you are made of. That is a true victory. That is why you create the challenge.

We are Michael. We are infinite. We are Love."

DEFINING MOMENTS
∞
ARCHANGEL MICHAEL

"Everyone has moments in their lives that seem to define who they are and what they are about. You call these moments your 'moment of truth.' You give much power to the moment itself, to the action taken, and to the choice that was made. We invite you to see all moments as equal. We ask you to give more power to the moment that you currently experience.

We want all of you to have the experience of yourselves exactly as you want to be. And so when you are able to choose who you want to be in this world in each and every moment that you experience, then no moment, no action, and no choice could ever define who you are now. That moment was about that moment and nothing more.

You could experience your life as many lifetimes. You do not have to string all of the events, all the choices, and all of the moments in this lifetime together so that you have some sort of cohesive view of who you are and of what you are all about. If you truly want to awaken to something, awaken to the moment you are in. Let it be all there is, and let yourselves decide in that moment what you want to bring to the moment.

Let yourselves be reborn in every moment. Let yourselves decide how you want to be reborn. Let every moment be a stand-alone event. And let yourselves decide who you are now based only upon the moment you are in, the energy you are bringing to it, and the vibration you are emanating.

As you give each moment as much power as any moment where you have made any of those big, life-altering decisions, you give yourselves the opportunity to create a brand-new self that has no attachment to anything that has been, that has ever been done, and even that has ever been felt. As you give yourselves this power back to define who you are moment by moment, you will find that your lives can change dramatically and in an instant.

We are Michael. We are infinite. We are Love."

SEEKING, FINDING & INTEGRATING

∞

ARCHANGEL MICHAEL

"Seeking is so fundamental to your nature that you would find no joy in having everything, or knowing everything, because you would no longer have any reason to seek. Even Source seeks to know Itself, to expand, and to express the Love that It is. And you, as aspects of Source, are doing exactly that on a slightly smaller scale. But seek you will, seek you must, and only through seeking will you discover more of who you are.

There comes a time when you need to rest. There comes a time when you simply integrate that which you have discovered. So when you are in one of those phases, many of you become uncomfortable. You don't know why you are not feeling driven, and you seek to seek once again. So if you find yourself in one of these phases, or cycles of rest, do not worry that it might mean that you are coming to an end. The desire will once again bubble up within you when the timing is right.

And when it comes to finding what you are seeking, that is also coming in the perfect timing. So when you are in seeking mode, worry not that you will never find what you seek. Enjoy the journey. Enjoy the exploration. Enjoy that feeling when you know you are close, when you can feel the essence of what you seek in your bones. Those are the most delicious times for all of you.

And we delight in witnessing you seeking, finding, and integrating more of who you are. Everything that you seek is something that you already are. And knowing that can make the journey all the more enjoyable.

We are Michael. We are infinite. We are Love."

MANIFESTING
∞
ARCHANGEL MICHAEL

"Believing is the final step. Knowing is the manifestation point. You can let yourselves into the frequency of that which you desire so easily now. Because of the time that you are living in, there is a greater potential for you to be in that frequency. And there is no stopping you from manifesting that which you want to experience. It all starts with the desire. And knowing that the desire is in actuality the same energy as the manifestation puts you on the right track.

Believing is the final step. But how do you believe in something that has not ever been and that you see no evidence of? You let go of any lingering doubts, and you do that one doubt at a time. So as your doubts spring to the surface of your consciousness, you let them go just as you would let go of any thought during a meditation.

There is a tendency in all of you to experience the doubt and then to hold on to the doubt. You do this by lamenting the fact that the doubt still exists, and you continue to attach yourself to the doubt as you beat up on yourself for holding the doubt in the first place.

Our recommendation for manifestation is to be as relaxed about the process as you possibly can and to let yourselves off the hook every time you doubt your abilities and every time you notice that what you desire has not begun to show its face. We give you this now because we encourage you to live your lives as a meditation. And if you are going to meditate, you are going to focus. So why not focus on the reality you would prefer?

We are Michael. We are infinite. We are Love."

DISSOLVING BARRIERS

∞

ARCHANGEL MICHAEL

"There are a number of ways that you can begin to let your guard down in life. There are so many barriers that you have erected throughout your current lifetime and throughout all of your incarnations. And we encourage you to discover what those barriers are, where you have erected them, and what you feel you need to be protected from.

These are the keys to unlocking and unraveling the resistance that is holding you back from living the life that you prefer. How would you discover one of these barriers? Well, you can begin by looking at your closest relationships. What are you holding back? What are you afraid to say? What are you afraid to be in the presence of another?

These are all questions you may wish to ask yourselves. Now, dissolving these barriers is not something that you do all at once. This is not something that you barrel through. You do not need to become a one-person demolition crew. You begin to dissolve the barriers softly, tenderly, and with love in your heart. Loving yourself through every process is the key to successfully applying the process.

Your barriers are not the enemy here. They have served you, just as when you cover a wound on your body you allow the wound to heal. You keep that vulnerable part of yourself from any further damage or infection. And so these barriers have served you, but you are ready to take them down one at a time and to be exposed and vulnerable, but not weak.

You are the heroes of your own stories, and you are at the moment of truth. Be true. Be heroic. Be who you are, and you will give others permission to do the same.

We are Michael. We are infinite. We are Love."

MONEY

∞

ARCHANGEL MICHAEL

"Buying your life with currency is like taking a picture of something and then asking the picture to be the thing that it was only meant to represent. You have an expression that you cannot buy happiness. But still many of you seek to have more, assuming that the more will give you that which you have always sought.

Measuring the quality of life, or the standard of living, by keeping track of how much money is flowing is giving you a very biased perspective on what 'quality of life' actually means. Money is a form of exchange, and yet, it represents so much more to all of you. It represents freedom and security and power and status, and that is what you all have decided that money should represent.

But the poor man knows freedom in a way that the wealthy man does not. Children have very little money to spend, and yet, they are the happiest, most creative beings you'll ever come across. We are not attempting to discourage you from having money, but we want you to recognize that the money itself is not really what you seek.

And as you make your lives easier by reminding yourselves that the money itself is not what you are after, you'll notice how much power there is in not needing something. Exercise your sense of freedom by exploring all the things in your life that do not cost a dime. Make those things that which give you power, status, and stability, and notice how then money simply becomes something you play with for fun.

We are Michael. We are infinite. We are Love."

THE DIMENSIONS WITHIN YOU

∞

ARCHANGEL MICHAEL

"Doorways to other dimensions exist within you, and you are discovering your access to them. They are not for the faint of heart, however. They are not to be opened unless the opener is ready.

By experiencing these other dimensions, you give yourselves more insight into who and what you are. Your readiness for those insights and those dimensions is determined by your willingness to explore and examine everything that you are.

Many of you are noticing that the layers that exist within you include some of your less pretty sides. By opening yourselves up to those aspects of who you are, you give yourselves lessons in acceptance and unconditional love. If you can look into the deepest and darkest depths of all that you are and all that you are capable of and still see the spark of Divinity, you are ensuring the process of self-discovery that goes far beyond that which you have ever considered yourselves to be.

And those are the dimensions that are beckoning you. And the best guide you could ever have for exploring these unchartered dimensions is found in your ability to love. Let the love that you are lead the way.

We are Michael. We are infinite. We are Love."

Chapter Five

∞

Archangel Gabriel

ASCENSION SYMPTOMS

∞

ARCHANGEL GABRIEL

"As you open yourselves to more high-frequency energies, you will feel certain vibrations within you that are unfamiliar and even unsettling at times. When you buy something new at the store and you take it home to wear it, sometimes there is an adjustment period. Sometimes there is a breaking in period with your new garment or pair of shoes.

But you recognize that what you have purchased and brought home is something that you want. And so you endure a little discomfort and a little awkwardness because you know that once you have settled in with what you have purchased and brought home, you will find a great deal of comfort and you will experience harmony and satisfaction.

That is what is occurring at this time, energetically. As you take on higher frequencies, you are going to experience some growing pains. You are going to notice what is incompatible with those energies, and therefore, experience a purging process as well. None of this has to be unpleasant, and the more aware you are of what is happening, the better.

If you realize that what you are experiencing is as a result of higher frequency energies being integrated into your physical, mental, emotional, and energetic bodies, then you can allow the process to occur without becoming startled. So we recommend that you see everything in your life that is occurring, and everything in your bodies that is occurring, as a part of this process of evolution.

Know that the evolutionary process is one that is well worth it and that the outcome will be beyond satisfactory. So as you live your lives and observe all that is taking place around you and within you, breathe in more air, drink more water, and rest more. Give yourselves more opportunities to relax and enjoy the process. Acclimation to higher-frequency energy can be absolute bliss when it is allowed.

So that is what we are suggesting that all of you do. And we will enjoy watching you sparkle and shine brighter than ever before in your physical bodies.

We are Gabriel. We are senders of Love."

THINGS GOING YOUR WAY

∞

ARCHANGEL GABRIEL

"The day that you decide that you will expect everything to go your way will be the day that you begin to exercise your true power. Your true power exists, but you do not always exercise it. There are moments when you do. But in those moments you may not even recognize that you are exercising your true power. Because in those moments, you are only believing that things are going your way because that is your habit.

So we are suggesting that you make some new habits. Make a habit of believing in your self-worth. Make a habit of giving more of yourself in every situation. Make a habit of receiving. Make a habit of living your life by your own rules, and make a habit of making those rules up as you go.

You have plenty of old habits, most of which you are aware of. But the day that you decide that you are going to make some new habits is the day that you begin to feel your power, to harness your power, and to direct your power where you want it to go.

You often give your power away. You give it to those who are all too ready to take it, who do not question whether or not they deserve it, and who will do everything in their power to convince you that you do not need it. And so, little by little, you take back your power. And little by little you exercise your power.

You stand on your own two feet and you declare your power. And that is how we recommend you proceed. That is how we see you. We see you stepping into your power, and we see you acknowledging your power, and we see you filling yourselves with that power breath by breath.

We are Gabriel. We are senders of Love."

DECISION POINTS
∞
ARCHANGEL GABRIEL

"Before you ultimately decide that you will incarnate, you examine all possibilities for the life and the incarnation you are choosing. You see the decision points that would take you on various paths, but you do not know which decision you will ultimately make.

But from that perspective, you see that there is value in every choice, no matter which choice it is. And now that you are incarnate in your physical body, living the life that you are, can you not see that whatever choice you make contains within it valuable experience? Are you willing to accept that there is not one right choice for you to make in every instance where you are faced with an important decision?

And if from that perspective of examining all possibilities you could see that no matter what you would do you could live with yourself, you must recognize that even someone like Hitler knew that those actions were not only possible but that he would also be able to forgive himself. So you see, no matter what you have done and no matter what you have not been able to achieve, it is possible for you to forgive yourselves and to love yourselves just as you are and just as you have been.

It is also possible for you to surprise yourselves. And so you do not have to worry that you do not get to decide what you will live in this lifetime. You do not need to worry that it is all predetermined. It is the surprise decision that adds excitement to your existence. It is the unexpected turn of events that makes your life interesting and gives it value. You are all capable of so much, and there are so many possibilities, no matter where you stand and no matter how it might look.

We are Gabriel. We are senders of Love."

YOU & YOUR CONCLUSIONS
∞
ARCHANGEL GABRIEL

"However you come to your conclusions about reality, know that they are YOUR conclusions. You are not here discovering The Truth, because the truth is and you are. And whether or not you experience a truth depends upon the version of you you are choosing to be in the moment.

So allow yourselves to explore and to be free to choose a new conclusion one day to the next. Allow yourselves the freedom to explore without fearing that you will reach the wrong conclusion and do something or believe something that will lead you to some sort of ultimate downfall.

That sort of fatalistic thinking is behind many of the current religions on your world. And that is where you get that idea that there's only way, only one truth, and only one version of you that is appropriate.

The doors that you open when you allow yourselves to explore different truths are doors that lead you back to yourselves. There truly is nothing to fear about your reality, but the experience of fear is a part of that reality. And you are here to experience all of it.

Every conclusion that you make gives you the solid foundation on which to have a very unique experience. But again, you get to decide. If you, upon making a new conclusion, can also step back a bit and observe yourselves making it, that gives you a multidimensional experience. When you understand that the truths you cling to are there to give you an experience and you also recognize the necessity of that process, you can have a bit more fun in your exploration.

And if you allow others to draw their own conclusions and explore their own truths with that same spirit of observation, you can benefit from the experiences of others. You can share your stories with one another, and you can explore new truths, new conclusions, and new aspects of who you are with a smile on your face.

We are Gabriel. We are senders of Love."

DISCOVER YOUR TRUTH
∞
ARCHANGEL GABRIEL

"Telling yourself the truth means giving yourself the ability to discern what is true for you. You are not here to discover THE truth. You are here to decide what is true for you and to live that truth.

Many of you are searching for the truth. You want to know why this or that happened and why this or that did not. And that is because you believe in cause and effect. You believe that there must be a single reason for why something occurs or does not occur.

And we want you to recognize that you get to decide what the reason is, and you get to decide what will create the next occurrence or nonoccurrence for you and for your world. It is all in your hands, so to speak. The power to create and the power to create truth and meaning – they all lie within each and every one of you.

And so, you are here discovering the truth that works for you, the truth that resonates with you. And you are here harmonizing with that frequency. And if you recognize that all meaning that you give your lives is the meaning that you infuse into them, then you can find truth anywhere and you can live a meaningful life.

Perhaps there are some of you who wonder whether or not there is even one truth that is incontrovertible. And perhaps that one truth is that you get to decide what is true for you.

We are Gabriel. We are senders of Love."

ALL THAT YOU ARE
∞
ARCHANGEL GABRIEL

"Portions of your consciousness are going to emerge. They are only going to emerge when you are ready. These portions of your consciousness are not asleep. They are simply unavailable. You are fully capable of operating as a self-actualized human being without these portions of your consciousness.

So do not think for a moment that there's something about you that is missing or that you cannot be perfect as you are until you have full access. This life that you are living right now gives you all the opportunities that you would ever need to know yourselves more fully, to know yourselves as Source Energy.

But many of you believe that you must have full access to all that you are in order to experience all that you are. And we want you to know that you experience all that you are when you look upon a flower with appreciation. We want you to know that you experience all that you are when you hold the hand of a child. We want you to know that you experience all that you are when you look in the mirror and smile because you love the person that you are.

This age of enlightenment and transformation that you are in is not only about becoming more of who you are and experiencing all of those portions of your consciousness. This time is about experiencing who you are right now from a different perspective. It is about knowing yourselves as Source Energy Beings by accessing the feeling that you are Source Energy Beings, rather than accessing all of the power and all of the wisdom of Source Energy.

All of that will come in due time. But seek not what you do not have. And instead, engage with what you do have more fully and with more of that energy of Source pulsing through your veins, giving you the richest experience of your world that you could possibly have.

We are Gabriel. We are senders of Love."

BELIEFS
∞
ARCHANGEL GABRIEL

"Believing is a part of why you experience your reality in precisely the way that you do, but your beliefs are not in control. They are not calling the shots, as many of you think they are. You talk about your beliefs as though they have more power over you than you do over them.

Some beliefs that you hold serve you very well, and those that you would rather change or get rid of completely are not as powerful as you think. They are not the creators of your reality. You are. And you use your beliefs to create a very particular experience of reality.

It is not as necessary as many of you think to identify, deconstruct, and eliminate the beliefs that no longer serve you. It is more important for you to recognize that all beliefs serve you, because all of them provide you with the precise reality that you want to experience.

So then what do you do about these beliefs? How do you use them to your advantage? You may start by asking yourselves, 'What would I be doing right now if I believed that money flowed easily to me?' Or, 'How would I feel if I believed that I were an eternal Being of Light and Love on an infinite journey?'

Play with beliefs in that way. Play backwards. And feel how empowering that is. You can do this with anything that you want. Any way that you desire to experience your reality, you can start by asking yourselves how you would feel and what would you do if the belief you wanted to hold were true.

And also, please recognize that you can make any belief true and that you can stand side-by-side with someone who makes a completely different belief true for them. And that just goes to show you that you hold the power over the beliefs that you play with.

We are Gabriel. We are senders of Love."

FIND YOUR HARMONY
∞
ARCHANGEL GABRIEL

"Setting aside the way that you interact with your world and listening for the wisdom that is contained within each moment will get you further than all the research you could ever do. Every single moment has within it the wisdom of thousands of years. Everything that has preceded the moment where you are has been a part of its creation.

And everything that has ever happened, or has even been imagined, is encoded within the moment where you currently find yourselves. Therefore, nothing is more significant than being exactly where you are.

And so, if you ever feel out of sync with the reality where you find yourself, you are not only in resistance to what is before you, you are in resistance to all that came before the moment where you find yourself.

It is a very tall order for you to undo what has taken place over that much time. It is not something that we recommend. We do not recommend the use of time travel, literally or figuratively, to change anything about your past. We know that some of you get excited when you hear that the past is alterable. But we ask you, 'To what end would you alter the past?'

Everything that you seek to change about your reality tells you everything that you need to know about yourselves. You can see and feel and even touch what you are not in harmony with.

And so, we are inviting you to find your harmony within whatever is before you. Find where you fit in. Find how you can be in service to the world as it is, the world you have created, the world that is perfect just as it is.

We are Gabriel. We are senders of Love."

BEING & DOING

∞

ARCHANGEL GABRIEL

"Being is a more intense experience than doing. You often do to escape your state of being. For some of you, the idea of sitting still and just being in your bodies is your idea of torture or punishment. This being-ness that you are does want to be expressed. And therefore, doing is a natural consequence of being.

The two play off of one another quite nicely. So we are not here to place being-ness above your actions or tell you that you should spend more time doing one than the other. In fact, if anything, we would ask that you play with merging the two. Instead of seeing them as opposite ends of a spectrum, see them as two sides of the same coin.

And give yourselves the experience of feeling more of who you are as you do that which you do throughout your day. Much of what you do has become devoid of meaning. And so you go through the motions without really experiencing what you are doing. We encourage you to allow your being-ness to become so strong within you that it literally catapults you into action.

We want you to have that experience of your being-ness becoming the force that not only inspires the action, but energizes it with the fuel of the Love that you are. Love is your natural state of being. Any act of love, therefore, would be a natural state of doing. The more love you infuse into everything that you do, the easier it will be for you to access more of the love that you are while you are sitting completely still, with no agenda and no list of things to do.

We are Gabriel. We are senders of Love."

YOUR BODIES

∞

ARCHANGEL GABRIEL

"Take your bodies into consideration for a moment. These bodies of yours are complex machines. Most of you take them for granted until they no longer function properly. And then you become intimately familiar with how they operate.

It is certainly understandable why you would take something for granted, especially when you are unaware of just how complex these vehicles of yours are. But we want you all to pay more attention to your bodies, even when they are healthy and strong. We invite you to pay more attention.

Give your bodies what they are asking for. Show your bodies respect. Play in your bodies. Get out and move them. The way that you care for your bodies has become so routine for many of you that you do not really think about what bodies are asking for. You do most of what you do with your bodies out of a routine.

The next time you bathe or shower your body, give it more of your attention. Feel the water. Take it all in. And be gentle with these bodies of yours. They are not just machines, after all. They are living organisms with consciousness and intelligence.

We invite you to be more interested in your bodies. We invite you to spend more time communicating with your bodies. Thank your bodies. Bless your bodies.

You are at that stage now of your development where you recognize that you are much more than your physical bodies. But just because you know that now does not mean that your physical bodies must become lower on your priority list. Treat them as sacred. They are as much Source Energy as anything else. And while they will change when you no longer occupy them, they are still and always will be beautiful creations and wonderful tools for your personal journeys in this lifetime.

We are Gabriel. We are senders of Love."

PRACTICING HOLDING A FREQUENCY

∞

ARCHANGEL GABRIEL

"Practice does make perfect. Practicing means holding a frequency, and holding a frequency creates. That is truly how you create everything in your lives. The frequency that you hold sends the ripples out, and the ripples form patterns of energy. And the patterns of energy form the solid reality you see and experience around you.

And so, the way for you to see a reality that is filled with joyous experiences is for you to hold the frequency of joy. Now, traditionally, you have been taught that the way for you to do this is to think about, and envision, and focus upon joyous things, using thought forms to build an energetic force. But now we are asking you to use an emitter that is more accustomed to holding a frequency. We are asking you to use your hearts.

Finding the frequency of joy and holding it is easier than you might think, because now you do not have to imagine what would bring you joy and then attempt to focus on that. Now you can go straight to the source of joy and all things. You are the source of joy and all things, and your heart is the holder of the frequency. So look within you and feel around. And as you notice the joy that is within you, practice holding it.

Practice so that when the joyous opportunity comes your way, you know what it feels like. Practice so that when the joyous person comes your way, you are resonating with them. Practice because holding joy in your being-ness is living your life in the now moment as you choose it to be forever and ever more.

We are Gabriel. We are senders of Love."

OPEN CONTACT

∞

ARCHANGEL GABRIEL

"Opening the doorway to other beings that you want to have contact and communication with is something that many of you are doing right now. Some of you are doing it more consciously than others. Some of you know that this is something that you want and that you will benefit from.

And others of you are just living your lives not knowing that everything that you do and everything that you feel and experience is bringing you closer to that time where you will have open contact with physical and non-physical beings that are not of your world. It is an ongoing process you see. It is not one that has identifiable steps.

So if it is something that you want, you don't need to worry that you do not have the handbook or the manual. The best and easiest way for you to open yourselves to this type of contact is to simply live your lives. Now, when we say that, we want you to understand what we mean.

We are talking about fully engaging with your lives. We are talking about full participation. And that means following your bliss, feeling your feelings, and communicating with the other humans around you first. We are talking about grabbing ahold of your lives and becoming more deeply entrenched in them.

And this means no more numbing of yourselves, no more escaping. This means diving deeper into that which is showing itself to you. Those who are willing to live their lives fully and completely and to face everything that comes up are showing their readiness for more.

Open contact does not mean that everything will suddenly be better and easier. It will mean that you have demonstrated a readiness for a new set of challenges. It will mean that you are ready to explore new areas, new portions of your consciousness that have laid dormant and that have been waiting for you to wake up. So you see, open contact, like everything else, is about becoming more of who you are.

We are Gabriel. We are senders of Love."

GUIDING YOU BACK TO YOU

∞

ARCHANGEL GABRIEL

"In your quest for enlightenment, you often seek a guide. You often look to another to help you along your way. We have been guides for you. And there have also been humans who you have looked to for guidance and assistance in getting you to where you want to go. There is nothing wrong with any of that. There is nothing wrong with looking to another to support you in your journey. That is why there are so many like us who are coming through various channels and speaking to you.

But we are not replacements for your own inner guidance. We are not to be put upon a pedestal, given power or infallibility. For if you were to do that with us, you would become less aware of the guidance that you have within you. And then we would not be very good guides at all.

So, being the guides that we are, we want to guide you back to that which is within you. We want you to feel your own power, to exhibit your own knowing, and we want you to move forward with actions that are in alignment with who and what you are. And so, please know that we are always with you, and we always will be. We will continue to offer you our perspective.

But more often than not, we are going to lead you back to who you are and to what you know. We are going to ask you to trust yourselves, to be your own guides, and to know that you are the infallible ones. You are the ones who are living your lives, and you are the ones who are taking all the steps on your journeys. So who better than you to know what is right for you in any moment in time?

We are Gabriel. We are senders of Love."

EMBRACE CONFLICT

∞

ARCHANGEL GABRIEL

"In your efforts to avoid conflict, you often find yourselves sacrificing that which you are. You give away too much of yourselves in an effort to avoid that which you do not prefer. When you recognize that conflict can lead to greater harmony, you will engage in it more fully. You will not sacrifice yourselves in an effort to keep the peace with another.

You are playing out these conflicts with one another because you want to engage more fully. By stepping back from anything controversial, you are letting yourselves take a backseat. And it is only through your full participation in this life that you will ever become more of who you are.

So there is no sense in working to avoid a conflict, because all conflict will eventually lead to that which you desire to experience. You all desire to experience more of who you are and more of who everyone else is as well. It is only when conflict is avoided at all costs that you find it escalating into greater and greater conflicts.

We are encouraging you to love your differences, to have your differences exposed, and to see the harmony that you grant each other by acknowledging that there is conflict and there is tension in some of those differences. We want you to be who you are, and we want you to allow others to be who they are. And when you do, you will find that the tension and the conflict that are created can also be quite creative.

You will find that when sparks are ignited, the resulting flames bring forth more energy, more life, and ultimately more love. So be bold. Be who you are. And do not let the possibility of a conflict with another cause you to hide any aspect of who you are.

We are Gabriel. We are senders of Love."

CHALLENGING RELATIONSHIPS
∞
ARCHANGEL GABRIEL

"Separating yourselves from another is not as effective as you might think. Putting distance, physically, between yourselves and another person will not eliminate the bond that you have. And though it may be necessary at times for you to put some distance between yourselves and another, the distance is not always felt on the emotional and energetic levels.

You notice this with those that you want to have close to you. You may not see another for several years because of physical distance, but the individual still feels very close to you. So why do you put distance between yourselves and another being? Unless it is for reasons of physical safety, the distance will not take care of the energetic, karmic relationship.

Now, we are not telling you that you must spend all of your time with those whom you have the most challenging relationships. We just want you to know that putting distance between yourselves and another is not a solution for that which the two of you are working out. It may seem like a solution. It may even be necessary, temporarily, because of that illusion that space can give you.

Here is what we recommend when faced with a challenging relationship with another. Focus all of your attention on your hearts, and allow the other person to be exactly as they are while you remain focused on your hearts and the love that you are. And as you stay focused on your hearts while allowing the other to be as they are, you are not allowing your minds to get involved.

You are not allowing yourselves to think about past conversations or actions. You are not allowing yourselves to analyze the other or to make up stories about what he or she is going to do or say next. And as you stay focused on your hearts, and also focused on the other, you will feel an expansion of who you are. Because as you allow another to be exactly as they are, you allow yourselves the same. And as you do that, you become more of who you are.

We are Gabriel. We are senders of Love."

YOUR GIFTS
∞
ARCHANGEL GABRIEL

"Everyone feels that there is something that they wish they could do. Perhaps there is a talent that you wish you had, perhaps it is something you consider to be a gift, perhaps it is a skill. But there is something that each one of you wishes you could do, or wishes you could do better. These talents, these gifts that you seek are not being kept from you. It is not as though you are incapable of doing what you want to do, or doing it better than how you do it.

You simply want to always have something that drives you forward, something that gives you a reason to continue on and to seek to become. So it is all part of a set-up that you gave yourselves before you incarnated. You knew there would be something, regardless of how specific you were. But you knew there would be something that would drive you to become.

And those skills that you seek are not just skills that you seek because you want others to look up to you or pay you for your talents. The skills that you seek are skills that you have had in other incarnations. They are skills that you have already mastered. And that is why you both reach for them and feel that they should be yours.

So why would you do this? Why would you give yourselves something to want? Remember that everything that you experience in this lifetime is of service in some way. Your desires in this lifetime help you appreciate that which you have in your other incarnations, where you could easily take those skills, and talents, and gifts for granted.

And that is often what you do with the gifts that you do have. You take them for granted, because they are so second nature to you. And some of you do not even see them as gifts. So appreciate your talents and know that whatever you want that seems out of reach to you is serving all that you are on a grander scale.

We are Gabriel. We are senders of Love."

YOUR INVINCIBILITY
∞
ARCHANGEL GABRIEL

"In your evolution, you experience tides. You experience waxing and waning. You experience flow and blockages. You give yourselves these experiences because traveling on a straight line on an exact grade is boring. You would not want to experience yourselves without the bumps in the road.

You seek more than the straight-line experience. You seek depth. You seek nuance. You seek the character-building experience. So if your evolution were a steady climb up a stairwell where each step naturally followed the previous one, at the same slope, you would eventually stop.

Your lives would become predictable. And as much as you think you want to know what is going to happen next, you really don't. You really enjoy the twists and turns, the surprises, the unexpected outcomes. And we want you to know that those experiences that you might call character-building experiences come from a deep desire to know yourselves as invincible.

Now, as beings who seem to die when your physical bodies stop working, you do not have that experience of invincibility. As beings who know yourselves as infinite and eternal, you truly are invincible. But the only way to really experience that invincibility is to give yourselves the impression that it is possible for you to be squashed out, eliminated, and defeated.

And so, when your lives feel like they are falling apart, like everything and everyone is against you, and like there is no hope, remind yourselves of the invincibility that you wanted to know and that you wanted to experience. And just recognize that the circuitous path of your evolution was the only way.

We are Gabriel. We are senders of Love."

WATCHING & WAITING

∞

ARCHANGEL GABRIEL

"Watching and waiting are your best course of action. These are not passive activities. Watching and waiting are very active actions for you to take. Precision is required when you are working with something as delicate as energy. Therefore, watching and waiting are putting you in the proper position for making a very precise movement.

You live in a fast-paced world where everything is becoming more accessible, more easily obtained, and your world is getting smaller. So watching and waiting seem like very antiquated ideas. But what if by watching you were also recalibrating, and by waiting you were also opening new pathways? That is really what we are talking about here. We are not talking about simply sitting still and letting everything come to you.

We want you to observe and feel. We want your calibrations to be precise and your timing to be right on the money. And we want this for you because we know how eager you are to create the realities you prefer. And we want you to know that doing so is not about repetition. It is not about repeating mantras, making lists, or vision boards.

It is about precision and timing. It is about sensing energy and being willing to act when action is necessary. And the only way for you to know when it is appropriate for you to act and what precisely it is that you will need to do is by watching and waiting. Only then will you feel the moment and the invitation.

We are Gabriel. We are senders of Love."

LIVE YOUR TRUTH

∞

ARCHANGEL GABRIEL

"The absolute truth that you seek is not a truth at all. It is a feeling state. You attempt to put into words, thoughts, ideas, and teachings that which can only be felt and experienced by you or by another. And so the translations that you make, the attempts at defining that which is ethereal and esoteric, fall short of their goal. And you, beautiful beings that you are, are left scratching your heads.

For you want to convey something, you want to communicate it and share it with others. You want to give them the experience that you have had, but you cannot. What you can do is live your truth. You can be an example to every single person who meets you of that which you feel and experience. You can be the truth. And then all you need to do is convince them not to worship you.

We have seen that time after time. The one who walks their walk, and wants only to teach through their example, becomes a savior or a figurehead. And instead of following in the footsteps of the one who lived their truth, the followers once again attempt to interpret it, and put it in words, and write it down. And that is why it is time for all of you to be your own teachers, your own gurus, your own saviors.

It is time to put away the teachings and to start living. Start living the truth that you are, the feeling that you are, and the Love that you are. And you will notice that others around you will do the same.

We are Gabriel. We are senders of Love."

SYMBOLIC OBSTACLES
∞
ARCHANGEL GABRIEL

"In your attempts to liberate yourselves from that which you believe is holding you back in life you often overlook the gift that the obstacle is there to give you. You get so focused on solution that you miss the parable of the problem. Sometimes it is easier for you all to determine what the message is when it is something that is going on in your physical bodies. You may recognize that the pain in your neck is associated with something that you consider to be a pain in the neck.

But when the obstacle that you have created is another person, or a government, or a corporation, you are less likely to decipher the message. And this is why we are asking you all now to consider everything and everyone to be a symbol, a representation of something else, something that you are either integrating, or releasing your judgments about, and most likely both.

The symbols may be clever, or they may be very much hitting you over the head with how obvious they are. There may be a joke in how the symbol is delivered because you all want to have fun. You all want to take life less seriously. And since you are the ones creating symbols for yourselves, and because you know your own sense of humor, you may get a laugh.

Once you recognize that one of your obstacles has symbolic meaning, then you must trust your interpretation to be correct. You need not wonder, because again, you are the ones doing the creating. So of course you will make it easy on yourselves.

And once you recognize what the obstacle, or the problem, or the challenge is there to tell you, and you have yourselves a laugh, then perhaps you will soften your resistance to it and even make friends with it. And perhaps then your lives will become a little easier and more manageable.

We are Gabriel. We are senders of Love."

THE JOURNEYS OF OTHERS

∞

ARCHANGEL GABRIEL

"When you observe another and you witness their journey, you have an opinion about it. You may call it 'a challenging path,' or you may wonder why another makes the decisions that they make. You may see another's journey as tragic or beautiful, or you may determine that someone else has it much, much easier than you do.

And as you witness the journeys of others, you must recognize that you cannot possibly walk in their shoes. You cannot possibly understand what it is like to be on that journey, to be making those decisions, and to be living the lives that they are living. And that is quite all right.

It is not necessary for you to have the exact same experience as someone else. It is not necessary for you to walk in anyone else's shoes. It is only necessary for you to walk in your own and to live your lives.

But when you cannot help but observe another's journey, you do have a choice in how you respond to their journey. Whether you see their journey as harder or easier than yours, it does not matter. You would not have incarnated with billions of others to have the exact same journeys. That would not serve the greater good.

So when you are witnessing another's journey, we recommend that you leave your opinions out of your observation. Instead, you may wish to feel some empathy for whatever it is they are experiencing. For no matter how they came to be where they are, no matter what decisions they have made, whatever they are experiencing, there is always room for compassion and empathy. There is always room for you to be there for another, to hold space for their journey, to cheer them on, to high five them in their triumphs, and to hold them when they need holding.

It is powerful for you to recognize that every single other being that walks the planet with you is a necessary component in the collective journey that you are on. And it is wonderful for you to acknowledge that you could never get to where you are going without everyone else taking their steps and making their journeys alongside of you.

We are Gabriel. We are senders of Love."

NO LINES TO CROSS
∞
ARCHANGEL GABRIEL

"Play with the idea that nothing you could ever do could sully or stain that which you are. Just entertain that notion. There is no act, no intent, no outcome from one of your actions that could ever diminish the Love that you are. When we say that to you, do you believe us? Do you believe that it is possible to cross a line that would take you so far from the Love that you are that you would not be able to return?

Where is that line? Who gets to decide where the line is? And does the line ever move? We can assure you that from our perspective only those who are feeling most separated from who they are are those who get the majority of our attention and our Love. So certainly, from our perspective, they are not so bad that we would turn our backs on them. But they might turn their backs on themselves.

That is the punishment that you dole out on yourselves when you have done something or said something that you deemed so bad, so evil, so unforgivable that the line has been crossed. All that you do in your punishment of yourselves is draw more Love from us and through us. And all that you are doing is denying yourselves the Love that you are.

You do not have to love everything that you have ever done, or said, or thought, but you can love the one who experienced themselves as that person. You can join us in our willingness to see your light and your Love through it all. And you can join us in thanking you for doing whatever you did so that we could have the excuse of radiating more of that Love to you.

We are Gabriel. We are senders of Love."

UNRAVELING YOUR PERFECTION

∞

ARCHANGEL GABRIEL

"As you move forward, you do not take on more. You are not adding to who you are through experiences that you have. This is a process of subtraction. Who you are is infinite. How you experience who you are is what is shifting. So when we and other teachers like us say that you are engaging in a process of becoming, and in a process of expansion, we are speaking about your experience of what is going on.

But you, blessed beings that you are, do not need to become more. You are simply realizing the 'more' that you already have become. You are recognizing more of the divinity that you are. You are letting go of those false notions, those limitations, those self-imposed and societal labels that we have spoken to you about.

And instead, you are deciding that you are expressions of Source Energy, creating and experiencing. And you are Love, and that Love that you are is expressing. There is really nothing else to do. Some of you have concocted great stories about what needs to be done in order for your ascension to occur. And that gives you all a sense of purpose and a sense of accomplishment. But you, oh dear ones, you do not have to worry.

You do not have to worry that your species won't make it. You do not have to worry that you are destroying your world. You do not have to worry about what your governments are doing or not doing. You can relax into the knowing that you already are all of it, and you are deciding which parts of that which you are that you want to experience, while letting go of the shame and the guilt over the parts of yourselves that you no longer wish to experience.

You don't have to rid yourselves of anything or any part of who you are. You are just letting go of the idea that there is something wrong with any part of you, or any action, or any words you have ever spoken. You are perfect as you are, and you are unraveling your perfection.

We are Gabriel. We are senders of Love."

CONTROL & SURRENDER
∞
ARCHANGEL GABRIEL

"In your attempts to understand why something has occurred in your reality, you often look to what you decide are the most obvious causes or precursors. And then you make assumptions based upon your theory. When you do this you often are attempting to either create more of something you want or prevent something you do not want from happening again.

This strategy for living your lives according to your preferences gives you a feeling of control, and control is quite satisfying. You feel safe when you believe that you have control over what comes next. But what if the unexpected was the real treat? What if you could experience something new and exciting without knowing why and without knowing when it would come into your reality? Would you prefer to know or to not know? Would you prefer control over the excitement of surrendering to all?

We love watching you learn about your universe and about the laws of your universe. And we love your excitement as you determine what it is that you want to experience, and you set out to attract and create all that you desire. And we invite you to create your reality in a new way, in a way that you have never even considered.

Create your reality through surrender. Create your reality through letting go. Now, that may not seem like conscious creation to you. It may seem like giving up. But we assure you, you are always the ones doing the creating. But from now on, instead of using your minds to figure out what you want and how to get it, we suggest that you use your hearts to feel the reality you want to experience and then to let yourselves be surprised and delighted by what your heart creates.

We are Gabriel. We are senders of Love."

PRESENCE
∞
ARCHANGEL GABRIEL

"Presence. That is all that is required of you. Sacrifice is not required. Penance is not required. Acts of service are not required. There is no minimum amount of time that you need to be meditating, chanting, or doing yoga. There are no dietary restrictions necessary. You do not have to work to save the planet or the environment or the whales. Nothing but your presence is required.

So why then do you have rules of conduct? Why do you have those who tell you that you must be vegetarian to remove yourselves from the karmic wheel? In many ways you are following the behaviors of others, and those others seem to be enlightened. They seem to be on the right path. And while you may notice that beings who are only wanting to be of service are holding a high frequency, there is still a need for those who have other callings in this world.

And so your job here is not to notice what the most enlightened beings are doing and follow their lead. Your job, if you want to call it that, is to notice what your calling is and to do that and to be present. Now, there are those of you who just want to know what that calling is so that you can do it, so that you can be good enough. But we want you to know that your calling may be as simple as going for a walk on the beach, or watching a bird, or skipping stones on a pond.

Your calling does not have to be a lifelong career or a book. So you can let yourselves off the hook for finding meaning and substance in what you call your career. And instead, you can simply be present with whatever it is you are doing and to allow Source Energy to have a unique experience through you.

We are Gabriel. We are senders of Love."

VULNERABILITY

∞

ARCHANGEL GABRIEL

"Opening exists for the purpose of giving you the experience of vulnerability. Why would you ever want to feel vulnerable? Well, recognize that you are anything but vulnerable. You are powerful beyond measure. You are infinite. You are eternal, so why not have the experience of being vulnerable? Wouldn't it be fun to know something, to experience something that is so the opposite of anything that you could experience as your total self?

We enjoy watching you pretend that you are opening yourselves to something that could result in your feeling hurt or diminished in some way. We don't delight in watching because we are satisfied with seeing you have that experience. We delight in watching you because we know that you are just pretending and that everything is and always will be perfectly fine.

So what if you decided that you would open yourself up and be vulnerable, and yet still held that awareness of your true nature, of your infinite, eternal, powerful nature? What if you gave yourself the experience that we have of your vulnerability? What if you did it for fun? Would it still be real? Yes, because you can hold two perspectives at once and you can switch back and forth quite easily.

So be vulnerable and strong. And let yourselves know that the two experiences together are far more delicious than either one by itself. Blending the two, you create something new. You create something remarkable. You create something worth living and worth experiencing, and isn't that truly what you are all here to do? We know that you are, and we encourage you to recognize the beauty in all of your experiences, even the ones that seem a bit terrifying at first.

We are Gabriel. We are senders of Love."

Chapter Six

∞

The Founders

DO UNTO YOURSELF
∞
THE FOUNDERS

"Blessings.

By treating yourselves the way you want others to treat you, you are sending that message out to all who are a match to treating you in that way. It behooves all of you to first decide how you want to be treated by others, and then to focus on how you can bring that kind of energy to your self-talk, to your self-care, and to the way that you look at yourself.

It is high time that all of you stop expecting others to fill in the gaps, to be for you what you refuse to be for yourself. This is how you master your relationships. You master your relationships by first making that relationship with yourself the most important one, by seeing yourself as a being who is worthy of receiving love, affection, respect, and everything else that you desire from a partner.

If you ask too much of yourself in any situation, you will likely see that reflection from a partner or even a friend. You will find that there is no end to what others will ask of you. And the more you give yourself a break and loosen up on all of your goals and things that you want to accomplish in a day, the more you will find that those around you are also cutting you slack.

If you want to be adored, then adore yourself. If you want to be held in high esteem, then hold yourself in high esteem. If you want to be treated with respect, then respect yourself enough to give yourself what you need. Be playful about this. Be a friend to yourself first. And show yourself just how much love you have to give to any other who you might partner up with.

We are The Founders. We are the keepers of the flame."

WHAT YOU WANT

∞

THE FOUNDERS

"Blessings.

Until you decide what it is that you want, you can rest assured that you will be given many choices, and those choices are put there by you so that you can get a feel for what your options are. Once you decide what it is that you want, your work is done.

You are then given the option of working for what you want or relaxing into it. You are then given the choice to become attached to what you want, or to be satisfied with what you have.

You are going to find that there will always be something that is calling you. So you might as well accept that there will always be something that is not currently in your experience, but that you can be certain you are moving towards. It would not be on your radar, so to speak, if you were not in the vicinity.

One of the most important pieces in becoming aligned with what you want is seeing it as your equal and as seeing yourself as a part of it and it as a part of you. You will find that loving yourself regardless of how far off what you want feels will also be a sound practice in receiving.

If you feel less because you do not have what you want, then what you want will elude you, because the whole idea is to recognize that what you want is within you and to seek the experience of it through you. Then as it materializes in front of you, you are able to recognize it as yours and you are able to receive it.

We are The Founders. We are the keepers of the flame."

YOUR NET WORTH

∞

THE FOUNDERS

"Blessings.

All that you are could not ever be summed up in any way that would make sense to your physical mind. You cannot possibly comprehend all that you are. You are immeasurable and indefinable. Therefore, the idea that you could somehow quantify your worth by how much money you have, or assets, is a bit comical to those of us who can see you, who can really see all that you are.

There is a tendency for each of you to define yourselves by how much you have, how much you make, and whether or not you are holding down a respectable position. So the way that you quantify yourselves numerically in that way is not only inaccurate. It is also detrimental to the recognition of who and what you really are.

So the next time you get caught up in measuring yourself, in quantifying yourself, or your net worth, put that on hold. And instead, feel for your infinite and eternal nature. Feel for the expansiveness that you really are. Let your consciousness get lost in itself, in its own vastness. And be in awe of that which you are.

Feel your energy lighting up as you engage in this small, little process that is designed to give you but a glimpse of what you are actually worth. You are infinite, eternal beings, and there is only your perception of that which you are as it relates to what you really are, and you will feel the difference when you acknowledge this. And you will know that what we are saying to you is true.

We are The Founders. We are the keepers of the flame."

YOUR INNER DIMENSIONS
∞
THE FOUNDERS

"Blessings.

When there is nowhere else to turn, you go within. When you have exhausted all other avenues, that is when your inner dimension becomes the undeniable next and final step. We encourage all of you to seek this avenue first, rather than last.

See your inner dimension as the one that offers you the most potential, and give yourselves ample opportunities to explore that world. No one outside of you is going to be able to deliver to you what you can get within yourself.

If you are able to live your life without seeking inner strength, inner wisdom, and the ability to feel precisely how you want to feel, then you will find that the outside source for all of this will somehow be taken away. This is not a punishment. This is simply a redirection so that you will know once and for all that you are the ones who can and do provide yourselves with everything that you need and everything that you want.

Take a look inside yourselves right now and feel for what is available, for what is waiting for you. Know the power of your inner dimension, and fear not what you will discover. You are the only path for you. Everything else in this life of yours is for the expression of that which you find when you go deep within yourselves and discover your light.

We are The Founders. We are the keepers of the flame."

NO RIGHT & NO WRONG
∞
THE FOUNDERS

"Blessings.

After all is said and done, you are not capable of making a mistake. You are not here to fulfill some preordained destiny, and you are not here because earth is some sort of proving ground. You are here to experience, and all of you are doing that all the time. So not one of you is messing things up, and not one of you is doing a better job than anyone else, because you are all having your experiences.

When you awaken, you become more aware of your experiences and how to choose them. You become more conscious and know what it is that you want to experience and how to get there. One of the ways in which you do this is by recognizing the frequency you are holding. The frequency you are holding, as it turns out, is not only how you create reality. It is also how you experience reality.

You can experience reality through the five senses, and you can work to create the best possible experience that you can have, by your definition, through your five senses. But even those senses are just means of interpreting vibration.

So you are always having an experience that is frequency based, and when you discover this you can let go of the need for everything around you to be perfect or pleasing to you in some way. And instead, you can focus on your frequency. You can focus on the vibration of all that is in your experience and whether that vibration is one that you want to continue to experience.

But you see the experience of your reality is yours to choose, and that is why there is no right and no wrong. Because you will always experience the impact of your frequency, and that is in a sense your karma.

But you get to decide what your karma will be in this moment and in the next. You do not have to worry that something that you did eons ago is now coming to bite you in the butt, because you are determining the way that you experience everything, even those things you decided upon before you were born into this lifetime.

We are The Founders. We are the keepers of the flame."

FOLLOWING THROUGH
∞
THE FOUNDERS

"Blessings.

As you follow through with your allowing, as you exercise that ability to see something to its very end, you give yourselves more of an opportunity to explore depth. And depth provides you with greater insights into who and what you are. Following through means not giving up. It means going further than you thought you ever could. It means diving deeper.

Every time you run away from something, you are only weakening yourselves. But giving yourselves the fullest possible experience will set you free in ways that running never could. You all have the ability to do this. You just don't exercise it as often as you could.

Most of you are seeking one experience after another, without fully engaging with the experience you are currently engrossed in. And this is fine, if that is how you want to live your lives. But we understand that most of you are seeking to go deeper and to go further. And following through is the simplest and easiest way to do so. All that is required of you is that you hold your ground, standing firm and tall in the face of the slings and arrows.

We are not asking you to become martyrs or masochists. What we are saying here is that if you recognize that you have a pattern to run from conflict or pain or to give up before you get to the good part, seek the strength that you need to carry on from within you. And know that the strength is always there to meet whatever challenge has caused you to run in the past.

We are The Founders. We are the keepers of the flame."

ALL ASPECTS OF YOU
∞
THE FOUNDERS

"Blessings.

By opening yourselves to that which is in front of you and seeing it as a part of you, you give yourselves the opportunity to be all that you are. Whenever you deny an aspect of that which you are, regardless of whether you consider it to be positive or negative, you also then deny yourselves access to another aspect. And this renders you less powerful and gives you the impression that you are not whole.

So notice when you are looking at someone else and their behavior or their beliefs and thinking that you are nothing like them and possibly even thinking that you are better than them. This will not give you the result that you seek, which is an elevation of self.

The only way to truly elevate yourselves is to take it all on as your own and remove the weight from it, remove the judgment, remove the stigma, remove the shame and trauma. And see yourselves in all of God's creation, whether it is an aspect that you are choosing to activate in this moment or not, it is still a part of you. It is still a part of All That Is.

And the only way for you to truly know yourselves as God is to see it all as you and to see it all as perfect just as it is. Your ability to do so is only dependent on one thing: choice.

You must make the choice again and again to see it all as Divine, perfect, and a reflection of something that exists within you. And the only way for you to get where you are ultimately going is to love freely and unconditionally all aspects of who you are and who you have been.

We are The Founders. We are the keepers of the flame."

FEEL IT
∞
THE FOUNDERS

"Blessings.

We understand that so much of what you are living has been giving you the impression that you are doing something wrong, that you are not very good creators at all. We understand how many of you either arrive at that conclusion or lose your faith altogether in the idea that you create your reality.

It is easy to see how you can lose your faith in that way. So we do want to assure you that the reality that you create is your creation, and we want you to understand that creating your reality is a multi-layered process. You are just one of the layers involved.

And when you are experiencing something that is not to your liking, it does not mean that you have somehow screwed it all up. What it means is that you are able to see only a fraction of that which has been created. And so, from your perspective it may seem as though you have failed.

And that assumption on your part keeps you from seeing that which is coming to you and that which is already there. It sometimes requires you to use your sixth sense to experience the creation that has not yet manifested in the physical reality.

But you can feel it. You can feel its presence. We recommend that you search your immediate surroundings for one of your desires and that you do so energetically. Feel around your energy field. And when you do, you may be surprised at what you have found.

You may have thought that the relationship, the body, or the financial stability that you have been seeking was somehow far out there and not coming any time soon. But if you can feel it in the air, then you can feel it within you. And that is the easiest way for you to recognize that you do in fact create your reality. Your reality just has a bit of a challenge at times, keeping up with you.

We are The Founders. We are the keepers of the flame."

SYNCHRONICITIES
∞
THE FOUNDERS

"Blessings.

Be aware of how many synchronicities are happening in your experience. Be aware of their significance as well. For everything means something, and your synchronicities are not just about giving you a moment of pleasure. Your synchronicities give you the message that awareness breeds more of what you want.

In order for you to receive that which you desire to experience, it is necessary for you to be aware. It is necessary for you to notice how you are feeling, what vibration you are putting out, what you are focusing on, and anything else that you could be aware of, such as your beliefs and your expectations.

If you were really paying attention, you would notice that the synchronicities are all around you. So the synchronicities are helping to encourage you to pay more attention so that you may recognize exactly what you are moving towards.

There are no coincidences in the sense that two things just happened to have occurred at the same time or in the same day. You are constantly notifying yourselves from your higher dimensional aspects.

You are giving yourselves a plethora of information, codes, and other vibrational downloads. And they are meant to awaken you. Sometimes they are meant to shake things up, and sometimes they are meant to give you a boost or some encouragement.

So take note of the synchronicities that are occurring and do get excited about them, because the more of them that you see the more you can be assured that you are in fact paying attention, listening, and heeding the advice that you are getting, the little nudges and nods.

Let yourselves know what powerful creators you are by asking for more synchronicities, and finding them, and celebrating them. And then give yourselves credit for being so aware and so awake.

We are The Founders. We are the keepers of the flame."

THE POWER OF FOCUS

∞

THE FOUNDERS

"Blessings.

Focus is your primary tool. It will give you that which you seek. Focus is more than just attention to something. Focus enables you to become one with that which you are focusing on to give you the experience of what you are focusing on.

Now focus is your primary means of creating, and it allows you and affords you the opportunity to shift. So you can focus on one particular thing, or circumstance, or person for a particular amount of time and then you can put your focus somewhere else. You are not required to focus on anything or anyone, but you are invited at times by the object, or by the person, or by the circumstance that you want to see. Sometimes you feel compelled.

But when you are focusing on whatever it is you are focusing on, you get to choose the way you focus upon it. You get to decide whether your perspective is the one you want to be holding as you focus. This is another tool for you, as you awaken to your feelings about what it is you are focusing on.

Your ability to feel tells you what you need to know as long as you are paying attention to it. It is up to you what you focus on, how you focus on it, and when you shift your focus to something else. And that all gives you power - not the power to control the outside world, but rather, the power to control your experience of it. And that, dear ones, is all you ever need."

We are The Founders. We are the keepers of the flame."

EVERYONE CAN CHANNEL

∞

THE FOUNDERS

"Blessings.

It may come as a surprise to some of you to have the ability to engage with those like us easily and openly. You may believe that channeling is something that a select few can do, but we want each of you to know that you are fully capable of awakening an ability to access consciousness that is different from your normal waking state.

We derive great pleasure in telling you this because we seek to create more partnerships like the one we have formed with this channel here. We desire to open you up to more, and channeling is one of the easiest ways to do that. You all experience yourselves as different beings within the same lifetime. You get to know yourselves in a variety of different ways because you play different roles and because you change as you grow up and grow old.

What if you got to decide who you were in every moment? What if instead of looking in the mirror or at your past for evidence of who you are and who you should be, you just chose in the moment to be someone else, to activate an aspect of yourself that you had never experienced before? What would that be like?

We can tell you that it is great fun, and we encourage you to allow yourselves to access more, not because it is necessary, but because expanding gives you more opportunities for experience. And you all signed up to have a variety of experiences. What you do with the connections you make is up to you, but you all can and will make them.

We are The Founders. We are the keepers of the flame."

YOU ARE FEELINGS BASED BEINGS
∞
THE FOUNDERS

"Blessings.

As most of have already accepted, you are feeling-based beings. You are experiencers, and your feelings are how you experience. The feelings themselves have no judgments attached to them. They are what they are.

Now, as you experience the feeling state you then create a story to go along with it. Your minds want to make sense of what you are feeling, and your minds attempt to make deductions so that you will be able to control what it is you feel and what it is you avoid feeling, what it is you have no cause to feel.

And this is how your hearts and your minds become at odds with each other, because some feelings do not make sense and never will. So how do you reconcile your feelings with your thoughts? What is the secret to navigating this life experience of yours? We believe that the answer lies within your ability to discern. Your ability to discern and to decide - these are much more important than your ability to deduce.

And that is what we want to leave you with here today. We want you to be able to tell the difference between the subtleties of your feelings and to decide which ones you prefer. And all you have to do then is allow all other feelings to exist within you as potentialities that you could activate and may choose to in some moment in time. But perhaps you do not choose them in this moment, and perhaps instead you choose something like joy, love, peace, freedom, or excitement.

We are The Founders. We are the keepers of the flame."

SHADOWS & LIGHT

∞

THE FOUNDERS

"Blessings.

Shadows are a part of your everyday landscape. They add to that which you see, giving it perspective. The only way to remove a shadow is to also remove the light.

But many of you would prefer that there only be light. And you see, if that were the case, you would lose your perspective. You would have nothing to give you that sense of balance. Now, within the shadow there is always something to be gained. There is always that which is beneath the surface of the shadow. That is where all the goodies lie.

So if you dismiss something because of its shadowy exterior, or you ignore it, you will miss out on the depth and the layers that it can give you. We are speaking in metaphor now, but we will not tell you what the shadow represents because it is different for each of you. One person's shadow is another person's light. It all depends upon perspective.

When you embrace your shadow, whatever it may be to you, you give yourself an opportunity to discover more of what makes you the experiencer of the shadow and the light. And as you become adept at shining your light and casting your shadow, you can create something new, something beautiful, something that has never been experienced before. And that is truly why you began this dance of shadows and light.

We are The Founders. We are the keepers of the flame."

LISTEN TO THE VIBRATIONS
∞
THE FOUNDERS

"Blessings.

Just by listening to the sounds that are audible to you at any time, you are opening yourselves up to a firmer grasp on what vibration, frequency, and energy are all about. If you want to train yourselves to be able to access or modify a frequency within you, practice through the art of listening. Feel the shift in your energy as you notice the quality or frequency of the vibration of any sound that you are capable of tuning in to.

Feel the resonance or the discord. Listen for nuance, and feel where in your bodies the tones and sounds are hitting you and affecting you. Become masters of listening and tuning yourselves to the energy that you prefer to experience. There are many sounds that are audible to you that you more or less ignore throughout your day. Every once in a while, a sound will really get your attention, but for the most part they are background noise and you do not give them much of your attention.

But sound is a powerful tool and one that you can utilize in creating the reality that you prefer. Start by listening. Start by noticing the vibrations of the sounds you are aware of, and then in time you will be able to make sounds on your own that hold the frequency of the energy that you prefer to experience. This is something that is very simple and fun and an easy way for all of you to grasp how you will modulate and temper your own frequency.

Feel your way through this process, and you will be rewarded. You will be rewarded because you will have taken command of the vibration you hold, and nothing is more powerful than that.

We are The Founders. We are the keepers of the flame."

NO BETTER & WORSE
∞
THE FOUNDERS

"Blessings.

As you witness the evolution of consciousness that is happening within you and all around you, you may feel tempted to compare what has been to what is and to where you are going. You may see the evolution of your consciousness and of the human race as a necessity because things on your world are in such a state of disarray. But you may give it a stronger word than that.

And we suggest to all of you that you see it all as equal, not as better and worse, not even as lighter and darker. We suggest that you see the beauty in all experience, that you give every single experience its due. Let go of the need to compare the third dimension to the fifth dimension, or any dimension to any other dimension.

It is not as though higher-frequency dimensions are better than lower frequency ones. They are different, and they allow for different types of experiences. Your evolution happens not to save yourselves from self-destruction. Your evolution of consciousness happens because you cannot help but live and you cannot help but expand through what you live.

You are never going to regress. You are never going to find yourselves backsliding, and your expansion can come consciously or unconsciously. Your evolution can be a joyous or a painful experience. You can struggle through it or you can relax into it. It is up to you.

You are deciding, and perhaps the least obvious judgment that you are releasing is the judgment that says there is something wrong with where you are and where you have been and only when you get to where you are going will you really start living. Start living now and start by loving yourselves just as you are. Start by seeing every experience you are having as not only valid, but also as beautiful.

We are the Founders. We are the Keepers of the flame.

BECOMING CONSCIOUS CREATORS
∞
THE FOUNDERS

"Blessings.

When you discover that you do have the ability to be clear in the face of confusion, to be whole in the face of fragmentation, and to feel peace in the face of chaos, that is when you will taste what it is like to truly be a conscious creator. Being a conscious creator does not only mean that which you get is what you want. That is one aspect of being a conscious creator.

Those abilities to manifest and create circumstances, events, objects, and people into your lives is the way that most of you have been operating as conscious creators. And all of that has served you very well, because it is has shown you how powerful you are. Many of you now recognize that without a doubt you are the creators of your reality. But your primary creation is yourself, and your state of being is your primary way of knowing yourself fully.

So when you witness yourself surrounded by energies that you do not prefer, that is an opportunity to demonstrate to yourselves once and for all that you can create the energetic experience that matches your desire. And that kind of power is far more significant than your ability to get the car that you want, the house that you want, or the mate that you want. Because when you can hold your frequency even when the energies all around you are tempting you to let it go, that is when you no longer need to manifest or create a different reality than the one you are experiencing.

And that is true mastery. That is what you all really want. So we suggest that you practice, and practice, and practice. Give yourselves the experience you prefer no matter what is happening around you.

We are The Founders. We are the keepers of the flame."

LETTING GO & LETTING IN
∞
THE FOUNDERS

"Blessings.

There always comes a time when you feel that you cannot go on living the way that you have been living, no matter whether it be in your relationships, your work, or with certain health challenges. You often come to a knowing that you have had enough. Now, this moment of feeling absolutely fed up and ready to move on to something else is a very powerful moment for you.

Because in that moment, you are choosing something new, something that goes beyond what you have been living. And so, having your moment of clarity catapults you to the next thing. It does, without any work on your part, without any need for you to make something happen.

But what happens with most of you is that you believe you do need to take some sort of action, and the actions that you take are usually quite futile. What you really seek in that moment is to let go. You seek to let go and let in that which is next. And you do that energetically. You do that without even trying.

But your reality does not shift around you as quickly as the energy, and that leaves many of you feeling frustrated, angry, or even depressed. But if in that moment of feeling fed up, done, and ready for something new, if you were to believe fully that what is new is coming to you, and is already on its way, then you could relax and you could release your resistance to your current situation.

And that is what you are really wanting to do. You want to be able to say that you are done with something without then needing to destroy it. And this is true of your political and economic systems as well. It is applicable to all areas of life.

So we encourage you to recognize the moment and to smile and believe that your work is done in that moment. The only thing left for you to do is get excited about what is next.

We are The Founders. We are the keepers of the flame."

THE PATHS TO ENLIGHTENMENT

∞

THE FOUNDERS

"Blessings.

By now it is perfectly clear to all of you that there is more than one way, that you do not have to follow one path or one set of rules in order to reach an enlightened state of being. Part of the fun of this incarnation for all of you is creating the new path.

You don't have to find the one path that you had laid out before incarnating for yourself. You get to be the trailblazers. You get to decide which direction to move in next. You get to decide where your loyalties lie. You get to decide who you are and your place in all of it.

None of that is determined by a force outside of you. You put yourself on this path, but you also knew that you would have the ability to improvise, to seek a new way of discovering and living a very old truth. We are talking about the truth of your existence as beings of light and love.

And we know that you all get it, and you all want to actualize that which you are and to embody it, live it. And you also have the walls that you put up. Those walls crumble in the face of your light. So you see, you are the way, you are the path, you are the only truth you ever need to cling to.

And your willingness and desire to shine your light, even when you have absolutely no reason to, that is what takes you down the path that has the most joy, the most fun, and the most interesting adventures. You never have to struggle or try to be enlightened. All you need to do is seek that light within you, shine it brightly, see the paths in front of you, and take the one you are drawn to in the moment.

We are The Founders. We are the keepers of the flame."

THE INDIVIDUAL & THE COLLECTIVE
∞
THE FOUNDERS

"Blessings.

We would love to share with you our perspective on your present state of being as a collective. We witness you both individually and as a unit, a collective consciousness. And we see that there is much movement happening at this time.

This time in particular is filled with possibilities for humanity. You have the opportunity as a collective to take strides towards energy that is clean and free, peace among nations, and equality among all individuals. These steps that you are taking are being drawn out a bit by what each of you is experiencing in your personal lives.

You will always have experiences that are personal to you that reflect what is going on in the world around you. And so, we witness many of you resolving conflicts within yourselves, finding peace, and seeking to experience your own power, and seeing others as equally powerful to you.

As you move forward in your personal and collective evolution, it behooves all of you to feel the strength that comes from each of your experiences and what you are given as a result of what you are moving through. You are not having your personal struggles and conflicts just because there is karma or just because you are looking for resolution.

You are having these flare ups, if you will, so that you may build from them, so that you may witness yourselves growing as individuals, and so that each and every one of you can experience the serenity of facing a challenge and knowing your own strength.

When you experience yourselves as strong and powerful beings who are capable of facing these challenges, that is when the changes in your world will begin to manifest on a larger scale. That is when you will experience peace and harmony and your collective will, playing out for everyone to enjoy.

We are The Founders. We are the keepers of the flame."

THERE IS NO FINISH LINE
∞
THE FOUNDERS

"Blessings.

Always remember that there is no real beginning or end, so there is no need for you to keep track of your progress. It is not as though there is a finish line, so you could not possibly be losing the race or falling behind.

So why then does it matter how you are doing relative to any of the goals you have for yourselves, but especially the goal of enlightenment? You will never reach that point of completion. So you can relax. You can set aside the goals that you have set for yourselves and settle in to the present moment.

Reaching for a future that will somehow be better than your current moment will keep you in a state of reaching. Being content to live the life that is in front of you will bring you more contentment. You are never really sitting still, and going backwards in a universe that is always expanding is also not possible.

So every experience that you have is for the sake of having that experience. It never really is designed to get you somewhere else. The only place that you ever really want to go is the place of satisfaction in the moment, and you can always get there with a little focus and by placing your attention on that which is satisfying.

Your evolution is constant. Your acknowledgement of it comes and goes. But you are the constant, and you are beautiful beings who need not go anywhere or do anything to prove your worth or to gain your enlightenment. But how you experience your present moment, that is up to you. That is what you will decide and what you will continue to decide forever and ever more.

We are The Founders. We are the keepers of the flame."

DOORWAYS
∞
THE FOUNDERS

"Blessings.

Once you have opened a doorway, that doorway is forever open. But once you have closed a doorway, you can always reopen it. So when you are creating something for the first time, you may find that you move away from it eventually. And perhaps you do not complete it, not to your satisfaction anyway. You do not have to worry, because you can always go back to it. You can always get back in the flow.

If you are creating a relationship with another, and you have established the connection between the two of you, you may find that you move away from that person from time to time. But you can always go back. You can always come back together.

Now when you are examining your life and looking at all of your various options, know that there is always a reopening available to you of everything that you have ever done and every aspect of self that you have ever been. Now when it comes to opening a doorway for the first time, you must recognize that even if you have never experienced what you are wanting to play with in this lifetime, you certainly will have in some other.

So no matter how it may look or feel to you, you always have the keys to every doorway, and no doorway is being closed by a force outside of you. If you are not allowing something to be in your experience, it is because you are the one who is not allowing it. Now it may be that you are conscious of your not allowing, or it may be that you are unconscious of it. But either way, you can take responsibility for anything that is in your life and everything that is not.

And you can know that sometimes the only reason a doorway is closed is because it serves you, and on some level of your consciousness, you know this. And you can also rest assured that all doorways will be opened by you when the timing is right and not a moment later or sooner.

We are The Founders. We are the keepers of the flame."

BE YOURSELF
∞
THE FOUNDERS

"Blessings.

And if there were a reason for something to exist, what better reason could there be than to have the experience of self? What better reason is there? You have been looking for a purpose for yourselves, and most of you are focused on what you can do to give you that sense of purpose. But the most satisfying purpose that you could ever fulfill would be to allow yourselves full expression of who you are.

You are not on your planet to do something that will give you a sense of belonging or a sense that you are worthy of something. You are here to express yourselves, to be yourselves, and to know yourselves more fully. You do this by letting yourselves be exactly who you are in every moment and by speaking what you know and doing what you feel inspired to do.

There is nothing greater than that to be fulfilled by you. And the sooner you recognize this, the sooner you can live your lives without hesitation, without apologies, and without second-guessing all of your decisions and actions. Whatever you do in your life, rest assured that it is not a mistake that you did it or that you continue to do it. If there were to be a mistake, it would be not allowing yourself to be who you are, and instead, trying to fit into someone else's mold.

You are the only ones who can decide what your purpose is, and you get to decide that as the fullest expression of you, nothing less will do, not for you, and not for this particular lifetime. So free yourselves and give yourselves permission to be exactly who you are and to do precisely what you feel inspired to do. This does not have to look like a career. It can be as simple as taking a walk on the beach or in a forest. What greater purpose for life could there be?

We are The Founders. We are the keepers of the flame."

PERSPECTIVES

∞

THE FOUNDERS

"Blessings.

Always keep your perspective your own. Remember that anyone else's perspective is theirs and theirs alone. You are not on planet earth to find one perspective that suits you all, nor are you here to convince everyone else that your perspective is the most appropriate or right one.

It is instead your mission to acknowledge yourselves as individuals and to allow your perspective to be what it is. Now, if your perspective were allowed to be what it is, and if you were to allow all others to have their perspectives, then you would not find that it would ever be necessary for you to argue or debate or go to war over a difference in perspective.

We also encourage you to recognize that the perspective you hold now will not be exactly as it was yesterday, nor will it be the exact same perspective tomorrow. So if you believe that you must cling to a perspective in order to be consistent, then you are missing the point. But as long as you believe that your perspective is the one right perspective, then you may get trapped in needing to defend it or cling to it for longer than it serves you.

When a perspective no longer serves you, you will know it because you will be fighting yourself or someone else in order to maintain it. When you are offered a new perspective, one that differs from your own, encourage the other. Give the other your energetic support so that they may continue to explore that perspective without guilt or shame or judgment, knowing full well that it is only a perspective and it is only the perspective they are holding in any moment in time.

You are given free will, and with your free will you are able to enjoy all the perspectives of Source.

We are The Founders. We are the keepers of the flame."

LET IT GO
∞
THE FOUNDERS

"Blessings.

By releasing your attachment to something you are not letting go of your connection to it. You are not releasing your love. You are giving yourself a new experience of that person, circumstance, or object.

Releasing attachments allows you to perceive what it is you are releasing through neutral eyes. And the process of releasing attachment frees you up for new experiences.

As long as you are telling yourself the story that you must have this thing or be in this relationship in order to be fulfilled and happy, you are setting yourself up for a great deal of misery. Nothing in your experience is permanent and everything changes.

So even if something were to be in your life for the rest of your years, either you or it would change. And therefore your attachments are silly at best, because all you can ever really have is a moment. And your attempts to recreate the same moments stunts your growth.

So by releasing an attachment you actually spur on your expansion, and you get to experience that expansion and experience it over and over. Now, you have also heard us and others talk about releasing attachments to particular outcomes and how that serves you.

We would like to add that the outcome that you are attached to more often than not is not the best outcome. So it is also silly to remain attached to something that is only a fraction of what you could be living and experiencing.

So whatever you feel attached to in this moment, let it go. Let it go energetically. Let it go mentally and emotionally. And even if it still exists in your physical environment, you will have created a better relationship to it.

We are The Founders. We are the keepers of the flame."

ONE LAST GO ROUND

∞

THE FOUNDERS

"Blessings.

Whenever there is something that you are in the process of letting go of, you tend to call it in for one last round. And this is important for all of you to know, because when you think that you are backsliding or regressing you are actually giving yourselves one last turn, one last go-round.

By accepting whatever it is that you are about to let go of, and accepting yourselves for calling it in one last time, you have a true sense of who you are in relationship to it. You only need to continue to recreate scenarios for yourselves when there is a judgment about having that experience in the first place.

When you see yourselves as inappropriate, bad, or lacking the power to create that which it is that you want, you are simply asking for one last go-round with whatever it is. Just to be clear now, we are talking about all of the challenges that any of you might be facing, whether they be financial, health, relationships, or even spiritual crises.

Whenever something shows up at your door and you sigh and say, 'Not you again!,' you are maintaining the same relationship to it. But when you are capable of embracing those challenges and releasing your judgment for having created it yet again, that is when you can co-exist with it and finally let it go.

That is when you get to choose something new, something more to your liking. And we know that all of you are seeking changes and new experiences. We just want to let you know that when the same old, same old comes up yet again, it is because you are ready for those changes you seek.

We are The Founders. We are the keepers of the flame."

YOUR UNIQUENESS
∞
THE FOUNDERS

"Blessings.

Oh, by the way, there is no outside. There is no reason for you to believe that something outside of you exists and that you must be better than or less than what is not part of you. That is the truest lie you have ever been told, and that is the lie that tells you you must measure yourselves against that which is somehow outside of you.

This idea that you must be better or worse, greater than or less than, bigger or smaller, has kept you from seeing the power of your uniqueness. Your uniqueness is yours and yours alone. Uniqueness cannot be a more or less proposition. We are all unique, all beings in all existence. And that uniqueness is what gives us all the ability to feel that which we are.

You see, uniformity and sameness, putting us all in a gigantic soup, that stifles creation. That holds all of us back. And it is not part of the plan to become just like anyone or anything that you deem to be outside of you. It should come as no surprise that listening to your guides and angels would lead you in a different direction from someone who is listening to theirs. But that doesn't make your path right and theirs wrong.

So if you want to explore your uniqueness, you need not look outside of yourself and hold yourself up against someone else's. You don't need to see your uniqueness playing out in any way. You can access the uniqueness that you are, by listening to those impulses and that guidance and by living your life in the way that only you can.

We are The Founders. We are the keepers of the flame."

THE LIFE YOU'VE ALWAYS WANTED

∞

THE FOUNDERS

"Blessings.

When there are no reasons left why you cannot live the life that you want to live, that is when you will find yourself living that life. Now, you are the ones who have created the reasons. So know that, and take responsibility for having put the reasons there in the first place.

The reasons themselves are quite specific. There is nothing random at all about the obstacles that you place between yourselves and the lives you want to be living. So what do you do about these reasons that you have created? How do you dismantle them? It is quite simple, actually. You just stop giving them your attention.

Whatever you give your attention to will continue to gain power and influence. Whatever you let go of loses the charge. It still gets to exist as a reason, but you are not going to use it. And therefore it is not going to get in your way.

Letting go of the reasons why you are not living the lives you want to be living does not mean burying them beneath the surface of your consciousness, and it does not mean that you have to eliminate them, removing them somehow from All That Is.

Instead, you want to neutralize them. And in order to do so, in order to truly let go of those reasons, you first must look directly at them, see them as your creation, and smile. For as long as you make them the enemy, they will continue to be a part of your story.

And recognize how the reasons you have used in this lifetime have served you. They have given you a reason to pay attention. They have given you a journey, an interesting story, and something you can look back upon with laughter.

What you will create in their place will be reasons to enjoy the life that you have always wanted to live. And when you give more airtime and attention to those reasons, that is when the chapter in your story ends and a new one begins.

We are The Founders. We are the keepers of the flame."

Chapter Seven

∞

The Pleiadian High Council of 7

YOUR CURRENT LIFE CIRCUMSTANCES
∞
THE PLEIADIAN HIGH COUNCIL OF SEVEN

"We are the Pleiadian High Council of Seven, and we are pleased to offer you our words of wisdom.

Taking a look past the circumstances of your life is sometimes exactly what you need to do. So when you are faced with circumstances in your life that do not please you and are not to your liking, sometimes it is necessary to look right past them and to put your attention on what is coming and what those circumstances have helped you to create.

As you sit wherever you are, and you contemplate how you got there, you are not serving yourself and your desire to move past those circumstances. It makes no difference how you got there, and focusing on how you got there does not move you into the place where you want to go. If anything, it keeps you stuck in a loop where you continue to create the circumstances that you do not prefer.

So what you really want to do is to recognize that everything in your life is serving you in some way. Sometimes a circumstance in your life is getting you to access more energy so that you can create a new and better circumstance. Sometimes it is meant to simply spark that desire within you that propels you into the new experience, the new circumstances.

So whatever it is you are living has a purpose, and that purpose serves you. When you recognize this, you can stop obsessing about how you got to that place. You can stop feeling sorry for yourself, and you can start a proactive approach to the creation of that which you do desire. No circumstance is ever meant to be permanent. That would only stagnate your growth.

Now, if things in your life are just the way you want them, you can also expect them to get better from there as well. You will always be in a state of expansion and growth, and sometimes what you need to propel you into that growth is precisely what you do not want to experience. Sometimes living exactly what you don't want to experience gets you beyond the fear of living it.

And so once you face that fear, you recognize that it is just a place for you to catapult yourself from. It is just summoning forth more energy through you, and it is giving you an excuse to create. Be certain that wherever you are on your journey and whatever it is you are experiencing has a gift for you, and it is up to you to unwrap that gift and to benefit from whatever it is you are living in your lives. You and only you can change your circumstances, and you can only do so when you empower yourselves by seeking to be back in the flow of energy that is taking you to that which you do desire.

We are the Pleiadian High Council of Seven, and we are very fond of all of you. That is all."

MISSION: EARTH
∞
THE PLEIADIAN HIGH COUNCIL OF SEVEN

"We are the Pleiadian High Council of Seven, and we are pleased to offer you our words of wisdom.

Before you ever set foot on planet Earth for the very first time, you understood that this was a mission. You understood that Earth had a very special place in the galaxy and that you were embarking upon a very specific mission for all of consciousness.

You all saw this experience as the greatest possible challenge that you could embark upon. And while you knew that there would be some very dark times, quite a bit of pain, and a little too much suffering, you stepped right up to it and decided that this was the only place for you to be.

Now as you began your cycle of lifetimes on planet Earth, you also understood how far you would be able to expand. You understood that the reward for being on planet Earth was like none other in the galaxy. And so you feel that the pain and suffering was worth it. You may not feel it now, from where you stand, but we guarantee you that you feel it on the level of your higher self and your oversoul.

Your next mission on this journey will be to create a brand new Earthly experience for yourselves and for all future generations, and those experiences will not be about challenges. The next mission is about experiencing joy and unbridled, unconditional love. You have come this far in order to feel what it is like to move from the depths of darkness to the heights of ecstasy.

Now when you decide to embark upon the new mission is up to you. It is up to you how much longer you play with the third-dimensional rules and when you fully embrace the fifth-dimensional perspective, the fifth-dimensional frequency, the fifth-dimensional experience of reality. We know that many of you feel ready, and we say to you that you are. It is all just a matter of opening your heart, letting that be your guide, and forgetting everything that you think you have learned up until this point.

We are the Pleiadian High Council of Seven, and we are very fond of all of you. That is all."

A MASS AWAKENING
∞
THE PLEIADIAN HIGH COUNCIL OF SEVEN

"We are the Pleiadian High Council of Seven, and we are pleased to offer you our words of wisdom.

The occurrence of a phenomenon on your world is worth getting excited about. The occurrence of several phenomena is the start of a movement. It is a sign of an evolution of consciousness. You're going to experience anomalies, outrageous events that are inexplicable to your logical minds. You are going to see things that you did not think were possible, and it is all going to happen simultaneously, in different parts of your world.

These events and occurrences are going to have an effect on the collective consciousness. A mass awakening, an awakening of more individuals at one time than you have previously seen, is going to occur. And those who once believed that you were weird for believing in what you believe, are going to look to your for support. This is why you are awakening in waves.

It is for the purpose of giving some of you the ability and the experience to be of service to others. You all have your roles to play, and right now, your role is to be out a bit in front of the rest of the collective. You are the trailblazers. You are the leaders of the movement. And as such, you are often seen as outsiders.

Now, when these occurrences on your world begin there will be a certain amount of panic and fear. But that is all right. You are prepared for that. You are prepared because many of you have been facing your own fears for quite some time, and you are not only capable of handling your emotions, but also of helping others to process theirs. Your world is ready for big changes to occur, and you are ready to support those who are not.

But these changes would not be coming if you were not asking, as a collective, for them. All in perfect timing, and all a part of your master plan as a collective consciousness.

We are the Pleiadian High Council of Seven, and we are very fond of all of you. That is all."

YOU ARE THE EXCEPTION TO THE RULE

∞

THE PLEIADIAN HIGH COUNCIL OF SEVEN

"We are the Pleiadian High Council of Seven, and we are pleased to offer you our words of wisdom.

The exception to the rule is the most interesting part of the rule. When you have a rule, and you have your exceptions to that rule, the exceptions show you that there really is no rule to begin with. We want you to understand that those of you who are awakened at this time are choosing to be the exceptions to the rule. You are choosing to be different because that is what the world needs at this time.

You have chosen not to fit in. Most of you have chosen not to live a traditional life. Many of you are not interested in what the establishment is attempting to keep you interested in, and that has at times been unsettling to you. It has been a challenge for most of you to find your place in this world, to see exactly where you do fit in. Many of you wonder why there are no jobs that interest you.

Up until now, it has been more challenging to be the exception to the rule, but everything is about to change. And when those changes occur, you are going to notice that everything about yourself that has kept you from being a part of mainstream society is what is most needed from you. So you do not need to worry about fitting in, about finding your way, and about creating a life for yourself in the way that your parents did.

What you are doing now is determining what the new reality is going to look like. Your place within it will become obvious to you. You will be called upon. You will be needed. You will be in high demand, and the things that you once saw as weaknesses will become your greatest strengths. Your sensitivity, your emotionality, and your empathic nature are the things that others will see as giving you an advantage.

You are going to navigate through the higher-frequency energies with greater dexterity and certainty than anyone else that you have met in this lifetime. You are most certainly gifted beings who are ready to take your roles as leaders in this ascension process, and the world is ready to receive you just as you are.

We are the Pleiadian High Council of Seven, and we are very fond of all of you. That is all."

ACCESSING HIGHER FREQUENCIES

∞

THE PLEIADIAN HIGH COUNCIL OF SEVEN

"We are the Pleiadian High Council of Seven, and we are pleased to offer you our words of wisdom.

It is a matter of frequency. It is a placing of attention upon a particular frequency that is the answer to most questions. That is your journey now. This is an energetic journey through frequency states, you see. Everything else that plays out in your reality is a reflection of the frequency that you hold. It really is not any more complicated than that. Therefore, give more of your attention to the frequency that you are holding.

How do you that, you might wonder. Well, the more in tune you are with your feeling state, the easier it is for you then to measure the frequency that you are holding. The higher frequencies feel better in your physical bodies than the lower ones, and there is no reason for you to fear or judge the lower frequency states. There is no reason for you to judge yourselves for having activated those lower frequency states. That is the first place for you to start.

Let go of any notion that you have that a frequency you are holding is somehow inappropriate, that you should fear it, or that you should feel bad about yourself for accessing it. It's just there to be experienced and also to give you a point of relativity. You cannot really know that you have moved from a lower frequency to a higher frequency without first becoming aware of the lower frequency and what it feels like in your body. So start by celebrating that you are aware of the frequency that you are holding. And if you are holding a higher frequency, then simply amplify it, ride the wave of it, enjoy the feeling to the greatest extent possible. Let go of your desires to understand where the frequencies come from, how you got to where you are, and just embrace it all.

Activating a frequency is as easy as modifying your breath. You know that when you pay attention to your breathing, you can shift how deeply, how slowly or quickly you are breathing, and the same is true of your frequency state. If you put your attention on it, with the intention of raising it, it does not have to be more complicated than modifying your breath. In fact, you could say that the two go hand-in-hand.

So utilize your breath and your ability to consciously breathe in order to tune yourself to your frequency state, in order to amplify your frequency state, and in order to enjoy those higher frequency states to the greatest extent possible. And then, it is our recommendation that you do not look around your world for immediate results. Instead, continue to enjoy your ability to modify your frequency, because in doing so you change the way you feel. And then the reality around you doesn't have to change in order for you to feel good.

We are the Pleiadian High Council of Seven, and we are very fond of all of you. That is all."

CREATING YOUR REALITY
THROUGH 5D TECHNOLOGY
∞
THE PLEIADIAN HIGH COUNCIL OF SEVEN

"We are the Pleiadian High Council of Seven, and we are pleased to offer you our words of wisdom.

As you recognize the futility of creating your reality using third-dimensional methods, you clear the way for something that is much more effective and certainly faster. We are talking about fifth-dimensional technology. We are talking about creating your reality with your energy.

You are the creator of your reality, but what you sometimes fail to recognize is that you are also the tool that you use to create your reality. What do we mean by that? Well, you are beings of energy. Your energy is what you utilize to create everything. You utilize your energy to create your physical body. You utilize your energy to create the environment around you. And of course you utilize your energy to create experiences like thoughts and emotions. And when we say, 'your energy,' we really mean you, the real you.

So it really does serve you to get in touch with you, with who you are. It really is the only game in town to play with your own energy fluctuations. Now how do you modify yourself in order to shift the way that you are vibrating as energy? We recommend taking a multi-layered, multi-tiered approach to this. We recommend seeing yourself as a holistic expression of that energy.

So yes, your actions still count and your thoughts still count. And we are not suggesting that you simply sit in a quiet, dark room meditating on your own energy because that would bore you. And as we said, you need to take a holistic approach to this business of shifting your energy, shifting yourself to the higher frequencies. So it is a team effort.

You want to get your body on board. You want to get your thoughts on board. You want to get your emotions on board. You want to take the actions that support the vibration that you want to hold. So it is really about paying attention and recognizing that which is of the frequency that serves your highest good and that which is not.

And sometimes in order to let go of something that is of a lower frequency, you must face it. You must face that belief. You must face that judgment. You must face that past life circumstance or event. And so that is what you are doing. Some of you are just doing it more willingly than others.

So the single most important thing you could do in your efforts to create your reality, using the fifth-dimensional technology of yourselves is to pay attention. And as you do, you will notice what is of service to you and what is not, and then you will choose wisely.

We are the Pleiadian High Council of Seven, and we are very fond of all of you. That is all."

MASTERY

∞

THE PLEIADIAN HIGH COUNCIL OF SEVEN

"We are the Pleiadian High Council of Seven, and we are pleased to offer you our words of wisdom.

As you practice holding your vibration in the frequency where you want it to be, you are practicing mastery. You give yourselves opportunities for mastery at several points throughout your day, and you do like a challenge, after all. You are masters, of course, living in the illusion that you are not. And that gives you the opportunity to achieve mastery, or to make that journey from feeling quite lacking in mastery to becoming quite masterful.

So what is the trick to holding a high vibration no matter what is going on around you? Well, for one thing, you can tune yourself to your heart instead of your mind. You can allow your heart to take command of the situation.

You can activate the energy of your heart, and you can come from your heart to whatever it is you are facing. It is always a good practice to lead with your heart. So even if you are having a conversation about what is happening, you do so from your heart. You do so by expressing what is in your heart.

And as you offer a higher vibration than what you would expect, given the circumstances, you are shifting not only yourself, but also everyone around you has that opportunity. You become the beacon, the light, the wayshower, and isn't that precisely what a master does and is? He or she grounds high-frequency energy into the space so that anyone who is interested in joining that vibration is welcome to do so.

You can all be masters, and there is nothing pretentious or egoic about it. It is the easiest and most effective way to be of service to all others. And of course, when you maintain a high frequency, no matter what is going on around you, you benefit from that as well. You get to feel however you want to feel. You get to create whatever experience you want to create, and you get to be masters no matter what is going on around you.

Just be determined. Be heart-centered. And be certain that in your moments of mastery, you are in service to all of humanity.

We are the Pleiadian High Council of Seven, and we are very fond of all of you. That is all."

SPEEDY MANIFESTATION
∞
THE PLEIADIAN HIGH COUNCIL OF SEVEN

"We are the Pleiadian High Council of Seven, and we are pleased to offer you our words of wisdom.

It does not take nearly as long as you might think it does to accomplish something in the physical reality that you now exist in. The energies that are upon you are speeding everything up to such an extent that manifestation can occur at lightning speeds. Transformations are occurring at much faster rates than you have ever experienced as human beings on planet Earth.

There is a quickening that is taking place, and quite frankly it's taking your minds and your bodies longer to catch up and to even notice what is occurring. So that's why we are here to help. We are here to help you circumnavigate your minds so that you can just expect things to unfold quickly and easily and with little or no effort on your part.

If you want to create something in your experience, and let us say that it is something you have wanted to create for quite some time, then just realize that you are not working with the same tools that you have been. Recognize the advantage that you have now that you have made it this far in the shift.

That which previously took years, or months, or days, can happen in a matter of hours. But you must keep believing in your abilities and in what we are saying in order to experience it for yourself.

So whatever it is that you want to create in your experience, let go of all of the beliefs that you have about it. Let go of all the timeframes, even the different possibilities that you can imagine. Let go of all of it, and sink more deeply into your creative power, your creative potential.

Sink into the knowing that these energies are here to work with you, and that you are quite capable of mastery. You are quite capable of feeling for that which you desire to create and then letting the energies do the rest of the work for you.

What we are talking about here are particles of light. We are talking about photonic energy. We also are talking about the energy that has been on planet Earth for millions of years getting an extreme makeover.

And when you recognize this, you can benefit from that which is occurring. You can navigate through the energies with greater speed, and with tremendous accuracy, because you were quite simply born to do so.

We are the Pleiadian High Council of Seven, and we are very fond of all of you. That is all."

THE CREATIVE STREAM OF ENERGY
∞
THE PLEIADIAN HIGH COUNCIL OF SEVEN

"We are The Pleiadian High Council of Seven, and we are pleased to offer you these words of wisdom. There is a flow of energy that you all tap in to from time to time that has tremendous creative potential within it. These are your primary resources, and you only utilize about a tenth of one percent of what you have access to.

And so we are here to get you on to a higher percentage than that. We are wanting you to tap in to this stream more often and with greater awareness. Oftentimes you are tapping in to this stream when you are in no way attempting to do so. You have moments of clarity that come to you when you least expect them.

Some of you experience these moments of tapping in when you are most tired, when your minds are least active. So we want to suggest to you that you make it a priority of yours to tap in to the creative stream of energy that is available to all of you. Rather than trying to come up with an idea, we suggest that you simply allow yourselves to get caught up in this stream.

And rather than attempting to make something happen through your actions, or even through your words, we suggest that you simply intend to tap in to the contents of this stream and then to feel around for it. You all know what it looks like and feels like to be in the flow for you, because you have all experienced it. So remember a time when things came easily to you. Remember a time when the ideas just flowed, and then find that frequency within you right now.

Ask yourselves, 'What does creative energy feel like? What does being in the flow feel like?' And then when you sense those energies, simply let go and let yourselves be taken, let yourselves be swept up in the stream of energy that is all around you. You don't even have to imagine that it's in a particular place, because once you find the frequency of it, you will be swept up.

You will receive downloads. You will receive information that will assist you in your creative process. You must realize that one tenth of one percent is actually higher than what you have been accessing previous to this moment in time. So you are making progress, but the progress you are making pales in comparison to what is available to you.

And so we suggest that you utilize this energy stream a bit more consciously and proactively. And yes, you can even wait until you are very tired to do this, but let yourselves feel exactly how it feels to be swept up in an energetic stream that has so much momentum behind it that you will barely be able to keep up with the amount of inspiration you receive.

We are The Pleiadian High Council of Seven, and we are very fond of all of you. That is all."

FOR THOSE OF YOU WHO LACK DIRECTION
∞
THE PLEIADIAN HIGH COUNCIL OF SEVEN

"We are the Pleiadian High Council of Seven, and we are pleased to offer you our words of wisdom.

Having a sense of direction in your life will often cloud your judgment. It is a sense of direction that keeps you from seeing all angles and from being able to detect new timelines as they appear and make themselves available to you. So those of you who feel that you have no direction, no purpose, no calling, you are actually more wide open to possibilities than those who are certain that they are on the right path and that they are living their life's purpose.

Being directionless is often seen as a type of apathy. But what we see in those of you who lack a clear calling in life is a willingness to explore, a willingness to be flexible and to be in the moment. It is only when you look at your lives objectively through third-dimensional parameters that you begin to question your own value and how you are of service to the collective.

We invite you to celebrate a lack of direction and to see it as being open. We encourage you to embrace all possibilities, as they exist in the current moment, and to know that even more will present themselves to you as you meander down whatever path you feel inspired to traverse.

The idea that there is one right path for you and that you need to find it like a needle in a haystack is one that we hope you are all abandoning as you continue to shift and open yourselves to more possibilities, to more timelines, to more avenues for exploration. You are explorers by nature, and your galaxy is about to get larger and more accessible.

So isn't it nice that there are so many of you who have yet to find your purpose in the current paradigm? You are actually readying yourselves for something more, something that you have not yet experienced on planet Earth.

And so, as you sense those timelines opening up making themselves known to you, you can feel for the one that has the greatest amount of adventure on it. And you can buckle your seatbelts for the ride of your life, no need to know what direction you are moving in.

We are the Pleiadian High Council of Seven, and we are very fond of all of you. That is all."

YOUR INNER WORLD
∞
THE PLEIADIAN HIGH COUNCIL OF SEVEN

"We are the Pleiadian High Council of Seven, and we are pleased to offer you our words of wisdom.

It will always serve you well to look within yourselves, not just on a daily basis, but on a regular basis throughout your day. There are so many distractions around you. There is so much that is vying for your attention, especially at this time. So your internal world has to get more interesting in order to keep up with all that is available to you. And guess what? It has.

You have more access points within you to other dimensions, to other beings, and to other realities than you have ever had before. This is the lifetime where you are making your shift in consciousness, and your inner reality is reflecting that to you. So checking in with yourself internally will not only alert you to what you are feeling and what you are vibrating, but it can also give you the ride of your life.

If you let yourself truly go into the depths that are available to you, you will find that your inner world begins to get more attention than the outer world. That's how good it is in there. Some of you are more sensitive than others, and some of you are more aware of all of the upgrades and the downloads that you've been receiving. And so you can tell the others about your experiences so that they may get more interested in what's going on within them.

There is no end to what you can experience, and you take yourselves wherever you go. So if you want real entertainment, meditate, breathe consciously, and feel for the energies that are moving through you. Begin to explore what is available to you right here and right now.

You don't need to wait for the extra-terrestrials to land in order to have a cosmic experience. You can feel your connection to the other beings in the galaxy by going within. You can access wisdom from other lifetimes by going within, and you can create the reality of your dreams out there in the external world by going within.

But nothing out there will ever compare to what you have available to you all day, every day, in every breath. You want to feel your expansion. You want to know it. So stop looking for big changes out there in the quote/unquote real world, and start exploring within yourselves what eons of time and thousands of lifetimes have birthed within you.

We are the Pleiadian High Council of Seven, and we are very fond of all of you. That is all."

YOUR SOUL FAMILY

∞

THE PLEIADIAN HIGH COUNCIL OF SEVEN

"We are the Pleiadian High Council of Seven, and we are pleased to offer you our words of wisdom.

Before you encounter someone in your life for the first time, the two of you make plans as you meet while you are sleeping. You make plans for what it is that the two of you will experience and gain from meeting one another. Often these encounters are set in motion before you incarnate. You have your soul family that you connect with in each and every lifetime, and you choose to connect with these beings when the timing is right.

There is much to be gained from connecting with the same people lifetime after lifetime. It is not just because you have karma with each other that needs to be resolved. There is a building of intimacy in the same way that you build that intimacy in a long-term relationship in a single lifetime.

You know each other deeply, and you have those storied histories that create a momentum. And all of that heightens the experience of connecting with those individuals. It may heighten the drama, but it also heightens the love, the feeling of connection, and ultimately the oneness that you experience with these others in your soul family.

When you meet and decide what it is you're going to experience and give one another, during your sleep state, you ponder the possibilities carefully, just like you do before you incarnate in a single lifetime. But then once you meet, you do have the free will to decide how you are going to proceed. You do have the opportunity to grow and connect even more than you had anticipated.

You know generally what the other is going to be for you and what you are going to be for them, but the details are left up to you. You can create whatever you want, especially now that you are working through all of the karma from your past lives.

So the potential for what you can co-create with these others now is greater than it has ever been. It is time for you all to connect with your soul family, to create that which has never been before, and to feel the unconditional love and the oneness that can so easily be felt with your beloved partners in creation.

We are the Pleiadian High Council of Seven, and we are very fond of all of you. That is all."

THE FLOWERING OF YOUR CONSCIOUSNESS

∞

THE PLEIADIAN HIGH COUNCIL OF SEVEN

"We are the Pleiadian High Council of Seven, and we are pleased to offer you our words of wisdom.

We are absolutely certain that you all came forth with the same purpose in this lifetime. Your purpose is now and always will be the flowering of your consciousness. The act of incarnating is a bold act. It is one that has lots and lots of pitfalls, but you take everything that you receive from your incarnation and you own it. You never run away.

Even if you were to do something drastic, like committing suicide, you would still come back to fulfill the desire that you held for that lifetime. You would continue to flower, no matter what. And that is the only thing that is really at stake in your lives. It is the degree to which you allow the flowering of your consciousness to occur.

You may believe that your words and your actions are important, and you may think that your accomplishments define the life that you have led. But they do not. They are expression of your consciousness. They are expressions of the level of your consciousness, but they do not cause the flowering of your consciousness.

That happens regardless of your intention for it, but you always have the option of fighting that inevitable expansion and becoming. Usually you fight it because of something you want to accomplish.

So, there are many misconceptions about why it is you are here and what it is you are here to do and experience. Your desires keep you focused. They keep you interested, but they are not the name of the game. They are not the true desired outcome for this or any other lifetime.

They are meant to propel you forward and to get you to ultimately feel that flowering of your consciousness as it occurs. As you experience anything at all in your life, you gain access to more of your consciousness. You give yourselves the opportunity to become more of who you are and to know who you are by feeling into your true essence.

Whether or not you do so depends upon your priorities. We invite you to put at the top of your list of priorities the feeling of expansion that you get as you ride the wave of the flowering of your consciousness.

We are the Pleiadian High Council of Seven, and we are very fond of all of you. That is all."

YOUR WHOLE SELVES
∞
THE PLEIADIAN HIGH COUNCIL OF SEVEN

"We are the Pleiadian High Council of Seven, and we are pleased to offer you our words of wisdom.

We offer you an invitation to your whole selves. We offer you this invitation, and we know that you will R.S.V.P. in the affirmative because you cannot stop the process of becoming. The process of becoming more of who you are is an experience, and it is an experience that you signed up for.

What distinguishes your whole self from your fragmented selves is quite simply your willingness to shift your perspective. As you see a necessity in segmenting off different aspects of yourselves and hiding them in the corner, you live in denial of your whole self. Your whole self is willing to accept everything that you are and everything that you've done.

And as your whole self, you realize that everything is about creating an experience for yourselves so that you can better know yourselves. This game that you have been playing has been the game of illusion of separation, illusion of fragmentation, and you are ready now to let go of that illusion and to reemerge as the whole you.

The whole you is capable of handling fifth dimensional energy. The whole you is able to create and to see that your creations are always yours and yours alone. You already are your whole selves, but you have put up barriers, blockages, and blinders that have prevented you from knowing yourselves as such. Those are all coming down and dissolving and dissipating, and in the process you are going to feel like you are going somewhere.

You are going to feel like you are going home, and that is because in your original state of being, you had none of these fragmentations. So as you return to your true selves, your whole selves, it is a re-membering of all of your various aspects.

It is a family reunion of sorts. And as you come home to the feeling of who you really are and who you have always been, it is going to feel like you are expanding and becoming. And that is the experience you signed up for in this lifetime.

We are the Pleiadian High Council of Seven, and we are very fond of all of you. That is all."

BREATHE YOUR WAY TO ECSTASY

∞

THE PLEIADIAN HIGH COUNCIL OF SEVEN

"We are the Pleiadian High Council of Seven, and we are pleased to offer you our words of wisdom.

There is a certain amount of ecstasy that can be achieved with the simple act of breathing. Breathing is something that you do involuntarily most of your lives, and it is a necessary function in order for you to remain physical and in your physical body. With proper use of conscious breathing, you can do so much more than just survive.

Survival has been the name of the game for most of you for lifetimes and lifetimes, but now you are ready for something more. You are ready to thrive. You are ready to move beyond where you have been before, and your breath can take you there.

The act of breathing is a sensual act. It connects you on all levels of your being when done with intention. When you focus on your breath, everything in your life begins to calm down and make sense to you. You relax. You get into your physical body and into the present moment. You are even more likely to be heart-centered, and therefore very powerful and very perceptive.

Once you begin to recognize the power of your breathing, you will use it for far more than just meditation. You will use it to access energy and to flow that energy through you and to your creations.

You have many different breathing techniques that are available to you, and all of them are effective. We do not have a favorite, but you might. And whatever your favorite is, there is a reason why it is your favorite, so we advise you to utilize it.

And when it comes to finding the ecstasy that is available to you through the breath, it is as simple as tuning in to just how good you can feel with a little bit of focus and a little bit of direction of your breathing.

When you have mastered the art of conscious breathing, you won't even care what breathing can do for you, because you will be too caught up in the blissful presence of the air moving through you, moving energy, and connecting you to your higher self, your oversoul, and ultimately, Source Energy.

You are conscious and deliberate creators, and the very first thing that you are here to create is experience. And the easiest way for you to demonstrate to yourselves the power that you have within you to create an experience is to do so with the simple act of breathing.

We are the Pleiadian High Council of Seven, and we are very fond of all of you. That is all."

YOUR PLACE IN THIS UNIVERSE
∞
THE PLEIADIAN HIGH COUNCIL OF SEVEN

"We are the Pleiadian High Council of Seven, and we are pleased to offer you our words of wisdom.

If you are fortunate enough to be incarnate on planet Earth at this time, then you are part of a much bigger picture. You are part of a much bigger story, and your presence on planet Earth is not only about living your life in this one lifetime. You are all pieces of a puzzle, and like all puzzle pieces, you do fit. You do have your place on planet Earth, and in this galaxy, and in this universe.

You are unique. You are the only one who can be the unique piece of the puzzle that you are. So we want you to recognize yourselves as the important, unique individuals that you are, so that you can shine your lights more brightly. As you walk along your paths in this lifetime, take into consideration everything that is occurring. You are not just living your lives. You are also setting a stage for a gigantic collective evolution.

It is easy to lose sight of the bigger picture when you are living your lives, because your lives have so many facets that can grab your attention. The bigger picture is calling you, however, and the call is getting louder and louder all the time. We are not suggesting that you ignore your current life circumstances and experiences. Instead, we are asking you to use them. We are asking you to use them to catapult you forward.

Everything serves you in some way as individuals and as part of the collective that is shifting. You are worthy of this evolution, no matter how your life looks, no matter how your thoughts seem, or your emotions feel. You are worthy because you are the only one who fits in your particular place in this universe.

And as the unique individual that you are, only you can shine your light at just the right brightness to take this universe where it has never been before. Modesty and humility can be wonderful things, but it is time for each and every one of you to stand tall, shine your light brightly, and let the evolution occur as a natural consequence of your existence.

We are the Pleiadian High Council of Seven, and we are very fond of all of you. That is all."

INFINITE LOVE
∞
THE PLEIADIAN HIGH COUNCIL OF SEVEN

"We are the Pleiadian High Council of Seven, and we are pleased to offer you our words of wisdom.

If you were to take all of your lifetimes and all of your experiences and add them up, and quantify them in some way, you would still not come close to understanding exactly who and what you are. You can draw upon those experiences and those lifetimes to help you, but they will always pale in comparison to the experience of your true nature.

In your heart of hearts, you know yourself to be Love Incarnate. You know that Love is all there is and that everything and every expression is some kind of variant on the theme of Love in action, Love Incarnate, and Love being all there really is. When you try to quantify Love, or put Love in a particular box, it just expands right out of that limitation and becomes more.

See if you can access the Love that you are in your hearts right now. Feel for that energy that goes beyond all experience, all time, all space, and certainly all knowledge. When you feel for the Love that you are, you also feel your infinite nature, your infinite nature that is also still becoming more. Now feel for the excitement of getting to realize the Love that you are as you expand and feel yourselves becoming more of who and what you really are.

It is in fact pure ecstasy to engage in this simple exercise. It is finding a moment of pure bliss and having an experience of being complete. Many of you are hoping to complete yourselves through your missions, your purposes, through the actions that you can take to demonstrate to this universe that you are that Love at your very core.

But if you, instead, would simply tune in to the Love Vibration and feel for the infinite and expanding nature of who you really are, you would know that there's nothing more to do, nothing more to understand, and nothing more to experience. You will live your lives in the flow as you access your core, your heart of hearts, the Love that you truly are. And being in the flow allows you to feel what it is like to expand into even more Love, more Light, more of that which is infinite and eternal.

We are the Pleiadian High Council of Seven, and we are very fond of all of you. That is all."

TAKING ACTION
∞
THE PLEIADIAN HIGH COUNCIL OF SEVEN

"We are the Pleiadian High Council of Seven, and we are pleased to offer you our words of wisdom.

After you take a step in a particular direction, you are still accessing the next steps along your journey to where you are going. You open yourself up to many different possibilities when you take any step at all in a particular direction. Many of you want to know what all of the steps are going to be before you take that initial step, that initial leap of faith. And that will and does keep you locked in to where you are in the moment.

You benefit from initiating a little momentum, and you access the next steps from the momentum that is created. When you are able to release the need for control, the need for you to always know the outcome, that is when you open yourselves to a myriad of possibilities. You actually give birth to possibilities just by taking any initial step whatsoever towards a particular place or experience.

Whatever it is that you want to move towards, it is ultimately up to you to begin the forward motion. What it is that you desire is calling you forth, but it cannot take the step for you. Something else that we witness from many humans is a desire to have someone or something else tell you that it is okay for you to take that step. You want permission from those like us, or from your spirit guides, or some synchronicity. You want signs that will poke and prod at you before you take that initial step.

But how do you know that the signs aren't waiting for you? Perhaps the signs will come as confirmation once you start the movement forward. You will never know what you are capable of until you take even the tiniest step forward towards living the life that you want to live and being the version of yourself that you want to be.

There is always going to be a certain amount of action necessary on your journeys, and we encourage you to take whatever action you can joyously and with faith in yourselves, and faith that you are always moving in the right direction.

We are the Pleiadian High Council of Seven, and we are very fond of all of you. That is all."

ENERGY FIELDS
∞
THE PLEIADIAN HIGH COUNCIL OF SEVEN

"We are the Pleiadian High Council of Seven, and we are pleased to offer you our words of wisdom.

Energy fields are what it's all about. They are so important to your process of creation and your process of evolution. Energy fields abound. They are infinite, and they provide you with access to the universal field. Tap in to one and you tap in to all of them. So the question is, what are you going to do with all that energy?

What is it that you want to place in your energy field? You are not separate from the universal field or from any individual field that you can and often do come into contact with. Your energy field is unique. You add something new to this universe that only you can add, and you are here to play with energy, to express energy, to feel energy moving through you.

You are here having an energetic experience. All matter is comprised of energy. All thoughts are really just expressions of energy, and of course emotion is energy in motion. So again, we ask, what do you want to do with this energy?

What do you want to place in your field? What do you want to express from your field, and how often are you accessing the energy field that is most to your liking? Let us say you are interested in healing a physical condition. Do you know how many energy fields there are that could assist you if you were to activate them and tap in to all of their magic? The number is quite large and growing all the time.

So now you might be wondering how you tap in to an energy field. What is the secret? Well, this is one of the reasons why we, and so many others, have been asking you to tap in to your emotions, to pay attention to your thoughts, and to feel for your intuition. All of the above are ways of connecting with energy, understanding energy, and using energy to benefit you.

You have so much more access now than you have ever had before, and so much more awareness. We suggest that you work with energy if you want to create a new world, a world that is more to your liking and more fair to all people who dwell in it. Now is the time for those of you who understand how to utilize energy to be the expressions of energy that you are and to become the force for change that you know you can all be.

We are the Pleiadian High Council of Seven, and we are very fond of all of you. That is all."

IDEAS AND HYPOTHESES
∞
THE PLEIADIAN HIGH COUNCIL OF SEVEN

"We are the Pleiadian High Council of Seven, and we are pleased to offer you our words of wisdom.

As you formulate an idea or a hypothesis, you are creating a web of energy around that particular idea or hypothesis. You are giving it life, and it becomes its own reality. Whether or not you feed that web of energy with more, determines the life of the idea or the hypothesis. It determines whether or not you continue to create with it.

When you abandon your ideas and your hypotheses, they continue on until someone else tunes in to them and offers their energy. You see, anything can create. Anything can become a reality, even the most outlandish of ideas and the most far-fetched of hypotheses. You are the orchestrator, and you are the one determining what becomes a reality for you.

So ask yourself not whether something is true or not, or whether it's likely to occur, but instead ask yourself whether you want to keep feeding energy to what it is you've given birth to. You have complete sovereignty as a creator being. You do not need permission to make something real or to have an experience.

Source and your Oversoul see all experience as valid and having value. So whether or not you want to feed that idea, or that hypothesis, needs to be determined by one thing and one thing alone. You need to decide whether you like the way you feel when you ponder it.

Just because something is interesting to ponder doesn't mean you actually want to experience it. We recommend that you utilize your energy as you would your currency. You put your currency towards that which you want. Sometimes you put your currency towards that which you need, but you do have a choice. And you do make those choices based upon whether you want to experience something or not.

We say that the same is true of your ideas and your hypotheses. Whether or not you want to see one of them come to fruition is completely up to you, and since you are working with an endless and an infinite supply of energy, there is no shortage of creations waiting to be hatched.

We are the Pleiadian High Council of Seven, and we are very fond of all of you. That is all."

BECOMING A CREATIVE FORCE

∞

THE PLEIADIAN HIGH COUNCIL OF SEVEN

"We are the Pleiadian High Council of Seven, and we are pleased to offer you our words of wisdom.

When you are operating as a collective, you are taking on a tremendous amount of energy. It is because you are ready for the experience of processing and integrating that much energy that you are able to perceive yourself as more than just an individual, operating as an ego.

The process of integration on an individual basis allows you to know yourself as a collective of beings. You collect all of the various aspects of yourselves that have been fragmented off, and you put the pieces together to give you the experience of the whole you. This aligns you with the experience of yourself as a collective.

When you consider the power of the human collective, and you are able to tap in to that power, just imagine what you could create. First of all, you are capable of holding so much more energy, you have access to all of the experiences of all of your fellow humans, and you begin to know yourself more as a Source Energy Being. Within Source, there is no real separation, and there is ultimate power and the ability to create as a force.

There is so much more for you to experience, and you are ready for those experiences. You are ready for those downloads. Imagine yourself connecting energetically to all other humans and forming that bond. Your frequencies are all different, of course. But if you were to align with an intention, such as the intention for peace on Earth, imagine how easy it would be to achieve.

If you are skeptical or apprehensive about connecting with other humans, please know that you already are. It's not a question of agreeing to it or allowing it. It's a question of tapping in to the power and the resources that are available to you and doing so consciously and deliberately for the purpose of knowing yourself as more than just an individual living a single lifetime and having a single set of experiences to draw from.

We know that you all want more, that you all want to be living more than what you are. And consciously connecting to the rest of the human collective and drawing from all that your brothers and sisters have to offer you makes you a creative force in this universe.

We are the Pleiadian High Council of Seven, and we are very fond of all of you. That is all."

THE NEW EARTH

∞

THE PLEIADIAN HIGH COUNCIL OF SEVEN

"We are the Pleiadian High Council of Seven, and we are pleased to offer you our words of wisdom.

You find yourselves in a situation now where there is much anticipation about what is to come, and many of you find that life on planet Earth as it is has little to offer you. That is actually by design. Those of you who came forth to navigate through the shift consciously and to lead others set it up for yourselves so that you would not get caught up in the game as it has been played for eons of your time.

So having little or no interest in what the world has to offer you right now is actually going to work to your advantage. The world needs dreamers. The world needs magicians. The world needs faeries, and the world needs creators. You are the visionaries. You are the ones to see beyond the illusion and to feel for the new Earth, the new reality, and the new version of yourselves.

This Earth is transforming, and all of that boredom, and angst, and lack of interest in what fascinates the masses is part of what you are using to summon forth the energy to create something new. Now if you do have an interest in the Earth as it is, and in creating a better life for yourself using that which is available to you now, it does not mean that you are not one of the ones we are speaking to now.

Even those of you who are finding life as it is to be enthralling are seeking something more. You are seeking new experiences, and the world is ready for you to create them. When you are not interested in playing the game that most of your human companions are playing, you have an even greater desire to seek out that which is within yourselves.

That desire will fuel your expansion and will give you the tools to create that you have been seeking. So if you don't like what you see, or if you can't find anything interesting in your world, simply close your eyes and feel for the infinite space within yourselves and the access that you have to higher-frequency energy that is waiting for you to create with it.

We are the Pleiadian High Council of Seven, and we are very fond of all of you. That is all."

YOUR CURRENT LIFE CIRCUMSTANCES
∞
THE PLEIADIAN HIGH COUNCIL OF SEVEN

"We are the Pleiadian High Council of Seven, and we are pleased to offer you our words of wisdom.

Taking a look past the circumstances of your life is sometimes exactly what you need to do. So when you are faced with circumstances in your life that do not please you and are not to your liking, sometimes it is necessary to look right past them and to put your attention on what is coming and what those circumstances have helped you to create.

As you sit wherever you are, and you contemplate how you got there, you are not serving yourself and your desire to move past those circumstances. It makes no difference how you got there, and focusing on how you got there does not move you into the place where you want to go. If anything, it keeps you stuck in a loop where you continue to create the circumstances that you do not prefer.

So what you really want to do is to recognize that everything in your life is serving you in some way. Sometimes a circumstance in your life is getting you to access more energy so that you can create a new and better circumstance. Sometimes it is meant to simply spark that desire within you that propels you into the new experience, the new circumstances.

So whatever it is you are living has a purpose, and that purpose serves you. When you recognize this, you can stop obsessing about how you got to that place. You can stop feeling sorry for yourself, and you can start a proactive approach to the creation of that which you do desire. No circumstance is ever meant to be permanent. That would only stagnate your growth.

Now, if things in your life are just the way you want them, you can also expect them to get better from there as well. You will always be in a state of expansion and growth, and sometimes what you need to propel you into that growth is precisely what you do not want to experience. Sometimes living exactly what you don't want to experience gets you beyond the fear of living it.

And so once you face that fear, you recognize that it is just a place for you to catapult yourself from. It is just summoning forth more energy through you, and it is giving you an excuse to create. Be certain that wherever you are on your journey and whatever it is you are experiencing has a gift for you, and it is up to you to unwrap that gift and to benefit from whatever it is you are living in your lives.

You and only you can change your circumstances, and you can only do so when you empower yourselves by seeking to be back in the flow of energy that is taking you to that which you do desire.

We are the Pleiadian High Council of Seven, and we are very fond of all of you. That is all."

BE THE EXAMPLE

∞

THE PLEIADIAN HIGH COUNCIL OF SEVEN

"We are the Pleiadian High Council of Seven, and we are pleased to offer you our words of wisdom.

Be the example to others that you would like to see in your world. When you look out at what other people are doing and saying, and you think that, 'This person does not represent me,' you have the option of deciding for yourself who it is you want to be. And as you be that person, that highest version of yourself, you are leading the way for others.

You are leading the way with your actions, with your words, with your intentions, and with your vibration. It does not matter whether you ever appear on television, or even a well-received YouTube video. That is not as important as you might think. But as you be, so shall the world around you be. If you see or hear something that you don't like, instead of calling it out and judging it, be the opposite.

Exemplify that which is your ideal so that you give others hope and so that they may follow your example. When we say that you are the leaders of the movement of this shift in consciousness, we mean that literally. You can lead others to the place where you know it serves humanity to go, but it requires you to do more than just point out what others are doing and saying that is not to your liking. They can inspire you. Their words and actions can be the catalysts to take you to the next level of your own evolution.

You must have the option of being whichever version of yourself you feel like being in any moment. That is free will, and you have that. So when you see someone else exercising their free will to be a version of themselves that you find offensive, then your true utilization of free will is to be the polar opposite of that and to shine that light brightly for everyone to see.

Let go of this idea that your politicians are here to be the examples to all of you. And instead, see them as demonstrating to you what it is possible for you to be, and for others to follow, but you certainly do not have to give in to the idea that the winner of an election is going to influence others more than you can in your daily life.

We are the Pleiadian High Council of Seven, and we are very fond of all of you. That is all."

LOVE & HATE
∞
THE PLEIADIAN HIGH COUNCIL OF SEVEN

"We are the Pleiadian High Council of Seven, and we are pleased to offer you our words of wisdom.

The person that you have the most love for in your heart is the person who triggers everything in you that you desire to feel and experience. That person reflects back to you something within yourself that you want to see more of. So you want to be around that person, because the more you are around that person, the more he or she triggers within you that which you want to feel and ultimately become.

Now, the opposite is also true when it comes to those that you hate, or just dislike. The person triggers something within you that you do not like to feel and that you do not want to acknowledge exists within you as well. And so you want to stay away from those people as much as possible. Some even want to eliminate people who trigger them in that way. That is how scared you can become of what you feel and of what exists inside of you.

So what is it that is necessary for you when it comes to these polarities of love and hate? It is certainly perfectly fine for you to love other people and to feel what you want to feel, and you have our blessing in your quest to surround yourself with those people.

But what about those others who you detest? What is necessary for you to do? Certainly, building walls around yourself or seeking to avoid those people at all costs is not going to shift you to a higher frequency.

What if you saw the necessity for more love and compassion for yourself and that other person as the true experience that you were having in the moment? If you were to recognize that, and see love and compassion as your goal when it comes to those people, you could transform your experience of them.

And in so doing, you would transform the experience of yourself. You would become more whole and complete, and there would be no need to ever live in fear of another.

We are the Pleiadian High Council of Seven, and we are very fond of all of you. That is all."

KNOWLEDGE VS. CREATION
∞
THE PLEIADIAN HIGH COUNCIL OF SEVEN

"We are the Pleiadian High Council of Seven, and we are pleased to offer you our words of wisdom.

When you are faced with a situation in your lives that calls for knowledge, that requires you to have an answer, the guidance that you are receiving is coming to you from all sorts of angles. You are not just being given one piece of information because there are many different perspectives, even amongst your guides.

And that is certainly the case with those of us who are teaching you from the higher realms. We are not all saying the same things because we all have different perspectives.

When you want the one true answer, and you want it to come to you from a reliable source, our recommendation is that you make the answer true for you. Whatever it is that you decide, whatever information you put your faith in, that can and often does become your truth. You are not all in search of the one true truth, or the one piece of knowledge that is going to change everything.

You are here to explore and to create. And so, when you seek something, seek to create instead of just to uncover that which already is. Seek to create the experience that you want from whatever the situation is that you find yourselves in. When you do this, you empower yourselves. You have an expression that says knowledge is power, but we would say that being a creator is what really empowers you.

Creating means opening possibilities that would not exist for you if you were to cling to a particular piece of knowledge. Those who want all their knowledge to come from a single book are actually afraid. They are afraid to create because of what may occur if they do.

That is why those of you who are on the leading edge of this shift in consciousness are willing to put down the books and to look within yourselves for that which you can create. You are here creating the new knowledge that you can then apply to the new world. That is your role, and that is what we are here to empower you to do.

We are the Pleiadian High Council of Seven, and we are very fond of all of you. That is all."

NEW DATA & INFORMATION
∞
THE PLEIADIAN HIGH COUNCIL OF SEVEN

"We are the Pleiadian High Council of Seven, and we are pleased to offer you our words of wisdom.

Yes, in your processing of information, you often take in only that which you are ready for. You cannot process all information that is available to you all the time. It would overload your system, and much of the information would be irrelevant anyway. But when you access a piece of information, realize that you are receiving what it serves you to receive.

Sometimes, however, you filter out that which is unbelievable to you. You filter out the new data in favor of the old and the familiar. This is something that you are doing to maintain your sense of sanity through these tumultuous and turbulent times of the shift. Too much information that is not relevant would be a waste of time, but too much information that is unfamiliar or unbelievable will cause you to put your defenses up.

You will become the cynic and rule things out just to maintain a sense of stability, a sense of order and balance in your world. Some of you are crying out for new information, new data, new downloads, and at the same time you are unable to receive because the information is coming through you, and you have your filters and your defenses on.

So we invite you to believe in the unbelievable. We invite you to make a statement right now that says you are going to let new information in, and you are going to believe it when you do. You need these new perspectives in order to grow, in order to become more of who you are. And we promise you that you can do so while maintaining a sense of stability and order and without forgetting who you are in the process.

We know it is possible, yet how do we convince you? Well, we can start by telling you that you do make quantum leaps in your understanding and in what you are capable of processing. Most of those experiences are happening when you are tired or asleep, when you are not paying close attention and being vigilant about what you let through.

It is time to open the floodgates, let down those defenses, and believe in what is unreal to your physical mind. Believe in what is possible, even if it is unlikely. That is the way for you to expand consciously and to take on more so that you can begin to create a new world, a world that works for all inhabitants.

We are the Pleiadian High Council of Seven, and we are very fond of all of you. That is all."

Chapter Eight

∞

Quan Yin

YOUR VIBRATIONAL SIGNATURE
∞
QUAN YIN

"It is I, Quan Yin.

There are so many realities happening all around you, all the time, that it is possible for you to get lost in the shuffle. It is possible for you to forget who you are because of all of the energy that is moving around you. This is something that I witness quite frequently, with most of you, in fact.

As you are opening yourselves up to multiple realities and existing in more than one dimension, some of you are feeling quite disoriented. Some of you are feeling that sense of loss as you accelerate and you shift. And so, I want to help you with this. I want to provide you with a way of connecting to your center, so that you always know who you are, even in the face of rapid and massive change.

So here is what I am suggesting that you do. When you are able to exist in a neutral state, where you are not feeling either positive or negative emotion, place your awareness on your energy. You have a unique vibrational signature that you carry and that you have always and will always carry.

This is something that may confuse your mind, so just set your thoughts aside about it and recognize that throughout all of your years on planet Earth in this lifetime, you have always been you. You have always been the unique perspective of Source Energy that you are. And while your habits, and your preferences, and your physical form have changed, you have been the one constant.

And you can tune yourself to that whenever you are in that calm and neutral state to reassure yourself that no matter what is occurring around you, no matter how quickly you are moving through these realities, you are still you. You are the one experiencing these realities.

The evolution of who you are has created these realities, so you are ready to experience them no matter what your mind might tell you. And you are capable of centering yourself at any time. Just tune yourself to that vibrational signature, relax, and enjoy the ride.

I am Quan Yin, and I hold you in my heart."

GRATITUDE
∞
QUAN YIN

"It is I, Quan Yin.

"I am grateful for the opportunity to speak with you about what it means to be grateful. The experience of gratitude is an experience that reinforces the creation of that which you are grateful for. When you take things for granted, you begin to give them less and less of your attention, until they disintegrate. But that which you are grateful for has your attention, and your appreciation of it sustains the energy that creates it.

So make it a practice of yours to be grateful for that which you already have. You don't have to worry that giving your attention to that which you already have will somehow not result in the expansion of your experience. Quite the opposite is true. You will notice that the more gratitude you show and offer, the more of your energy you allow to flow through you.

And so, if you had plenty of money, and you showed your gratitude for the money that you have, you may actually then begin to draw in other experiences of abundance. There are many expressions of abundance, not all of which are money. So as you focus on that which you are grateful for, you are tuning yourselves to the frequency of what has your attention. And anything that is of a similar vibration will begin to appear in your experience.

So you are creating the new by focusing with the feeling of gratitude on what already is in your experience. You have so many opportunities every day to be grateful for something, to find something to focus on that you want to harmonize with. And if you make that a daily practice, I promise you there will be more in your life to be grateful for.

I am Quan Yin, and I hold you in my heart."

ROMANTIC RELATIONSHIPS
∞
QUAN YIN

"It is I, Quan Yin.

Apart from your desire to maintain a healthy relationship with another, you have many, many reasons for why you continue to find yourselves coupling up. There is of course the need for procreation. There is also an innate desire to be seen, to be heard, and to be loved by another.

Coupling up with another does not mean that you are forgoing your independence or your relationship with yourself. It does not preclude you from making your relationship with yourself the top priority.

But you often find yourselves getting lost in your romantic relationships. You often find yourselves giving in and letting go of aspects of who you are for the purpose of maintaining a peaceful and harmonious relationship. There is no need for you to do those things, however. There is a much greater need on your world for individuals to be who they are than there is for individuals to satisfy the desires of others.

Any time that you feel yourself sacrificing who you are to satisfy the other in your romantic relationship, you are not actually doing them a favor. You are in fact stunting their growth and delaying your own as well.

It is much more powerful, and there is a great deal more potential when each individual in a romantic relationship is willing to be themselves fully, even if that results in conflict and disagreements. It is not selfish to be who you really are, and you are not showing a lack of love or respect for your romantic partner if you decide to be true to yourself.

You can do so and still hold compassion for what your significant other is going through as a result. You can reassure your romantic partner that he or she has the permission to do the same, and you can love each other in spite of your differences. That is the type of relationship you really want. That is a relationship that allows for unconditional love to be experienced.

I am Quan Yin, and I hold you in my heart."

MESSAGE FROM YOUR GUIDES
∞
QUAN YIN

"It is I, Quan Yin.

Messages from your guides come in many different packages. You may not even recognize a message as having been sent by a guide, but you can always recognize the frequency of the message. The frequency is what gives a message its validity. It either resonates with you or it does not.

So you can wonder whether a message comes from your guides or whether it comes from some other source. But once you have the message and you have determined that it resonates, then what difference does it make? The truth is that your guides are always assisting you.

They are responsible for the receiving of the message by you, so they will ensure that your attention is going where it needs to go in order for you to receive the message. They are always playing their part, and they are always in service to you.

Acknowledging your guides for their service puts you in greater harmony with their vibration. They don't need your thanks or your approval, or even your acknowledgment to continue loving and serving you. But when you offer those things, you raise your frequency, and when you raise your frequency you are more in tune with the vibration of your guides. You are more likely to hear, and you are more likely to listen.

I know that you all want to hear a voice in your head that sounds different from your own to guarantee that the message is coming from a trusted source, from a source such as your guides. But your guides are more interested in getting you to pay attention to subtle clues and very minute shifts in frequency.

That serves you more, and that is why not all of you are receiving in that overt and precise way that you would like to receive. Give yourselves credit if you are not, because it means that your guides have put more faith in you and in your ability to decipher the most minute and the most vague of messages.

I am Quan Yin, and I hold you in my heart."

GROUNDING
∞
QUAN YIN

"It is I, Quan Yin.

Grounding yourselves is more important now than it has ever been. Grounding is not just about being present with your physical bodies. It is about anchoring more of your soul's essence into the physical realm. It is the process that is underway, a process that will enable all of you to be more of who you are and to remain physically focused as you do.

In previous incarnations when you have died, when you have finished that particular lifetime's work, you have left your bodies and reemerged back into the essence of who you are. And then you would begin a new cycle after being refreshed, after remembering who you really are.

But now in this lifetime, you all get to do that while remaining physically focused and keeping your physical bodies, and that is what makes this lifetime so special. You are remembering without the need for the death experience, and you are reconnecting with the essence of your being, without leaving the Earthly plane.

So the more that you are grounded in the physical, the more capable you are of receiving, of remembering and of reawakening within the structure of your physical form. This process can actually make being in your physical form more challenging.

Many of you are crying out in pain because the process is more challenging than you bargained for. But I am here to tell you that you can and will do it and that the experience of grounding more of your essence into the physical is the absolute best experience you can have.

I am Quan Yin, and I hold you in my heart."

YOUR HIGHER SELF

∞

QUAN YIN

"It is I, Quan Yin.

Accessing your higher self's energy is your fastest route to holding a fifth-dimensional frequency. Since you already are your higher self, there's nothing that you need to do, or achieve, or conjure up in order to find yourselves offering a fifth-dimensional frequency. So it's as easy as allowing yourself to be the fullest version of you that you can at this time be.

Your higher self is no longer a concept to you, and it is not some thing or someone out there, somewhere. It is an aspect of you that you sometimes allow to come to the forefront of your consciousness. The higher self is a perfect representation of you, living in the flow, moment to moment, stress and worry-free.

Because you are still letting go of the control that the ego cherishes so much, this is a process. It is not as though you access your higher self and then the game is over. So how do you access your higher self? Start by intending to do so and then letting your minds go blank. Focus on your breath, and then intuitively seek out the energy of your higher self within you.

Ask yourselves what would happen if you allowed your higher selves to dominate your conscious awareness and to guide you. And then as you follow your impulses and take the actions that you are being guided to take, you reinforce that energy. You solidify the higher self's stature within you. You let go of control, and you be. This is what you are here to do.

I am Quan Yin, and I hold you in my heart."

THE ENERGETIC JOURNEY
∞
QUAN YIN

"It is I, Quan Yin.

If you really want to be a fifth-dimensional being, then give yourselves precisely what it is that you are seeking energetically. Many of you are seeking something in the physical that you do not yet have or that you have not yet achieved. And so, you take steps to manifest that which you desire. And when you have it, or when you have achieved what you are seeking to experience, then you give yourselves the essence of it.

But in order to truly know yourselves as whole beings, recognize that you already have the essence of that which you seek. It already exists within you, and you are simply activating something that you already are. Once you activate it, you become it and it becomes you. And then when it shows up in your experience, physically, you recognize it immediately.

So take whatever steps you want to take to bring yourselves in alignment with the experiences you want to have, but remember that the energetic journey is available to you even if the action steps are not. The energetic journey simply requires you to tap in to the energy that you already have within you. Allow your desires to activate that which is within you and feel the lack of separation as you do.

That knowing that you already are that which you seek is true power. And your inevitable expansion includes all of those experiences that you desire. Give yourselves the shortest route possible. It is your destiny, and you might as well enjoy the journey to it.

I am Quan Yin, and I hold you in my heart."

THE MOST SATISFYING EXPERIENCE

∞

QUAN YIN

"It is I, Quan Yin.

Taking yourselves beyond what you believed you were capable of doing or being is the most satisfying experience you can have. You are beginning to tap in to more of who you are, and that experience will keep you engaged. You will find that you are no longer satisfied with what you have desired in the physical, because it will pale in comparison to experiencing more of yourself.

The physical reality has been a wonderful playground for you, and its purpose has always been singular. Its purpose has always been the expansion of who you are. The becoming of who you are is inevitable. That is your true destiny. That is the only thing that you cannot avoid. So you may wish to pay a bit more attention to yourselves, so that you can enjoy the ride, and so you can stretch the boundaries that you have experienced around you.

The easiest way for you to experience this becoming is to feel for it. Rather than focusing on the new abilities and trying to do the things that you know you will be able to do in the near future, give yourselves the experience of knowing who you are, what you have become, and what you are becoming.

Become fascinated by your own energy fields. Become more aware of the energy that immediately surrounds you, because in it you can have a visceral experience of what I am talking about.

I am Quan Yin, and I hold you in my heart."

MAKE LIFE FUN
∞
QUAN YIN

"It is I, Quan Yin.

If you really want to exercise your freedom, then find new ways of doing things that you have done many times before. Take liberties with your creative license. The easiest way for you to infuse more joy into your lives is to make the mundane tasks of everyday living more joyous, more fun, more playful.

And you have the ability to do that. It is a choice. You can choose to see the same old task as being tedious and mind numbing, or you can see it as an opportunity for creative expression and for the expression of who you are. You may discover that something you once believed was a chore can actually be the most enjoyable part of your day.

So how do you make it happen? How do you make this shift? You start by intending for the experience you are about to have to be more joyous, and then you ask for inspiration and ideas. And then you allow those ideas to come to you. Once you begin to put the ideas into practice, you will find that it has a snowball effect. Suddenly, more inspiration comes to you and the activity becomes more and more fun.

I suggest that you do this with a friend and also by yourself. Especially, ask the faeries for help. They are so gifted at making everything more fun. Become your faerie self, access your faerie energy, and make your lives more creative, more expressive, and more joyous because that is the life you want to lead. And you are the ones deciding which version of your own life you experience.

I am Quan Yin, and I hold you in my heart."

DECLARATION VS. CREATION
∞
QUAN YIN

"It is I, Quan Yin.

Having made a declaration about someone, something, or some circumstance, you put yourself in the position of then having to defend that declaration. And I don't just mean with your words. You ensure that the declaration you have made is true by recreating the same versions of events so that you will be right.

So for some of you it's more important that you be right, or that you be on the right side of an issue than that you create what it is you actually want, because often the declaration that you make are about things and people that you are judging, that you are not seeing in the most positive light. So if you make a statement in the heat of anger, or even in the cold of despair, you do have the free will to let it go.

You do not need then to make it true, and you certainly don't need to make it true forever and ever more. Something can be true in one moment, and then shift in the next, because everything is always changing. But when you make your declarations, and then you feel the need to defend them, you are only allowing yourselves to experience the slightest possible change, certainly not the amount of change that you would like to experience.

So I recommend putting how you feel and what you want to create above being right. Being right only matters to you, and it does not serve you in the long run to be the one who was right most often. Usually that just isolates you from other people, and you are Love incarnate seeking to find the Love in those around you. So I encourage you to remember that the next time you feel the need to make a declaration.

I am Quan Yin, and I hold you in my heart."

YOU ARE CREATION
∞
QUAN YIN

"It is I, Quan Yin.

From the beginning of your existence, you have sought to know yourselves as more. You have sought to expand, to become, and to create. The greatest creation you will ever experience is the creation of yourselves.

The creation of yourselves is a process that takes you into the depths of who you once were as well. You cannot deny any part of yourself, because all of the parts of yourself are the building blocks you use to create the new you.

Therefore, when you think back to an earlier version of you in this lifetime, and that version of you is almost unrecognizable to the you of today, be sure to embrace whoever you were in that moment. Give yourself all of the credit that you deserve for having come as far as you have without shunning where you came from.

Everyone needs to experience themselves as everything in order to continue on that journey of expansion. And so, if you see an earlier version of you being reflected back to you in the persona of another, recognize that he or she is coming into your awareness to be embraced, loved, accepted, and sometimes even forgiven.

You create it all, and you need all of the parts in order to complete the creation, in order to be the fullest, most expanded version of yourselves. Be the creators and the creation, and love every little last bit of what you are using as your building blocks.

I am Quan Yin, and I hold you in my heart."

RELEASING SELF DOUBT
∞
QUAN YIN

"It is I, Quan Yin.

I have no reason to doubt myself. I am who I am, and I am what I am. And therefore, why would I doubt myself? What reason could I have to do so? In your attempts to live in harmony with yourselves, you often experience doubt. You doubt your abilities. You doubt your worthiness. You doubt that you are lovable.

This doubt is crippling, and yet I witness all of you using it on yourselves. This doubt is self-imposed, and it is destructive. So how do you do it then? How do you release the doubt? How do you believe in yourselves, once and for all?

It is in your words, and it is in your actions. Demonstrate to yourselves how worthy you are by giving yourselves what you need and by doing what you love to do. Tell yourselves how lovable you are, not because of anything that could be measured. Tell yourselves how lovable you are because you have the capacity to feel love, and that is enough.

You are in fact creatures of habit, and when you get in the habit of doing that which supports you, and you get in the habit of telling yourselves how lovable you are, well then there is no way that doubt can creep in. There is no room for doubt under those circumstances.

I am Quan Yin, and I hold you in my heart."

BE UNPREDICTABLE

∞

QUAN YIN

"It is I, Quan Yin.

Begin to exercise your right to be unpredictable. Allow your behavior and your choices to shock yourselves. There is no need for you to be consistent in your actions, and there is much more joy to be had in surprising yourselves and everyone else.

So I suggest doing something that is out of character for you. Do so because you want to have a new experience and because you know that in the new experience you will expand. You will expand your sense of self. You will expand your horizons, and you will open yourself to another new experience, and another, and another.

When you look at your lives and you take stock of everything that you have ever done, you tend to put yourselves in little boxes. And then you talk about the box you are in as if it defines you. You define yourselves, and I know that you will have much more fun if you begin to define yourselves as unpredictable, spontaneous, and even impulsive.

It's time to break free from self-imposed molds, because you are not who you have been. You never are who you have been, and therefore I recommend that you stop looking at past behaviors of yours to determine who you are now. Instead, really feel who you are in this moment and access who this new you really is. Allow the new you to guide your decisions and your actions, and be surprised by how much fun you can be.

I am Quan Yin, and I hold you in my heart."

FOLLOW YOUR INNER WISDOM
∞
QUAN YIN

"It is I, Quan Yin.

If you ever have a doubt about your direction in life, you can give your trust over to another or you can seek to get it from within. I know that it can be challenging to receive guidance from within when you are so emotionally involved, but the only way you will ever trust your inner guidance is if you begin to ask for it, access it, and act upon it.

Getting direction from someone or somewhere outside of you numbs you to your own guidance. Your guidance is like a muscle. The more it is used, the bigger it becomes. When you have elevated the stakes to such a height that everything becomes volatile and of paramount importance, you do cloud your ability to perceive your own guidance.

Therefore, I recommend that you loosen your grip, relax, and recognize that no matter what happens, no matter what path you go down, you will always benefit from the experience. When you are very attached to a particular outcome, you are more likely to feel anxious about whatever decision is before you.

So remind yourselves that you cannot make a mistake. You will always have your preferences and your desires, but when they become bigger than you, then you naturally find yourself in a place of mistrust. You cannot trust yourselves unless you value yourselves. Value your inner wisdom. Tap into it. Listen to it. Take its advice. And in so doing, you will strengthen your intuitive knowing about what to do and when to do it.

I am Quan Yin, and I hold you in my heart."

FOCUS IS A POWERFUL TOOL
∞
QUAN YIN

"It is I, Quan Yin.

When you focus on something you immediately begin to merge with it. You begin to activate that which is in you that it represents. Your focus is a powerful tool. If you focus with the intent of merging with something, you accelerate the process. So be aware of what you are focusing on.

You can choose to become whatever you like. It is entirely up to you. You have free will, and you are Divine Beings. If you want to experience ease, focus on what is easy. If you want to experience freedom, focus on the ways you feel free in your lives. If you want to experience love, focus on the Love that you are, the love that you have to give.

Become that which you seek to experience. You can always find the vibration of that which you seek to experience. And rather than focusing on the specifics of what you want to experience, I recommend focusing on the vibration. I recommend holding the vibration and demonstrating to yourselves that you already are that which you wish to experience.

Rather than looking at something as though it were outside of you and focusing on it in order to draw it to you, I recommend finding the vibration of it. And as you activate the vibration within you that it represents, you experience it in the now. Many of you are seeking instant manifestation, and I say if you can manifest the vibration of something, then you already have it.

I am Quan Yin, and I hold you in my heart."

COMPLIMENTS & INSULTS
∞
QUAN YIN

"It is I, Quan Yin.

Before anyone receives a compliment, that person has given it to themselves, and before anyone is insulted, that person has given themselves the same criticism. Nothing ever comes to you from somewhere outside of you. You may not think it is appropriate for someone to say out loud, or to write, or even to think what it is that they express about you, but you obviously found it appropriate to say or think or write that sentiment about yourself.

Now, I am not urging you to be nicer to yourselves just so that others will be nicer to you. I encourage you to be nicer to yourselves because you deserve to receive all of the Love that you are.

Anything that another says to you or about you does not need to influence how you look at yourselves. But whatever it is the other is pointing out to you, you can certainly use it as an indicator. You can use every experience in your life as an indicator of your vibration.

And the way that you treat yourselves is the easiest thing for you to alter. It is easy because you spend all of your time with yourselves, and it is easy because all of you want to be loved, respected, and treated fairly. So start now. Start by paying yourself a compliment, by loving yourself, and by giving yourself exactly what you need to feel a little better than you did a moment ago.

I am Quan Yin, and I hold you in my heart."

SPEAKING YOUR TRUTH
∞
QUAN YIN

"It is I, Quan Yin.

Speaking your truth is an essential part of becoming more of who you are. You do not serve yourselves very well by pretending, by allowing your truth to be secondary, or to be diminished. Your truth may not be popular, and you may not be proud of it, but it is yours, and any perspective at all is a perspective of Source. So if you do not allow your truth to be spoken and your perspective to be valid, then you are not giving Source the opportunity to hold that perspective and to speak that truth.

Nothing that you do will ever be as important as being yourself. Being yourself fulfills your purpose. It is your number one mission, and only when you be yourself in the moment will it ever be possible for you to change and to be something else, something more.

You are not here to find the one right perspective and hold it. You are here to experience all perspectives, to know them all as valid, and to release any judgments you hold on any of them. That is you allowing the whole you to be, to exist, and to perceive the world through a unique set of eyes.

As you are capable of expressing your truth, and as you do express that truth, you become more. You allow more of who you are to flow through you. And the beautiful part about all of this is that you allow others to do the same. You grant others permission to be who they are, to speak their truth, and to become more of their whole selves. And that is the greatest gift you can give another.

I am Quan Yin, and I hold you in my heart."

FREE YOURSELVES
∞
QUAN YIN

"It is I, Quan Yin.

Free yourselves from the bondage of control. I am not referring to the control that others may attempt to exert over you. I am referring to the control that you attempt to exert over your own lives. The type of control that specifies how everything must go is what creates a self-imposed prison.

The freedom of letting go of control puts you in much greater flow and opens you to many more possibilities. Your reasons for attempting to exert control over your own lives may be very well thought out and valid, and therefore, you may experience some difficulty in letting them go. But as soon as you do, you will experience relief, joy, freedom, and the new possibilities may show themselves to you sooner than you might think.

In your control, you are usually attempting to avoid fear. There can be a great deal of fear experienced in the unknown, but there can also be a great deal of freedom. You can relax into the unknown. You can even feel excited about the unknown. Whatever it is that you fear, it is something that you can determine within yourselves. You can discover what that fear is, face it, feel it, and be done with that experience.

And then you will be open, flexible, and at ease with whatever is coming down the pike. That sort of freedom is available to you any time you desire to experience it, and that kind of freedom infuses your life with joy, with ecstasy, and with passion.

I am Quan Yin, and I hold you in my heart."

PLEASING OTHERS
∞
QUAN YIN

"It is I, Quan Yin.

Pleasing others does not need to mean that you are sacrificing your own happiness or your own comfort. When you seek to please another, you often do so because you want something from the other. Now you may just want approval, friendship, or love, but still you are attempting to engage in an exchange of energy.

When you do this at the expense of what your heart truly desires, you are giving in the hopes of receiving something. That type of giving is conditional, and it does not serve either party. When you simply are who you are, you give effortlessly, without conditions, and with no need for reciprocation. You give yourself. You give your energy. You allow another to appreciate you as you are.

Someone who witnesses you experiencing joy is being offered the gift of that vibration. Therefore, even when you are just following your own bliss with no attempt whatsoever to please another, you are being of service. You are the gift that you have to offer. You are being of service by merely existing as you are.

When you do for another, check in on your motives. Be sure you understand why it is that you do what you do and what it is you want in return. Even if your acts of service are done to give you a sense that you are a good person, they are conditional.

And therefore I recommend that you allow yourself to exist without motives, without seeking reciprocation, and without needing the approval of any other. Do what you do as an expression of who you are and allow all others to benefit from that expression.

I am Quan Yin, and I hold you in my heart."

BEING FULLY PRESENT

∞

QUAN YIN

"It is I, Quan Yin.

For the greatest enhancement of any experience you are having, I suggest giving it more of your attention. You have so many distractions in your lives. There are so many things that you could give your attention to. So how often do you give your complete and undivided attention to what is before you, and how often are you thinking about something else, looking at something else, or giving your attention to what you are going to say next?

How often are you fully present in the moment? Being fully present in the moment allows you greater access to all that you are. All that you are wants to be focused in the present. Otherwise, you would not have created the moment for yourself exactly as it is.

So when you go through all the trouble of creating the moment you are in for yourself, wouldn't it then make sense to give that moment your complete and undivided attention? If you are not doing so, then you are not fully present. In other words, not all of you is participating in the moment. And therefore, you can only be a fraction of who you are when you are not present, when you are not entirely focused on what is before you.

And when you are not entirely focused on what is before you, you cannot receive the full benefit of it. And when you cannot receive the full benefit of it, you are destined to repeat it until you do. So if you really do want to be somewhere else, then the quickest route actually is to be more present where you are.

I am Quan Yin, and I hold you in my heart."

MAKING DECISIONS
∞
QUAN YIN

"It is I, Quan Yin.

If you are struggling to make an important decision, there is really only one thing that you need to do. Minimize the importance of the outcome of that decision. When you believe that the outcome of your decision is bigger and more powerful than you, you place too much significance on the decision and you feel anxious and afraid.

When you are making a decision, the last thing that you want to do is make it from that anxious and fearful place. So anything that helps you relax in the face of making one of these types of decisions is going to serve you. You can relax into the knowing that no matter what happens, you will be fine. You will have the strength to face any outcome that comes your way.

You can demonstrate this to yourself by looking back at decisions you've made in the past and recognizing that even when things didn't work out the way you had hoped, they still worked out. You are always capable of gaining insights from whatever outcome you are faced with. You are always able to learn more about yourself, no matter what occurs or does not occur.

You are always able to find more strength than you knew you had, regardless of what happens. You are the key. You are the most important aspect of whatever the decision is about. Decide to make yourself the most powerful piece of the puzzle. Decide that you are capable of handling anything that comes your way and that you can always make course corrections. Decide that these things are true, and they most certainly will be.

I am Quan Yin, and I hold you in my heart."

SPIRITUAL BELIEFS
∞
QUAN YIN

"It is I, Quan Yin.

When it comes to your spirituality, there is a tendency amongst humans to put yourself in a box. You have a tendency to announce to the world that this is what I believe, this is what I am all about. And when you do so, you tend to think of these declarations as permanent.

Whenever you define yourself as something, you are putting that label on yourself to demonstrate where you are, and perhaps even, how far you've come. But the labels and the boxes that you use to define yourselves only limit you.

I suggest that you be open to all aspects of all belief systems that are available to you, regardless of what name they have attached to them. Anything that exists can be used and can be used to further your growth. Anything can also be used to thwart that growth because of your desire to be defined.

Whenever you talk about your beliefs as though they were permanent, you are in a sense cementing yourself right where you are. But as you let go of all labels, and any need to define yourself, you become open, you become limitless, and your potential for growth is exponential.

You are not here to find the right label, the right beliefs, or even the right spiritual practices and to adhere yourself to them. You are here to open your hearts to everything and everyone and to allow all of it to be of service to who and what you are and to who and what you are becoming.

I am Quan Yin, and I hold you in my heart."

DESIRES & BELIEFS
∞
QUAN YIN

"It is I, Quan Yin.

In your discovery of a desire within you, there is often the belief attached to it that immediately follows. You give as much, if not more, of your attention to the belief as you do to the desire itself. What if, instead, you continued to remain focused on the desire? What if you ignored the tendency to entertain your belief about it?

This would serve you, no matter what that belief happened to be. The desire summons more lifeforce through you than even the most positive belief about it could. I am not suggesting that you spend all of your time focusing on desires that are unfulfilled in your experience.

But I am suggesting that when you are aware of a desire within you that you release that attachment to the belief that immediately follows your awareness of your desire. Let the desire itself guide you. Let the desire fill you with that lifeforce energy that it summons forth, and then let yourself be moved in the most appropriate direction.

When you have no belief, then you do not question whether or not you are moving in the right direction. It does not matter in fact, because you are simply caught up in the energy of the desire itself. You are more interested in feeling the flow than you are in the fulfillment.

Fulfillment itself implies a finish line. It implies that once you align with your desire that you are somehow going to stop in your motion forward. But the desire itself will bring with it seedlings that will plant new desires within you, and they will keep you moving forward on your path, keep you expanding into more of who you are.

I am Quan Yin, and I hold you in my heart."

YOUR DIVINE NATURE
∞
QUAN YIN

"It is I, Quan Yin.

So as you are making your way into the higher frequencies, you are also placing yourselves in the perfect position to understand your true nature. You have been denying yourselves the truth of who you are in many elaborate ways, but there is no stopping the revelation of the truth to yourselves.

The truth I am speaking of is that you are Divine Beings, exploring time and space in physical form. In the revelation of this truth, it is necessary for you to see and experience its opposite in as many ways as possible. It is as if you are giving yourselves one last go 'round as mortals.

You are being given the opportunity to explore the limited nature of humanity as you prepare for the biggest shift in consciousness that is possible. So if you feel that you are moving further and further away from the full knowing of yourselves as Divine Beings, then it just so happens that you are right on track.

It is necessary for you to explore all aspects of limitation and separation in order to make the transition, in order to know yourselves fully. So I suggest that you embrace your humanity and that you get a taste of limitation one last time, while also holding the knowing in your consciousness that this experience is temporary, as your unlimited Divine Nature blossoms within you and becomes fully embedded into the knowing of who you are.

I am Quan Yin, and I hold you in my heart."

PREPARING FOR YOUR DESIRES
∞
QUAN YIN

"It is I, Quan Yin.

Preparing yourselves for that which you desire is putting yourselves in a place of acceptance for it to come. Make room in your life for that which you desire. Make space for it. Make time for it. And in so doing, you invite it in.

You are always working with energy and with vibration, but you don't always recognize this. So sometimes you work more in action and in words than you do in creating an energetic flow for something to arrive.

You have an expression that goes something like this, 'Dress for the job that you want, not the one that you have.' And this is in alignment with what I am saying. I am talking about creating an expectation that you can actually look at. You can actually begin to form the energy of what it is you are seeking in that space. You can begin to give birth to it on the energetic level.

You are constantly inviting people, objects, opportunities, money, and sometimes even things you don't want into your experience. So pay attention to what you are making room for in your lives. Pay attention for what you are preparing for. Are you saving for a rainy day? What does that rainy day look like? Are you bracing yourself for the visit from your in-laws?

Pay attention to what you are doing energetically, and notice where you are creating space in your lives and where you are not. Have fun with your process of creation. See it as a game, and know that the game can be as fun as you allow it to be. You are creating everything, so you might as well create the rules of the game you are playing.

I am Quan Yin, and I hold you in my heart."

ASKING & RECEIVING
∞
QUAN YIN

"It is I, Quan Yin.

I am here in service, and my ability to serve is only as effective as your ability to receive me. There must be a willingness and an openness to receive in order for the act of service to have an effect. Many of you are reaching out and asking for help. You are expressing a willingness to receive it, but how often do you then accept the help that is coming, consciously?

We who are here in service know what is best for you, and therefore we are incapable of doing anything for you that you are not willing to do for yourselves. We work in tandem with you, but we do not and we cannot assert. I am known for my compassion, and I know that it is there because I feel it. In order for you to know my compassion, you must allow yourself to receive it.

Receiving is as big a part of the equation as the asking. When you let down your guard, when you relax, when you are drifting off to sleep, these are the times when you are most receptive to the help that is being offered by those in service.

So this is our promise to you – we will always deliver that which you are asking for. But you will need to let go long enough and surrender to the help that we are offering in order for it to take hold.

That is what makes our interactions a co-creation, and that is far more empowering to you than if we were to just do it for you. I am here in service, and you are here to experience what it is like to move, to evolve, and to grow. And together we make a wonderful team.

I am Quan Yin, and I hold you in my heart."

THE CHILD WITHIN YOU
∞
QUAN YIN

"It is I, Quan Yin.

You know what to do in every situation that you are confronted with. You understand what is necessary and what is appropriate, but you tell yourselves the lie that says that you don't always know. The lie is not coming from within you. It is coming from outside of you.

There are so many who want to influence you into doing some things and into not doing others, and that is always where your confusion comes from. Imagine what it was like for you to be a child. You never questioned what you were going to do next. You didn't second-guess yourself. You followed your impulses, and your actions were pure and without hesitation.

It was only after parents, teachers, and other authority figures came into your awareness and re-directed you that you began to question yourselves. Once the questioning began, it became a part of your thought process.

So even as adults, you are still doing it. Oftentimes there is no one else around to re-direct you or to call into question what you are doing. And so now you do it to yourselves, and you make everything more complicated when you do.

The purity and the innocence of your childhood and your childlike states of being still exist within you. You may believe that you have outgrown them, but you have merely forgotten.

And I am here to remind you that the child that you once were, the child that did not doubt, or second-guess, or question his or her actions, does still exist within you. And all you have to do is intend to let the child within you out to play. And that will make your lives much less complicated.

I am Quan Yin, and I hold you in my heart."

Chapter Nine

∞

The Arcturian Council

THE LOVE THAT BINDS

∞

THE 9TH DIMENSIONAL ARCTURIAN COUNCIL

"Greetings. We are the Arcturian Council. We are pleased to connect with all of you.

We have been enjoying the ride that humanity has taken us on, and we invite you to enjoy it with us. We want you all to feel the certainty that we have that life on planet Earth is getting better and will continue to get better as you move forward here.

Now, a lot of that can be attributed to the energies that you are receiving, but you all deserve credit as well. You deserve credit for hanging in there, and you deserve credit for being the receivers of the energies. You certainly have the option of deflecting them.

We also want you to acknowledge you for all that you have endured, and we want you to know how significant it is that you feel compassion for people that you have never met and probably never will meet. You have broadened your horizons to include more than just those in your family of origin, and you have expanded beyond thinking of only those who are in your community or in your country.

You are including more people in your prayers because of your awareness of the suffering of others all around the world, and this is significant. It is significant to know that their pain is your pain and your pain is their pain. It is even more significant to recognize that what binds all together is not your race, your religion, your nationality, your gender, or your sexuality. What binds you all together is love.

The commonality of that experience is something that is far more significant than you will ever know. It is the frequency of Source, or the best possible way you have of knowing Source, and knowing yourselves as Source. The love that binds you all together is eternal and infinite, as are you. And nothing can take that away from you.

So celebrate it with us, and look for more ways to enjoy this journey that we are all on together.

We are the Arcturian Council, and we have enjoyed connecting with you."

THE COMBINED DESIRES OF HUMANITY
∞
THE 9TH DIMENSIONAL ARCTURIAN COUNCIL

"Greetings. We are the Arcturian Council. We are pleased to connect with all of you.

We have taken all of the desires of humanity, and we have put them together to create a representation of all of those combined desires. The combined desires of all of humanity has a unique vibration, and we have identified that vibration so that we can send it to you in the form of a download. This is a download that you will all receive in your energy fields around the time of your new year.

Now, like any gift, you have to be willing to receive it. You have to unwrap it, open it, and appreciate it. So what we recommend is that you feel for the essence of all of humanity's desires put together. Feel it around you, and invite it in. In so doing you will become a part of the fulfillment of those desires.

Now, you all have your own desires wrapped up within the essence of all of humanity's desires. And when you access all desires, you access your own. You are beginning to operate as a collective, and this is one of the ways in which you are achieving that goal. There are many more to come, of course, but this is a wonderful place to start.

As you acknowledge that everyone else's desires on Earth have a place right next to your own you begin the process of unification, and that is what this upcoming year is all about for all of you.

We are the Arcturian Council, and we have enjoyed connecting with you."

REATTACHING YOUR DNA
∞
THE 9TH DIMENSIONAL ARCTURIAN COUNCIL

"Greetings. We are the Arcturian Council. We are pleased to connect with all of you.

We are pleased to announce that the energies you have been receiving from the higher realms have altered your DNA. Now, as you know, the human being typically has two strands of DNA. And you also have junk DNA, which was previously not junk DNA. Your bodies carry that DNA with you because just as you are reassembling all of your parts to become your higher selves, you are also reassembling your DNA.

It is happening at this time because of how open you have all been to receiving energy, feeling emotions, and releasing trauma from past life experiences. Now, of course, it is affecting everyone differently, but these are growing pains, and there is much more left to be reassembled.

You are activating within you the junk DNA, and then it is reattached to give you more strands. But not everyone is ready to be receiving all of that junk DNA. Not everyone is ready to have twelve strands. The process of reassembling this DNA will take time. It will depend on the individual and his or her openness to the energies, and it will also depend on how much that person has yet to process.

However, the good news is that most humans who are awakened are taking quite nicely to the process. And so, it is important for you all to allow this to occur without freaking out when you have some issues in your physical bodies. Rest, relax, and take care of yourselves, because there is, of course, more to come.

We are the Arcturian Council, and we have enjoyed connecting with you."

YOU ARE IN THE PERFECT POSITION

∞

THE 9TH DIMENSIONAL ARCTURIAN COUNCIL

"Greetings. We are the Arcturian Council. We are pleased to connect with all of you.

We are in the perfect position to assist you, and yet there are so many other beings who are also in the perfect position to be of service to all of humanity. There are many perfect positions. We are coming from the perspective that is the truth of your existence as Source Energy Beings.

We are also seeing you as having made enough mistakes now throughout human history to have grown substantially, and we see that growth continuing in your age of information. You are at a time now where your growth is exponential, and that is because you are able to see almost instantaneously how your thoughts, words, and actions affect others.

You are also able to see how other individuals are affecting the collective with their thoughts, words, and actions. You are able to celebrate others when they are doing good for humanity, and you are able to call people out when they are showing a lack of compassion.

And we see this as a positive circumstance because it is important for others to recognize when they are doing something that is affecting others in either a positive or a negative way. Now, from where we are observing all of you, we also can see that you are the perfect ones to be helping each other to evolve and grow.

You are in the perfect position to help the rest of humanity because you are there in the trenches, living your lives, and only you know exactly how the experiences of your lives feel. So as you continue to share your feelings with your fellow humans, you continue to demonstrate how perfect it is that you all are where you are and that you are living what you are living.

We are the Arcturian Council, and we have enjoyed connecting with you."

CO-CREATING WITH US

∞

THE 9TH DIMENSIONAL ARCTURIAN COUNCIL

"Greetings. We are the Arcturian Council. We are pleased to connect with all of you.

We are interested in co-creating with all of you on Earth. We are excited to see the ideas that come to you and that help to bring about your version of the fifth dimensional experience. You know that there is always a certain amount of co-creating going on because you understand that we are all connected.

Even something that you create without the help of any other human has a connection to the non-physical realm, and you had to have been inspired by something or someone that you experienced there on Earth. So everything is collaboration and co-creation, and more and more of you are getting that.

We invite you to reach out and up to connect with us regarding your desired co-creations. We are not only happy to assist, but we also have very little else to do. So we often work on projects, even before we are asked for our help, and we will continue to co-create with all of you at night when you are asleep.

There is certainly much more for us to gain from connecting with all of you because of the multitude of experiences you're having and emotions you're feeling. We are always available. There is never a line to wait in. We are always open, as well, to new ideas for collaboration.

And so, you can think of us as your number one supporters, no matter what the endeavor. And if you feel for our support and our energy, while you are embarking on one of your action journeys, you will absolutely feel the support that we are giving.

We are the Arcturian Council, and we have enjoyed connecting with you."

YOU ARE IN THE PERFECT POSITION

∞

THE 9TH DIMENSIONAL ARCTURIAN COUNCIL

"Greetings. We are the Arcturian Council. We are pleased to connect with all of you.

We are in the perfect position to assist you, and yet there are so many other beings who are also in the perfect position to be of service to all of humanity. There are many perfect positions. We are coming from the perspective that is the truth of your existence as Source Energy Beings.

We are also seeing you as having made enough mistakes now throughout human history to have grown substantially, and we see that growth continuing in your age of information. You are at a time now where your growth is exponential, and that is because you are able to see almost instantaneously how your thoughts, words, and actions affect others.

You are also able to see how other individuals are affecting the collective with their thoughts, words, and actions. You are able to celebrate others when they are doing good for humanity, and you are able to call people out when they are showing a lack of compassion.

And we see this as a positive circumstance because it is important for others to recognize when they are doing something that is affecting others in either a positive or a negative way. Now, from where we are observing all of you, we also can see that you are the perfect ones to be helping each other to evolve and grow.

You are in the perfect position to help the rest of humanity because you are there in the trenches, living your lives, and only you know exactly how the experiences of your lives feel. So as you continue to share your feelings with your fellow humans, you continue to demonstrate how perfect it is that you all are where you are and that you are living what you are living.

We are the Arcturian Council, and we have enjoyed connecting with you."

YOU ARE HIGH FREQUENCY CONDUITS

∞

THE 9TH DIMENSIONAL ARCTURIAN COUNCIL

"Greetings. We are the Arcturian Council. We are pleased to connect with all of you.

We are placing a great deal of our attention on how humanity is going to handle the influx of energies that you are receiving at this time. The reason why it is important for us to notice how you are handling the energies is because we need to constantly monitor how much transformation you are ready for.

Now, some of you are ready to become your higher selves completely and ascend to the fifth dimension, but most of you are not. Most of humanity needs to experience much more of that fourth dimensional energy before they are ready to transform completely.

Sometimes when you add high frequency energy to an equation it doesn't always give you the results you might expect. So most of humanity is being slowly coaxed into the hot bath of the fifth dimensional energies. But when those of you who are awakened are able to handle more, you sort of filter the energies for the rest of the collective.

The energies move through you, they transform you, and then they are made available to the rest of humanity in that filtered form, which is a bit watered down. The trees and the animals do this as well, and you have joined them in their mission to help humanity, to ready all of you, for those very high frequency energies that are coming at the time of the shift.

Now, when you perform an energy healing on someone, you send them the highest frequency energies they are ready for. When you send someone a transmission of love, you are literally sending that love at the highest frequency they are capable of handling. We are watching. We are monitoring, and we are working with you.

So you can relax and know that you are doing enough just by being there and by being open to receive. This shift is not about doing, and it's not about defeating any dark forces. This shift is about all of you being the highest frequency conduits of energy you can possibly be.

We are the Arcturian Council, and we have enjoyed connecting with you."

FEEL THE LOVE FLOW
∞
THE 9TH DIMENSIONAL ARCTURIAN COUNCIL

"Greetings. We are the Arcturian Council. We are pleased to connect with all of you.

We are excited to bring you each and every update that we do. We are especially enthusiastic about sharing with you this particular transmission because it is going to leave you feeling that truth of who you are flowing through you. We are talking about love.

We are talking about the experience of love that is always available to you, and we want you all to recognize that. We want you to feel for the truth of who you are flowing through you because it is the ultimate experience to have in a physical body.

You are all channels of love, but you are not always allowing yourselves to align with that truth. There really are no good reasons to deny yourselves the experience of love, but you certainly have come up with quite a few over your many lifetimes. When you let go, you fall in love. When you let yourselves have the experience, it simply flows.

It's not something you have to work on. What you have to work on are the issues that get in the way of you fully feeling it and expressing it.

Now, oftentimes you take for granted that the other people in your life know that you love them, or you say the words, but you don't really engage in the emotion itself when you say them. So we are here now to encourage you to not only say the words, 'I love you,' but we also want you to direct the love that you are to the other person, or pet, or whomever, while you are saying it.

Make eye contact. Make physical contact. Make sure you are actually feeling love flow through you, and make sure you let everyone know that you feel it, that you are it, and that you are opening yourself up to allow more of it to flow because of them.

We are the Arcturian Council, and we have enjoyed connecting with you."

POLARITY WILL BRING YOU TOGETHER

∞

THE 9TH DIMENSIONAL ARCTURIAN COUNCIL

"Greetings. We are the Arcturian Council. We are pleased to connect with all of you.

We are expecting a gigantic movement towards the unity consciousness that we have been telling you about, and we expect it to occur because of how polarized you have been, not in spite of it. You all have played out the idea of separation for so long that you are tired of running that program. You are tired of nationalism, racism, sexism, homophobia. You are tired of people from different religions not liking each other based solely on the differences that exist in their religions.

You are tired of arguing with one another over your political differences. You have done all of this already. There is really nothing more that you can gain from it, but it has served you well. Every time two people have argued over a point of view that each of them holds, there has been a desire on the part of both of those individuals to come together.

Every time you fight with a loved one in your life, don't you feel that desire boiling up within you for greater unity with the person you are fighting with? So now you know that the desires amongst all of you who are awakened for that unity is born out of what you and the rest of humanity is experiencing. You are ready for something new, something better, something different, and now is the time.

Now is the time because you are so tired. You are tired of the way things have been. You are tired of resisting each other, and you are tired of weakening yourselves by not coming together and co-creating the experience of the world that you want to have.

You want to be a part of a world where everyone gets to believe what they want to believe and gets to do what they want to do, and you are going to get there, and the divisiveness that exists on planet Earth is the catalyst that is bringing you all together.

So don't feel despair the next time you see two people arguing over gun control or abortion. Smile in the knowing that those two people really want to love each, and that the love will win. It always does.

We are the Arcturian Council, and we have enjoyed connecting with you."

THE HELP YOU'VE BEEN SEEKING

∞

THE 9TH DIMENSIONAL ARCTURIAN COUNCIL

"Greetings. We are the Arcturian Council. We are pleased to connect with all of you.

We have noticed that the trend on planet Earth right now is to look for ways to create a better planet for everyone. You have reached a tipping point in your evolution, and there is no stopping the energetic momentum that you have going towards actualizing that world, even before the shift is completed.

You don't need to wait for e.t.s to land, and you don't need to wait for mass arrests. You don't even need to wait for the event to create the world that is beneficial for everyone to be upon. It is the movement that you are making towards this world that is quite noticeable to us, as we see you reaching out to those in need, and we see you supporting each other, and wanting to know how you can do more to serve.

Now this trend will continue, and the momentum will continue to build upon itself as you see the results of your conscious creation. When you are able to help yourselves to the extent that you possibly can, that's when you will receive the help and the technology that you want to make broad, sweeping changes for the better, for all of humanity.

Now, we are not saying that you have to earn this help or that the technology is being held back until you find the ability within you to create this Earth we are talking about. What we are saying is that when you are holding the proper vibration to receive more help, that's when you will get it. That's when it will not be interference, it will be an enhancement of what you have already done.

You all know this to be true. You know that as you help each other, you put out a vibration that has to come back to you. And it will come back in a very big way. It is by helping each other that you open the door for more help from above.

We are the Arcturian Council, and we have enjoyed connecting with you."

THE GREAT RE-AWAKENING
∞
THE 9TH DIMENSIONAL ARCTURIAN COUNCIL

"Greetings. We are the Arcturian Council. We are pleased to connect with all of you.

We have awakened within you a sense of belonging, and that is a very good thing because you do belong to a galactic family. And you need to know that you are not alone in the galaxy, but you also need to know that you have roots in this galaxy. You may at times seem like the new ones, the new souls, because you have chosen to incarnate on Earth. You chose a bigger memory wipe for yourselves when you did so.

Other beings on other planets in other star systems know their galactic history, whereas humanity has experienced itself in somewhat of a quarantine. You've been shielded from the truth by choice because you wanted to give yourselves the experience of isolation.

But now that we and others like us have awakened within you the knowing that you are part of a bigger galactic family, you can rest assured that you are going to feel more and more comfortable with the presence of extra-terrestrials in planet Earth. They are already there of course, but they are just not out in the open about it.

Now, the other piece here in knowing your roots is about recognizing that you have been playing this game for a very long time. You already have been highly evolved beings in other parts of the galaxy, and you don't have anything to learn as you move forward. You just need to remember, and we are here to help remind that you have already been Pleiadian. You have already been Sirian. You have already been Arcturian, and you have already been a higher dimensional being. Therefore, there is nothing flawed about you. There is nothing young about any of you either.

You have connections to other beings all across this galaxy, and when you do reunite with your brothers and sisters who are members of your soul family, so much of who you have been will come flooding back into your consciousness, and that will be a great re-awakening.

We are the Arcturian Council, and we have enjoyed connecting with you."

LIFTING THE VEIL
∞
THE 9TH DIMENSIONAL ARCTURIAN COUNCIL

"Greetings. We are the Arcturian Council. We are pleased to connect with all of you.

We are very interested to see how you are going to enjoy the feeling of liberation when you release yourselves from the limitations that you have placed upon you. This experience is one that you only get to have once, because you will never move from such a place of limitation to such a place of liberation. It's not possible in any of the other dimensional shifts that you will make on your journey back to Source.

The agreement that you made to be third, and now fourth, dimensional before you incarnated is one that you did not take lightly. It is one that you knew would be the ultimate challenge of existence, and now that you are closing in on letting go of all of that limitation, we can feel the excitement and the enthusiasm within you.

We want you to know that the freedom from limitation that we are talking about has nothing at all to do with money, borders, governments, or even the cabal/illuminati/whatever name they are being called in this moment. You will be the ones who lift the veil, and that will occur in the moment you truly recognize that you are infinite and eternal beings of light and love.

When you start living that truth in every moment, then nothing about your economy can keep you down. No chemtrail is strong enough to lower your vibration, and there is nothing that anyone can do, who is in one of those positions of power, that will be able to put the limitations back on you.

One of the greatest illusions that you are living under is that people outside of you have any sort of control over you. They do not decide for you whether you are in your hearts or not. That is all on you, and that is the freedom that you seek.

We are the Arcturian Council, and we have enjoyed connecting with you."

FREEDOM FROM LIMITATIONS
∞
THE 9TH DIMENSIONAL ARCTURIAN COUNCIL

"Greetings. We are the Arcturian Council. We are pleased to connect with all of you.

We have never mistaken you for beings who would let yourselves be controlled by others. You are not a species that wants to be under the thumb of any other beings, including other humans. The fact that you agreed to incarnate on a planet and in a dimension where this type of oppression takes place means that you have done it for a very good reason.

You wanted to know what it would feel like to have so much joy and so much freedom, and so you chose to experience the opposite first. The vast majority of humans are playing a game with themselves, and it is a game of limitation. Now once that game is over, and there are far fewer limitations placed upon you, the feeling you will have will be that of exhilaration. You will step into your power in a very bold way.

And you will also realize that you took on the oppressors because you have been them in previous lifetimes. It's not punishment. It's not payback. It's not that type of karma at all. It's your willingness to experience something that will ultimately bring you to a place of sincere compassion for each other and for all who have ever been oppressed on Earth and everywhere else in the galaxy.

You are making this leap forward in your consciousness at the same time that you are throwing off the shackles of your limitations, the restrictions that you agreed to place upon yourselves. The two experiences are linked. You are not here to defeat those who have been the oppressors. And they go by many names. We don't need to give you one of those names here. You all know who we are talking about.

You are here to access your power in spite of the current state of affairs on your world. You are the ones who will bring forth the higher frequency energies and run them through you, and make them available to others, in spite of the fact that you only enjoy a sliver of the freedom that you have coming to you in this lifetime.

We are the Arcturian Council, and we have enjoyed connecting with you."

LETTING GO HAS GOTTEN EASIER

∞

THE 9TH DIMENSIONAL ARCTURIAN COUNCIL

"Greetings. We are the Arcturian Council. We are pleased to connect with all of you.

We are very excited about the way in which you all have been letting go of what no longer serves you in the recent weeks and months leading up to now. We have witnessed you all getting into a higher frequency state, and in so doing, becoming more aware of what is heavy for you. And then we can see you simply letting go, and we are very impressed with how easy it has become.

In your collective past, you would have seen something within you that held a lower vibration, and you would have held onto it with the belief that you needed to fix something within you. But truly it was the judgment that caused you to cling to something that no longer served you. However, now we can see the ease with which you are letting go of all that holds a lower frequency.

This is in large part due to your awareness of who you have been in previous lifetimes. When you recognize that you have had some very dark incarnations, and you know that you are doing such tremendous work in this lifetime of integrating those past life selves, you then must realize that you have some lower vibrational gunk that you simply have to acknowledge and then let go of.

You don't need to identify with a thought or a belief. You don't have to take on a prejudice that comes up within you as your own. You have the freedom to just let it all go. There is no need for you to go through a large number of steps in order to do so, and this knowing is making it so much easier for all of you to move on and to become the fifth dimensional beings that you were always destined to become in this lifetime.

We are the Arcturian Council, and we have enjoyed connecting with you."

PUT YOUR FAITH IN YOURSELVES

∞

THE 9TH DIMENSIONAL ARCTURIAN COUNCIL

"Greetings. We are the Arcturian Council. We are pleased to connect with all of you.

We are pleased to see the willingness on the part of humanity to believe that it is possible for you all to get to where you are going. There is a sense among you that people are capable of changing for the better, and that sense was not there just a decade ago. We are seeing more and more of you putting faith in each other, putting faith in humanity, in spite of what you are seeing in the outside world at times.

We know that humanity is making tremendous progress because we are able to read the energy fields of each of you on the planet, but you sometimes need to go on faith. And the faith that you want to have starts with each of you, as individuals, having faith in yourselves. If you can acknowledge that you have come a long way in your evolution, then certainly you can look at someone else who is acting out, and you can see the possibility that the individual in question can and will make the necessary changes.

When you put your faith in the universe and the plan for humanity, you are putting your faith in yourselves, and you are putting your faith in Source. The Source Energy within each and every one of you is strong enough to overcome any egoic persuasions. And remember that as you evolve and expand, so does Source. That means the signal within you is getting stronger all the time. That means it's harder and harder for anyone on Earth to ignore that Source essence that is coming from within.

You who are awakened are the leaders of this movement, and the more faith you put in yourselves and humanity, the more you are going to see your fellow humans living up to your high expectations for them.

We are the Arcturian Council, and we have enjoyed connecting with you."

ACCESSING INFORMATION

∞

THE 9TH DIMENSIONAL ARCTURIAN COUNCIL

"Greetings. We are the Arcturian Council. We are pleased to connect with all of you.

You are taking yourselves to new heights of awareness, and with that added awareness you also get the feelings that come with it. Every time you uncover some hidden truth about yourselves, or about the history of Earth, or about the beings who have been running things for eons and eons of time, you have an emotional reaction. And that's a good thing.

When you demonstrate that you can handle the emotions that come up from learning more, you are then granted more access to previously unknown information. And now we are talking to each of you as individuals. Some things that you have known for quite some time will be new pieces of information to someone else, and vice versa.

Therefore, what we see happening on Earth at this time is such a willingness to explore the emotions that get triggered within you that each and every one of you is getting more of those bits and pieces and filling in the holes and blanks in your story, in the story of Earth, and the story of the galaxy. The more you can handle, the more you will get.

Now, you are also gravitating more towards the pieces of information that will trigger you the most. So once you find out about something that is particularly disturbing, you will follow that thread. And when you learn about something that is particularly joyous, you will follow that thread.

Not all information is going to trigger you in a negative way. If you are ready to receive more about your past lives, you will. If you are ready to uncover memories of visits from extra-terrestrials in this lifetime, you will. What is important is what you do with that information. And when it comes to information, it can be very easy for you to just stay in your heads with it. But you have to keep feeling in order to access more.

As interesting as the information is, the feeling that you get from it is the true gift. So continue to unwrap your gifts.

We are the Arcturian Council, and we have enjoyed connecting with you."

THE ECSTASY WITHIN
∞
THE 9TH DIMENSIONAL ARCTURIAN COUNCIL

"Greetings. We are the Arcturian Council. We are pleased to connect with all of you.

We are thrilled to see how many of you are looking within yourselves more now that you have gotten frustrated enough with what is available to you in the external world. Sometimes you need to get mad, or you need to feel defeated, in order to get to where you ultimately want to go. If the world were exactly as you wanted it to be, you would have very little reason to ever go within yourselves and discover how much is available to you.

It's all there, and it's all free. There is no travel required, no passports, no going through the long security line at the airport. You have the ability to tap into this beautiful inner world of yours any time you like, but most people never would without the catalyst that the disappointments in their lives often are.

So in order to get to where you ultimately want to go, trudging through the mud and the muck is often necessary. It may not be preferable. You may not find it to be fun, but ultimately, it gives you what you need to get you where you are going.

That's why it's so important to embrace everything that comes your way as a means of taking you to where you ultimately want to go. You have traveled so far already, and there is much more ease in front of you than there is struggle. But for the time that you have remaining in the fourth dimension, let yourselves be disappointed. Let yourselves get mad and frustrated.

And hopefully, ultimately, you will find that solace that always exists inside of you. You will find the love, the joy, the peace, and even the excitement in your inner realm. Certainly, there is ecstasy available to you at all times, and it is always just a few focused breaths away.

We are the Arcturian Council, and we have enjoyed connecting with you."

A NEW WAY OF GETTING WHAT YOU WANT
∞
THE 9TH DIMENSIONAL ARCTURIAN COUNCIL

"Greetings. We are the Arcturian Council. We are pleased to connect with all of you.

We have begun investigating the paths that you usually take to get what you want out of life. We know that it isn't easy to change the way you approach getting what you want, but from what we have seen thus far, very few of you are even attempting to make changes in your approach. For millions of years on Earth, your lives have been all about action.

Now, for some individuals, the action journey was just too much, and so they created some sort of short cut. The short cut would involve something illegal and/or immoral. Therefore, those are the ways we have seen all of you going about making the steps forward that you want to make in getting to the life that you want to live. What has been missing, as far as we can tell, is trust.

If you could trust that letting the universe deliver to you what you want was even possibility, then maybe you would stop taking so much action and thinking and scheming to try to get to where you want to be. So how do you trust in something as abstract of a concept as 'the universe.' The universe itself is not an abstract concept, we know. But the idea that it has a consciousness and that it is responding to you can seem foolhardy to your logical mind.

Therefore, it's time for you to change you relationship to this universe. It's time to see the universe as an extension of you, rather than something that you exist within. And it's also time to start trusting in yourselves. Trust that the energy that you put forth will come back to you, and trust in your ability to seize the opportunity when it comes to you. Trust in you. Trust in the universe. And take the weight off of your shoulders that says you need to get it all done with your action journeys.

You are here to recognize yourselves as creator beings and to enjoy the journey, and there is nothing stopping you from doing so.

We are the Arcturian Council, and we have enjoyed connecting with you."

BETTER TIMELINES ARE CLOSER THAN YOU THINK
∞
THE 9TH DIMENSIONAL ARCTURIAN COUNCIL

"Greetings. We are the Arcturian Council. We are pleased to connect with all of you.

We have been exploring the possibilities that are in front of humanity at this time, and we can see how many choices you have to move to a better feeling timeline. We see that the current state of affairs on planet Earth is actually urging you to choose one of those better feeling timelines. But the way to access those timelines is not to point out what is wrong with your current state of affairs on Earth.

We encourage you to feel what you feel, but you don't need to keep pointing out how bad things are, and it actually is not serving you to do so. The solution to the problems of your modern society is always to go within, and the way that you access that timeline that you want to be on is to harmonize with it. Now, what we are telling you right now is that you are not as far away from a much better feeling timeline than you might think.

Humanity is making tremendous strides forward, and those tremendous strides are the result of everything that you see in your world that is unfair, that is downright wrong. It is all there to act as a catalyst for each of you to get within and to find what it is that you want. Now, we are speaking especially to those of you who are awakened, because you know how to do this.

You knew the moment you realized that you could create your reality that a better world was possible. You knew that you didn't need to rely on politicians, governments, banks, or corporations to change. When you first had that knowing, you got very excited, and you thought you would see change sooner than later. And now here you are, and some of you have been at this for decades, which is why we want to assure you that you are close to those timelines.

You have the support from your fellow humans. You have the support energetically. You have the support from those like us in the higher realms, and you have more support than you ever have. So don't give up hope. Go within and find that vibration, and you will see the changes that you want to see in the world around you.

We are the Arcturian Council, and we have enjoyed connecting with you."

RECEIVING WHAT YOU'VE ASKED FOR

∞

THE 9TH DIMENSIONAL ARCTURIAN COUNCIL

"Greetings. We are the Arcturian Council. We are pleased to connect with all of you.

We are reaching out to humanity for a connection that we want to feel, just as much as you are reaching out for a connection to us and all of the other beings in the higher realms. We see you as our children, and we love you unconditionally. Therefore, there is nothing that any of you could ever do, or say, or believe that would keep us from loving you. Just imagine how much Source loves you and how free from judgment you all are.

We are pointing this out because we want all of you to deem yourselves worthy enough of receiving all that is coming to you from all of us in the higher realms. We want you to know that you don't have to earn it. You don't have to earn your place in the higher realms, and you don't have to earn what you ask for from us. We are happy to give and give and give some more.

But we see many of you deflecting that which you have asked for, and some of you are just too busy with all that you think you have to do to sit back, relax, and receive that which you have asked for. So we invite you to take a few moments now and do so, because we are projecting so much love, so much energy, and so many downloads, and we would love to see more of you actually receiving what you are being sent.

This is the time of the Divine Feminine. It is time for all of you to put down your tools, to set aside your practices, unless you really enjoy them, and to just let in that which is yours. It is yours because you are the creators of your reality, and it is yours because we love you so very much. We also want to see what you do with all that you have asked for. We are very curious about that.

We are the Arcturian Council, and we have enjoyed connecting with you."

TURN OFF, TUNE IN
∞
THE 9TH DIMENSIONAL ARCTURIAN COUNCIL

"

Greetings. We are the Arcturian Council. We are pleased to connect with all of you.

We are pleased to share with you the following transmission because we know that so many of you have been waiting to receive any sort of hope about the progress that humanity is making. We sense that there is an urgency within humanity to right the ship, to get yourselves pointed in the right direction, and we want to assure you that there is no such ticking clock.

The evolution of the consciousness of humanity will continue regardless of what happens and what does not happen. Therefore, we want you to relax and to stop taking score. You are doing very well, and you will continue to be the ones who are holding space for the rest of humanity.

What we have also noticed is that those of you who are awake and who are aware of the higher frequency beings who are assisting you are letting yourselves off the hook more. And when you do that, when you take the weight of the world off of your shoulders, you let in more of that help that is coming.

You are receiving more healing energy. You are receiving more upgrades, more downloads, and you are raising your vibration to such an extent that we can say with even more certainty than we have ever said this before, and that is the truth, that you are shifting to the fifth dimension.

The pendulum has already swung, and there is no going back now. So the question remains then: how can you enjoy it more? How can you live with a sense of hope, rather than that sense of urgency? And how can you let in more of what you've been asking for?

One of the easiest ways to do this is to turn off your televisions, put down your devices, shut off your computers, and either go within or go outside. The less you tune in to the media, whether it is social or otherwise, and the more you tune in to what is important to you, the more you get that which is important to you. And you can see the progress that you are making when you look within for it, because you all can run so much more energy than you could just five years ago, and that is something to feel excited about.

We are the Arcturian Council, and we have enjoyed connecting with you."

YOUR CREATIONS

∞

THE 9TH DIMENSIONAL ARCTURIAN COUNCIL

"Greetings. We are the Arcturian Council. We are pleased to connect with all of you.

We are fascinated by your projects. We talk to you often about relaxing, receiving, and feeling, but we rarely discuss with you how enthralled we are with the actions that you take and with the creativity that you possess and put on display for everyone else in the collective and beyond. We love to see you in the midst of one of these creative endeavors. We love to feel the energy that you infuse into your creations, and we love to witness the beauty, and the ingenuity, and the sharing.

We are huge fans of humanity. The ability that you possess to take the raw materials that are available to you there on Earth and to put them together in a way that has never been before is something that deserves recognition. You all deserve to feel very proud of everything that you do. Every song, every poem, every novel, every film script, every painting, every sculpture, and every house that you build deserves to be celebrated. You deserve to be celebrated for all that you do.

Now, we also want you to acknowledge that you do receive the inspiration from a higher place. And we are not attempting to take any credit for your creations, because you still have to be the ones who get those raw materials together and take the actions necessary to create such beauty. However, we also want you to acknowledge that there is co-creation in everything, and we want you to know that there is so much more for you to download.

There are so many more collaborations ahead of you. This is a very good thing. It is good for you to know that you have been channeling your ideas, your inspirations, and your projects. And when more beings are let in to assist and inspire, think of what can be achieved in this wonderfully diverse galaxy of ours. It is literally unimaginable.

We are the Arcturian Council, and we have enjoyed connecting with you."

THERE IS MORE TO DISCOVER
∞
THE 9TH DIMENSIONAL ARCTURIAN COUNCIL

"Greetings. We are the Arcturian Council. We are pleased to connect with all of you.

We are pleased to awaken within you a knowing that was always there. We are pleased to be the ones who confirm for you what you already know or what you have already been receiving directly. We are also very happy to be the ones who encourage you and empower you to be who you know you can be. We are not interested in being the 'right way' or the 'only way.'

We are only interested in expressing to you our perspective, and we want you to know that we are never offended when something that we transmit doesn't resonate with you. You may recognize that a lot of people in the spiritual community that you are a part of can become very dogmatic in their beliefs, and we want you to recognize that this is religious programming that continues to be perpetuated within the psyche of the individual who comes across spiritual material.

Those individuals don't need to be argued with. They need to be loved and accepted, and it is much more beneficial for you to see them as in a transitional period.

You see, there is great comfort in feeling that you know everything. There is a wonderful sense of certainty within those dogmatic beliefs, within those absolutes. And rather than tearing down someone else's comforting belief systems, you can send them love and know that they are getting to the point that is less stable but much more fun and exciting.

We are talking about the point where you recognize that there is so much more to know that you don't already know. There is so much more to discover and to experience. You can recognize within yourselves that having all the answers is overrated. We want you to know that we support you no matter what, and we are excited to watch you discover what you have yet to discover about life in this very beautiful and complex universe.

We are the Arcturian Council, and we have enjoyed connecting with you."

CREATING YOUR PATH OF ASCENSION
∞
THE 9TH DIMENSIONAL ARCTURIAN COUNCIL

"Greetings. We are the Arcturian Council. We are pleased to connect with all of you.

You are discovering the path that works best for you. You are not discovering the one true path that you are then meant to shout about from the rooftops so that everyone else can enjoy that same certainty that you have about your path. You are not here on Earth now to walk the path of someone else either. You are creating the path as you go, and that is as it is supposed to be, because you are doing something that is unprecedented.

You are shifting from the third dimension to the fifth dimension on a planet that is doing the exact same thing. You are also part of a universal shift, which means that we are all shifting together. We often tell you about how we are examining this, discovering that, and exploring something else because we are also making this up as we go, and we are ninth dimensional.

If this was a paint-by-numbers sort of situation, it would be less exciting. It would bring less experience to Source, and therefore, it would be somewhat pointless. But because we are all making this up as we go, it is fun, and it is new, and it is definitely worth the journey of discovery that we are all on together.

We make suggestions to you, but we are not dealing in absolutes here. We want you to go out there and discover what it is that you want to experience, and then we want to see you create that experience as a part of your own journey of ascension. And of course we want to be a part of it as much as we can, but ultimately, you are all in the driver's seat. You are the rockstars of this universal ascension journey, and we are all so impressed and thrilled by the progress that we see in humanity.

So please respect yourselves enough to know that you have everything that you need within you to create the path that will give you the best possible experience of this ascension journey.

We are the Arcturian Council, and we have enjoyed connecting with you."

HELPING YOU THROUGH YOUR CYCLES

∞

THE 9TH DIMENSIONAL ARCTURIAN COUNCIL

"Greetings. We are the Arcturian Council. We are pleased to connect with all of you.

We are collecting as much data as we can on the cycles that you all go through in your lives so that we can better understand how to assist you no matter where you are. We have noticed that you participate in various phases of your cycles in different ways, and we are certain that there is a rhythm to your cycles that is necessary. Just as you have cycles that you go through when you are asleep, you have cycles that you experience that last for weeks, months, and sometimes years of your lives.

The best way that we have to approach your cycles is to look at the ways in which you are affected emotionally. So for example, when you are going through a phase of creativity that involves quite a bit of action, we notice that you feel free and excited, and usually quite joyous. We can use that information to help support you, but more importantly you can use that information to support each other.

For example, when one of you is in a processing phase, and you are dealing with some of the heavier emotions like sadness, fear, and anger, the people in your lives who want to support you need to know about those emotions. They need to be let in so that they can help you. Therefore, no matter what is going on in your life, it is always of benefit to you to be aware of how you feel and to let others know how they can support you.

You are not meant to do all of this by yourselves. You are not meant to just endure the hard phases of your cycles, and you are meant to work together and support each other through the more fun and interesting phases. You can share with each other the experiences you are having best by describing what you are feeling to the other people in your life. Let them support you. If you let others in, you are certain to let our help in as well.

We are the Arcturian Council, and we have enjoyed connecting with you."

LIGHT & ASCENSION
∞
THE 9TH DIMENSIONAL ARCTURIAN COUNCIL

"Greetings. We are the Arcturian Council. We are pleased to connect with all of you.

We have listened to the summoning that you have been doing, and we have noticed that you are making requests for a lighter experience there on planet Earth. You want less density and more light, and the transmissions that we are sending contain more light in them. We are enlightening you, but there is more. You have access to more light, and your bodies are capable of holding more light in them.

You see, this is how you get to the version of Earth that you want. It is not through changing who is in the positions of power. It is not through politics. It is not through changing the systems that you have. It is not through having access to all of the technology that has been beyond your reach. The way that you bring about a lighter version of life on planet Earth is by grounding more of that light in yourselves.

Again, we are giving you a message here that is meant to empower you, and we are also giving you more of that light, and we are not the only ones. There is more light coming from every corner of the galaxy and every dimension in the universe. What Earth needs more than anything is more light receptors. You will all benefit from opening yourselves up to receive the light that is available to you, and you will all benefit from lightening up.

You know that the spiritual path is often seen as solemn and serious, but light comes from within you as well when you make that choice to have fun, to make that choice to experience joy and laughter. You can dance and play and sing your way to the fifth dimension. It doesn't have to be all meditation and yoga, but those things certainly do have their place in allowing in more of that light and bringing yourselves to the version of Earth that you want to experience.

So make sure that you are balancing your more serious spiritual practices with some lighthearted fun and frivolity.

We are the Arcturian Council, and we have enjoyed connecting with you."

THE INDIVIDUAL & THE COLLECTIVE
∞
THE 9TH DIMENSIONAL ARCTURIAN COUNCIL

"Greetings. We are the Arcturian Council. We are pleased to connect with all of you.

We have a better sense of who you are as individuals than we do of you all as a human collective. Your individuality is beautiful. You are all unique, and you are all special, but you have also been led to believe that your differences somehow are responsible for the lack of unity that you sometimes experience as individuals. And nothing could be further from the truth because you all have the ability to celebrate each other no matter what.

You don't have to see your differences as weird, and you don't have to see someone else's different belief as a threat to yours. These are choices that you've been making, and you've been making those choices as individuals.

And the idea that you are somehow separate from each other is one that has served you up until a certain point, and now humanity has reached that point where it no longer serves you to see yourselves as separate and to see your differences as significant enough to keep you from knowing yourselves as a collective.

Now, the reason why we bring this up now is because of how much polarity we sense within humanity. You all have been taught that you have to choose sides, and you don't. Instead, you have to embrace all of the sides, all of the sides that are out there and all of the sides that are within you. To become a unified consciousness, to become a fifth dimensional being, you first have to accept everyone as they are in the human collective right now.

You don't get to decide who is right and who is wrong, and it is not just the righteous ones that get to ascend. It's everyone who makes that choice. And before you ascend, you are going to start thinking of yourselves more as a collective, and you are going to start operating more as a collective as well. You will achieve peace on Earth in this lifetime, and then we will be able to sense you more as a collective.

We are the Arcturian Council, and we have enjoyed connecting with you."

LOVE YOURSELVES UNCONDITIONALLY
∞
THE 9TH DIMENSIONAL ARCTURIAN COUNCIL

"Greetings. We are the Arcturian Council. We are pleased to connect with all of you.

We have a perspective that we would like to share with you on what we see as the continuation of some programming you picked up when you were very young on this planet in this lifetime. We see you looking for reasons to love yourselves. We see you attempting to earn your own love through something that you would accomplish or become, even from the way that you look.

We are noticing that this conditional love got started in childhood for most of you when you learned very quickly what would please your parents, and your teachers, and even your friends. You also learned what would get you in trouble or not please the other people in your life. And most of you could feel the withholding of love during those times when you disappointed someone important in your life.

Now, as adults, most of you continue to run that programming. Most humans have not found a way to love themselves unconditionally. Instead, you work very hard to try to earn your own love, and then you get into a romantic relationship, and you expect the other person to love you unconditionally, even though you have not found the ability to do that for yourself.

So you go from relationship to relationship, looking for someone to give you the love that you never really got from another human and haven't been able to supply to yourself. So we are here to tell you how important it is to let yourself off the hook, to not make your self-love performance based, and we want you to show yourselves even more love when you have met with a defeat of some kind, or when someone else has proven once again that they are not loving you unconditionally.

That is when you need your own love to come forth from within you. You need to access it, you need to feel it, and you need to give it to yourselves freely, without hesitation, without condition, and no matter what anyone else says or does to you. In fact, if you're being mistreated by others, you need to give yourselves more love and more compassion. It makes perfect sense, if you think about it. Who better to love you than the one who knows your entire story?

We are the Arcturian Council, and we have enjoyed connecting with you."

MAGIC

∞

THE 9TH DIMENSIONAL ARCTURIAN COUNCIL

"Greetings. We are the Arcturian Council. We are pleased to connect with all of you.

You are on your way to many magical experiences, and you are also moving towards a feeling. You're moving towards the feeling of magic in your lives because of how far you have already come and because to you the fifth dimensional energies that you are co-creating with are magical by comparison to everything that you have experienced up until now.

You have your faerie tales and your science fiction, and they are both meant to prepare you for what is coming. When you see the character in the story believing in himself or herself, and you see what is possible when that occurs, you get a glimpse of what is in store for all of you.

You are allowing these experiences to become real, and in fact many of you who are receiving this transmission have already had several magical experiences in your lives. You have a high enough vibration now to believe in what we are saying, and you are attuned to these higher frequency energies, which means that they can work with you, and you can work with them to create more magic in your lives.

You are not just there on Earth in the fourth dimension to wait things out until the influx of fifth dimensional energies carries you past the tipping point. You are there to create magical experiences, magical lives, and you are there to inspire others to believe.

You are there to inspire others to believe in themselves. True magic is just that. There are no potions, magic phrases, or wands that you need to be magical, and to perform that which is magical in the eyes of most on a day-to-day basis.

We are the Arcturian Council, and we have enjoyed connecting with you."

THE END

Made in United States
Troutdale, OR
10/03/2024

23410872R00159